Janet Ruhl's

ANSWERS

FOR

COMPUTER
CONTRACTORS

How to get the highest rates and the fairest deals from consulting firms, agencies, and clients

TECHNION Books

Published by Technion Books
P.O. Box 171
Leverett, MA 01054
technion@realrates.com

Additional copies of this book may be ordered from the publisher.
Please include $2.50 for postage and handling. For information
about volume discounts please contact the publisher at the address
above.

This publication is designed to provide accurate and authoritative
information in regard to the subject matter covered. It is sold with
the understanding that the publisher and author are not engaged
in rendering legal, accounting, or other professional services. If legal advice or other expert assistance is required, the services of a
competent professional person should be sought.

LIBRARY OF CONGRESS CATALOG CARD NUMBER: 98-90524
ISBN NUMBER: 0-9647116-2-1

Printed in the United States of America

10 9 8 7 6 5 4 3

ACKNOWLEDGMENTS

This book could not have been written without the help of the many thousands of computer contractors and consultants who have sent their rate reports to the Real Rate Survey since 1995. The data they have provided makes it possible, at last, for contractors to get accurate and unbiased information about what their skills are worth.

I am also heavily in debt to the many contracting experts who hang out at *The Computer Consultants Message Board* at http://www.realrates.com/bbs. Their lively discourse, breadth of knowledge, and willingness to share what they know with others impresses me daily. Their many thousands of postings over the past year have greatly improved my understanding of computer contracting.

Special thanks to the following message board participants whose contributions enrich these pages: Charles Crizer, "Dinosaur," Brian Harris, Scott Horne, Bob McIlree, Elizabeth P., Ben Prusinski, James V. Reagan, Lisa the Recruiter, "Swamy," Don Wallace, and James Ziegler. My grateful thanks go out, too, to everyone else whose messages I've quoted here, including the many people who posted anonymously.

I'm deeply grateful to computer consulting legal expert Frederic Wilf, Esq. for reviewing the chapter on contract clauses, and to Harvey Shulman, the NACCB's legal advisor, for answering the questions I posed him about the NACCB model consulting firm contract. Thanks also go to the helpful insurance experts at http://www.techinsurance.com, and to Tony Grace, William Redmond, and the other consulting firm principals who answered my questions about how their businesses operate.

My beta readers provided invaluable feedback that greatly improved the text you'll find here. Hats off to Larry Keyes, Jeffrey Cai, and Tracy Barnett!

Huge thanks, too, to Peter Atwood, for his fastidious proofreading and many useful suggestions, as well as for his ability to astonish me daily and make life fun.

Finally, my heartiest thanks go out to all the readers who have contacted me over the years. Your many tales of business success encourage me to believe that these books of mine do help!

TABLE OF CONTENTS

What is a computer contractor? What kinds of work do computer contractors do? How much do contractors earn? Who hires contractors? Why do clients use contractors? Do clients save money by hiring contractors? How is a computer contractor different from a computer consultant? How many computer contractors are there in the US? Are all computer contractors temps? What are working conditions like for contractors? What kind of status does a contractor have on the job? What percentage of contractors work through consulting firms? What are the advantages of contracting? What are the drawbacks of contracting? How many people make a long-term career out of contracting? Where does contracting fit into long-term computer career planning? Can I work part time as a contractor? Can I do contract work for remote clients from my home? What is the single most important thing to remember about contracting? Will contracting remain a viable career option for the next twenty or thirty years? Can you recommend any magazines I could subscribe to in order to learn more about contracting? My goal is to become a real consultant, the kind who sells advice. How does contracting fit into these plans?

What are the minimum qualifications you need to become a contractor? What kinds of skills are most valuable? How important is it to have paid experience? How much total experience do most contractors have? Can I become a computer contractor by taking a mail order course? How do consulting firm recruiters evaluate skills? How technically savvy are the recruiters who read my resume? How do I determine if there is a market for my specific technical skills? Where can I find out more about conditions for contractors with skills like mine where I live? Can I be a contractor if I am not a programmer but have other computer-related skills? Is it a good idea to begin contracting straight out of college? Do some types of personalities do better than others as contractors? I have a lot of bills. Could I pay them off faster as a contractor? Is taking a salaried job with a consulting firm a good way to break into contracting? Won't I learn more about the consulting business working as an employee of a successful consulting firm? My spouse isn't crazy about the idea of my giving up a steady job. Will they change their mind when the money starts rolling in?

Do I have to establish my business in a particular legal form? What is a W-2 Contractor? What are the advantages of working as an employee contractor? What formal steps are required to work as an employee contractor? What is a sole proprietor? What is an 1099 Contractor? What are the benefits of being an independent contractor or sole proprietor? What legal steps do I have to take to become a 1099 contractor? What do I do if a company sends me a 1099 statement with an incorrect amount on it? What is involved in incorporating? What is the difference between a C-Corporation and an S-Corporation? Can I start out as a C-Corporation and then change to an S-Corporation later? If I have to incorporate should I use an online service that promises to incorporate me in my home state for $200? Is it a good idea to incorporate in another state where incorporation is cheaper than my home state? What is a Limited Liability Company? Would it make sense to form a partnership?

How do you decide which form to use? Why do firms vary so much in what employment status they demand? What exactly does Section 1706 do? What happens if you violate the IRS guidelines and work with the wrong status? Where do you find consulting firms that will work on a 1099 or corp-to-corp basis? Does my employment status make a difference in how much I earn? Should I hold out for independent status? Will 1706 be repealed? Can I change my status from W-2 to 1099 or become a corporation in the middle of an existing contract? Have thousands of independent computer contractors been reclassified as employees as an agency recruiter told me? Why did the consulting firm tell me I need to buy expensive insurance before they'll let me work as an Independent? Does my homeowner's policy cover my computer equipment at home? What is disability insurance? Where can I buy the business insurance I need? Will I have problems finding health insurance if I'm working as a W-2 contractor? Is it easier to buy insurance if I am incorporated? What about continuing in my old employer's plan under COBRA? Can I get health insurance through a consulting firm if I am an hourly rate W-2 employee? Do I have to choose a business name if I am a contractor? How can I ensure that my business name is unique? What business expenses can I treat as tax deductions as a W-2 contractor? What business expenses can I claim as tax deductions as an independent contractor? Can I deduct the cost of my health insurance? Can I deduct the expenses of maintaining a home office? Would I save money leasing a car for my business and then deducting the expense on my taxes? Will I have credit problems if I become a contractor? Can I get the benefits of independence working as an employee of an umbrella company?

4 WHAT RATE?

How do I set my rate? Can I believe what other people tell me about rates? Can I believe what consulting firm recruiters tell me about rates? How useful are surveys? What does your Real Rate Survey tell us about rates? Is there a simple way to come up with a rate? What kind of income does a rate of $70 per hour translate into? What cut does a consulting firm get when they place a contractor? Where does the consulting firm's cut go? What percentage raise can I expect when I get a new contract? What kind of raise can I expect when I extend a contract? Are there situations where I'd earn more as a salaried employee? Can't I get a salaried job that pays what I'd make as an hourly rate contractor minus the cost of benefits? Wouldn't I have more job security as an employee? As an employee, won't I get paid for "bench time?" How does salaried work as a contractor differ from salaried work elsewhere?

5 WHICH CONSULTING FIRM?

What is a consulting firm? What is a broker? What is an agency? What is a Big Six Consulting Firm? What are Vendor Consulting Firms? What about the consulting firms I see in the magazines and online? What about the traditional temporary and employment agencies now placing technical contractors? What about smaller, local consulting firms? Do consulting firms earn obscene profits? How do consulting firms pay their recruiters? Are the most successful consulting firms those that best understand technology? Who keeps the consulting firm in business, the client or the contractor? What kinds of problems do contractors cause consulting firms? How do I find a good consulting firm? What about consulting firms that post jobs on Internet job boards? How do I find a good out-of-town consulting firm? What kinds of problems should I be looking out for? The reputable consulting firms in town won't interview me because I'm currently employed by a large area firm they have contracts with. What can I do? How paranoid do I have to be?

6 HOW DO I WORK WITH CONSULTING FIRMS?

When should I contact consulting firms? How many consulting firms should I contact? Should I first contact firms whose employees recommend them? Should I look for consulting firms that pay a sign-on bonus? What is the best way to approach a consulting firm? What should be my goal in the initial contact? What kinds of questions should I expect the recruiter to ask? Should I discuss rates during the initial contact? Should I tell them what rate I want? Should I ask about tax status at this point? What should I do if the consulting firm wants a face-to-face interview? How should I dress for an interview? How do I handle the consulting firm interview? Should I deal with a recruiter who is a technical idiot? The recruiter gave me a contract to sign at the preliminary interview. Should I sign it? Can I ask to see their regular contract now? What kind of résumé should I send a consulting firm? What comes after the first contact? The recruiter has an interview for me. What now? What happens at the client interview? Who will be interviewing me? Should I discuss rates at the client interview? Should I discuss the start date at the interview? How much can I find out about the contract at the interview? This is just a six week contract, so why worry? The contract they've got for me is "temp to perm." What does that mean? How can I optimize my chances of getting the contract? What should I do if I can't find out much at the interview? I'd like to interview for more than one contract before I decide on one. Can I do this? What should I do when I get an offer? What should I do if the recruiter tries to lowball me? I can't make up my mind about this offer. How do I handle this? How can I improve my negotiation skills? Do I have to negotiate? Besides my rate and status what else must I negotiate? How do I accept the offer? When should I give notice on my old job or contract? Should I start working for the client before I sign the contract?

7 WHAT'S IN MY CONSULTING FIRM CONTRACT?............. 133

Do all consulting firms use written contracts? Who supplies the contract? What parties are bound by this contract? Since I'm not contracting with the client, what contract binds them? What should I do if the consulting firm doesn't send a contract? How negotiable is the consulting firm contract? Do I have to accept everything in the contract to take the job? How do I negotiate a clause? How do I modify a contract clause? What clauses should I expect to find in a contract? How do W-2 contracts differ from 1099 and corp-to-corp contracts? How does a corporation's contract differ from that of a 1099 IC? Are computer consulting contracts covered by Federal law? The consulting firm is located in a state other than the one I work in. What state's laws prevail? The consulting firm representative says that theirs is the standard NACCB contract and that they cannot change it. Is this true? What if I can't figure out what a clause means? Can you show me a sample of each clause I can expect to see? I've heard that overly broad clauses will get thrown out in court. Does this mean I can ignore the most abusive ones? How frequent are lawsuits by consulting firms against contractors? What happens to my contract if another firm buys the firm I sign with?

8 HOW CAN I WORK DIRECT? 151

Do I have to be an entrepreneur to work without agencies? How do I market myself? What's the easiest way to find direct clients? How can I get old employers to hire me? How can I work direct for clients I met through consulting firms? How can I make the most of my existing contacts? How do I find new clients? What kinds of companies will hire contractors directly? What is a preferred vendor? Can I become one? What kinds of firms don't use preferred vendors? Why do clients hire from body shops when they can get better talent hiring direct? Why do so many companies prefer to hire from agencies and consulting firms when they can find my resume on the Internet? How do I find out which companies in my area will hire direct? Is it worthwhile to send a mass mailing to area managers? How do I present myself as an expert? I've found a manager who is interested in hiring me for a direct contract. What now? What status should I work under? The client insists that I work through a pass-through agency. What's that? How do I negotiate my rate? What should I watch out for when negotiating directly with managers? Who provides the contract when I work direct? What should my contract include? What do I do with the contract? Can I work without a formal signed contract?

What is an invoice? What should I do when I get paid? What should I do if I don't get my check? How do I terminate the contract?

9 HOW DO I HANDLE THIS?

How do I give notice at my old job once I've found a contract? How do I start my new contract? How long do I have on a new contract to figure out what's going on? The work isn't what was described at the interview. I'm out of my depth. Help! There's nothing for me to do! The employees here work a thirty-five hour week. Does that mean I can only bill for thirty-five hours? The manager asked me to compete in the United Way Bowlathon. Do I bill for the time I spend on that? This project is headed for disaster. Help! I could save this project. Why won't anyone take my advice? With my high rate, it's hard to justifying taking time off. How can I stop working so many hours? The client wants to hire me as an employee. Should I do it? I am going to miss my deadline. How should I handle the situation? I have been assigned to work with another contractor who is an imbecile. How can I keep his mistakes from making me look bad? I've been assigned to work with a client employee who is an imbecile. What do I do now? In a few weeks the term specified in my contract will end. What should I do? I'm stuck in a contract that just seems to go on and on. Should I take a third extension? Can I ask the client about what they are paying before I negotiate an extension? What kind of paperwork should I expect to see if I accept an extension? Today, without warning, the client terminated me. I had five months left on my contract. Can they do this? Can a client or old employer give me a bad reference? I just discovered that the rate the consulting firm is billing my client is four times what they are paying me. Can I do anything about this? Is there any way I can get out of my consulting firm contract? The recruiter says I'll be blacklisted if I leave this contract early. Can they do this? The client wants to hire me direct and cut out the consulting firm. Can we do this? I found a new contract that pays a lot more than my current one. When I told the consulting firm I was leaving they offered to match the new rate. Should I stay? The project is over and my client is very pleased with my work. How can I make the most of this? I want to take a vacation before I begin my next assignment. How do I do this? The consulting firm won't pay my last invoice. How can I make them pay me?

10 HOW CAN I DO BETTER?

How can I improve my earnings as a contractor? I need new skills. Can I get them by signing on as a consulting firm employee? It costs a fortune to buy all the hardware and software I want to master! How can I pick up new skills? I already know an in-demand language and operating system. So why should I worry about upgrading? What about the packages you can't install and teach yourself? What is certification? How useful is certification? What does the Real Rate Survey data show about the value of certifications? How can I find out if it is worth getting an expensive certification? Why does it sometimes seem like the biggest b-s artists get the best rates? How can I improve my communications skills? How important is image? What are some ways to build a better image? I'm finding that my programming skills aren't good enough for me to make it as a contractor. What do I do now? Would relocating to another city be a good way to revive my contracting career? How can I decide if I'd like living in a distant city? What specific dangers are involved in relocating to take a contract? Can I get paid extra for taking a temporary contract away from home? How can I find a contract overseas? Do I need to speak a foreign language to work abroad? Do I have to be a gypsy to get the best rates and opportunities? Does it ever make sense to go back to being a regular employee? How can I convince employers I'd take a salaried job? They say my contractor's earnings are too high! I'm burning out on contracting but I don't want to be an employee. What are my other options?

INDEX

CHARTS

FACT SHEETS

INTRODUCTION

This book is for anyone who has ever wondered what it would be like to be a computer contractor. It is also for the thousands of professionals who make their livings as contractors now. Its goal is to answer the important questions that contractors ask: questions about their career prospects and employment status, about what rates to charge and how to deal with consulting firms, about the contracts they sign and their problems on the job.

In the pages that follow you'll find hundreds of topics presented in a FAQ format. Each topic is introduced by a question similar to the questions you see posted on online bulletin boards. Each question is followed by a comprehensive answer. These answers draw on my personal knowledge of contracting, on the interviews I've held with contractors earning rates of $100 per hour and more, and on the many thousands of messages about computer contracting that I've collected over nearly a decade spent running online bulletin boards on CompuServe and, more recently, on my own Web site at http://www.realrates.com.

SLICES OF LIFE

Many of the issues that are discussed in this book are accompanied by excerpts from messages that were posted by visitors to *The Computer Consultant's Message Board* located at http://www.realrates.com/bbs.

I have printed these messages exactly the way they were posted except for minor spelling corrections and cuts to remove material irrelevant to our discussion here. Where the writer of the message has given a name I have used it. Otherwise I have tagged the messages with the screen names or aliases that the posters have used or with tags of my own.

Scatteerd through the text you'll also find shaded boxes highlighting important facts or giving lists of useful resources.

Both the use of message board material and the highlighting of resources is similar to the approach I used in my earlier books about independent consulting, *The Computer Consultant's Guide* and *The Computer Consultant's Workbook*. But what is new in these pages and what, I hope, will greatly add to the value of what you read here is the wealth of hard data about actual computer contracts that we've collected using the Real Rate Survey.

This survey uses a form located at `http://www.realrates.com/rate_sur.htm` to collect information from visiting contractors about their current contracts. Fields on the form allow contractors to tell us about their current rate, what rate they earned on their previous contract, and, if they are working through a consulting firm or broker, what rate the client is paying for their services. To put this information in context the Real Rate Survey also asks for information about the languages and platforms the contractors work in, the location of the contract, the contractor's job description, their industry, their experience, what their tax status is, whether they got the contract through a consulting firm or other broker, how long the contract is expected to last, and whether the contract was an extension of a previous contract. Our site also hosts a separate Real Salary Survey which collects information about employee salaries in the IT field, including those of salaried computer consultants.

Visitors to our site can browse through all the survey data we've collected, using various sorts, or they can search the data for the specific skills, location, status, or job description that they are interested in seeing. At the time of writing this, we had collected information about over 4,000 actual contracts. Over 2,000 of these had been reported during the past year. This data came from all over the world, from contractors working on every platform in every industry. It came from beginners and veterans, from independents and consulting firm employees.

Because we have this Real Rate Survey data we need no longer guess at the answers to many of the important questions contractors ask. Our data can tell us things like what kinds of rates W-2 contractors are earning in comparison with 1099 contractors or what the ranges are for rates for various platforms. With access to this data we are also freed from having to trust the word of consulting firm staffers when they tell us what constitutes a standard consulting firm cut or which languages, locations, or industries pay the best rates. Our data shows us exactly what size of cut hundreds of consulting firms are taking and gives us a very good idea what the ranges are for rates for a host of specialties in a great number of locations.

Best of all, because this Real Rate Survey data is freely available to the public, readers do not have to worry that the data they find in this book might go stale. The Real Rate Survey is updated weekly, and readers of this book can always find the latest data by visiting us at `http://www.realrates.com`.

Like the writer of any FAQs, my goal is to get you oriented as quickly as possible. When you finish this book you should have a very good idea of whether contracting would make sense for you right now. You should have an even better idea of how you can strengthen your appeal to clients and consulting firms. You'll have a good grasp of the business issues you'll find yourself discussing with clients and consulting firms as well as a heightened awareness of the many things you need to watch out for. Best of all, you should come away from this book with a clear understanding of how to find high-paying contracts using reputable consulting firms or on your own and how to conduct yourself on the job so that you get further contracts.

Read these pages, consider the data, and then come visit us online at http://www.realrates.com where you can view our latest data and share any questions you may still have with the hundreds of contractors active on our message board.

There's a lot of information in the pages ahead, but as you read you can take comfort in knowing that there has never been a better time to enter the marketplace with your computer skills. The demand for contractors outstrips the supply and predictions are that this will remain the case for at least the next decade. There has never been a better time to be a contractor than now, nor has it ever been easier to learn about the contracting industry. So once you master the information you'll find here, you should be able to put it to immediate use. The opportunities are waiting!

ABOUT OUR REAL RATE SURVEY STATISTICS

The statistics you will find scattered throughout this text are drawn from the July 1998 Real Rate Survey Report.

This report analyzed the 887 computer consulting rates that were contributed to the Survey by contractors working in the United States between January 1 and June 30, 1998.

To make our analysis more useful, we followed the standard statistical practice of throwing away the five highest rates, which ranged from $150 to $350 per hour, and the five lowest rates, which ranged from $9 to $16.

Unless otherwise noted, on our charts we graph all categories reporting 5 rates or more.

CHAPTER 1

WHAT IS CONTRACTING?

What is a computer contractor?

Computer contractors are highly skilled, highly paid temporary workers who design, develop, install, and maintain computer hardware and software for clients. They are called "contractors" because a written contract usually defines the conditions under which they fill their temporary positions.

The computer contractor's contract is almost always time-oriented, not task-oriented. The contract describes the contractor's assignment in terms of how long it will last rather than what tasks the contractor will accomplish. These contracts generally include a provision that lets clients extend the time period covered by the contract if they need more of the contractor's services.

Computer contractors are *paid* on a time-defined basis too, with most contractors charging clients an hourly rate for each hour they work no matter what they accomplish in that time.

What kinds of work do computer contractors do?

Most computer contractors are programmers. As you can see from the chart on the next page, 60% of the contractors who reported their rates to the Real Rate Survey in 1998 described themselves as being a "Programmer," "Programmer Analyst," "Developer," or "Software Engineer." A much smaller number took on a managerial role. Eight percent of our Real Rate Survey respondents described their role as "Team Leader" and 3% as "Manager." Computer contractors also do network support, database administration, high level design, software testing, quality assurance, and end user training.

Contractors frequently work on projects whose goal is to develop new software. They may be deployed to do nothing more than simple coding or they may be brought in to manage the entire project. Indeed, there are corporations where contractors not only design the system architecture, but also hire the other contractors and employees who staff the development project.

Contractors may be brought in to convert older systems to newer technologies or to do Y2K work. Clients also hire contractors to run end-of-the year processing or maintain legacy systems.

In fact, you are likely to find contractors doing just about any job that a regular employee might do. But unlike employees, contractors always know that their relationships with the people who pay them are temporary and that they'll be working somewhere else when their current assignments are done.

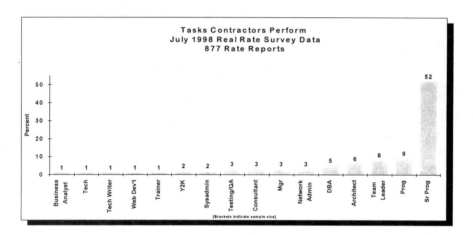

How much do computer contractors earn?

Computer contractors are usually paid by the hour. The hourly rate they receive depends on a number of factors. Among them are what languages and platforms they work with, the geographical area in which they are located, the industry they work in, whether they are working as an employee or an independent, and whether they got their contract through a consulting firm or other middleman. We will discuss how all these factors influence rates in Chapter 4, "What Rate?"

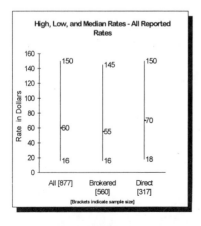

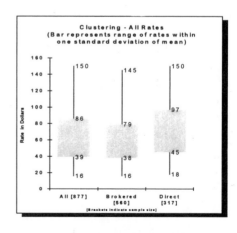

Our adjusted Real Rate Survey data shows that in 1998 rates for all contractors ranged from $16 to $150 per hour, with rates concentrated most heavily in a range extending from $39 to $86 per hour. The median rate for all contractors reporting was $60 per hour. The median rate for contractors working through middlemen was $55 per hour. Rates for contractors working through middlemen ranged from $16 to $145 per hour and clustered most heavily between $38 per hour and $78 per hour. The median rate for contractors working directly for clients was $70 per hour. Their rates ranged from $18 to $150 per hour and clustered most heavily between $45 per hour and $97 per hour.

Who hires contractors?

Most contractors work at large corporations in IT-intensive industries like Insurance, Banking, Finance, Government, Manufacturing, and Telecommunications. Many more work in the Computer industry itself at hardware and software development firms. Computer contractors are much less likely to be found working for smaller companies like local retailers or service firms, because to stay viable contractors must charge rates of $40 per hour or more and find contracts that last anywhere from three months to a year. This makes their services too expensive for most smaller firms to afford.

Only a minority of contractors are actually paid by the companies for whom they do their work. Most operate through middlemen: consulting firms, placement agencies and brokers. Sixty-four percent of the contractors who reported their rates to us at the Real Rate Survey in 1998 worked through middlemen. These Middlemen find clients for contractors. In return, they take a hefty percentage of the contractors' billing to cover their expenses and provide their profits.

Why do clients use contractors?

Clients hire contractors for a number of reasons. The most common one is that they need people with fully developed skills who can be productive immediately using brand new technologies. They are willing to pay whatever it takes to hire these skilled contractors because the highly competitive nature of the high tech marketplace makes it dangerous for them to wait the amount of time it would take to train their existing employees.

Clients also hire contractors when they have short term needs that don't justify hiring full-time staff or when they can't find qualified candidates willing to hire on as full-time staff.

Corporate clients may also hire contractors when they are under pressure from stockholders to cut costs and trim their payrolls. For example, during the late 1980s and early 1990s when Wall Street applauded every time a large corporation axed a healthy chunk of its work force, corporations would announce huge IT layoffs, their stock prices would rise, and then, because the work that the programmers had been doing did not go away when the programmers did, the company would quietly hire contractors to replace the fired programmers. These contractors were often paid rates that were more than twice as high as the employees' old salaries. But this strategy satisfied stockholders because the company paid their contractors with funds that were not charged to payroll on the company's earnings statement, making it look as if headcount had been trimmed.

Clients may also hire contractors to circumvent the protections provided to employees by labor law. Since contractors are not the client's employees they can be fired at a moment's notice for no reason at all without the client having to go through annoying HR procedures. At interviews clients can ask would-be contractors nosy questions about their family lives, religion, or other topics that would be strictly forbidden if they were interviewing prospective employees. But since the contractor is either self-employed or is the prospective employee of a consulting firm, they lose the protection the law affords regular employees in job interviews.

In a similar vein, clients may also hire contractors to free themselves from the pesky requirements of equal opportunity employment law. Executives unwilling to hire women, minorities, or legal immigrants can make it clear to a consulting firm recruiter that they are only interested in seeing the résumés of contractors who fit their prejudices. Since the contractors are not interviewing for jobs with the client, they can't turn to equal opportunity employment law for protection against discrimination.

Do clients save money by hiring contractors?

In the past, management often turned to contractors as a cost cutting measure. Not only would they save money because they didn't have to buy benefits for their contractors, but since contractors don't participate in the company's benefit plans, a company could staff up with older, experienced contractors without having to worry that the contractors' ages would push up the cost of the company's health and life insurance. Hiring contractors could also help cut costs because contractors don't participate in company 401(k) plans or require severance packages, company picnics, Christmas bonuses, or scheduled raises.

However, the contractor shortage that has existed throughout the late 1990s has driven up rates to the point where it is often cheaper to hire full-time employees than contractors. As a result, many companies would now like to replace their contractors with employees, but because of the bad will created by the downsizings of the past decade, they often find it impossible to find experienced computer professionals willing to trade the high rates they can earn as contractors for the dubious "job security" offered by full time employment.

How is a computer contractor different from a computer consultant?

While we will be using the term "contractor" throughout this book, in the workplace the people we are referring to are just as likely to be called "consultants" as they are to be called "contractors." This generates a great deal of confusion, since the term "consultant" is used to describe people whose functions in the workplace could not be more different. Indeed, it might be applied to the recent college graduate who types in Web page text or the ex-CIO who advises the CEO on strategic planning!

Within the consulting community itself, there is a tendency to distinguish between contractors and *independent*, or entrepreneurial, consultants. These independent consultants may be programmers, systems integrators, VARS or IT-oriented management consultants. What they all have in common is that they do their own marketing, find their own clients, work from their own offices, and usually work for more than one client in a given time period. Their contracts are often written on a task-defined basis, rather than the time-defined basis characteristic of computer contractors. By this we mean that because they are brought in to solve a specific problem or deliver a specific solution, their contracts are written so that the contract term ends only when the problem is solved or the solution delivered.

Consultants who consider themselves to be entrepreneurial independent consultants often claim that they are the only "real" computer consultants and that computer contractors who call themselves "consultants" are deluding themselves and dragging down the professional image of consultants as a group.

However, the line separating the different kinds of consultants is not always clear. Many "real" consultants flesh out their schedules with contract programming, and many contractors who work on time-based contracts also do their own marketing and develop their own clienteles. By the same token, many people calling themselves "contractors" do high level design, strategic planning, and project management, while entrepreneurs calling themselves "consultants" may do nothing more than code up simple HTML pages or Visual Basic routines.

How many computer contractors are there in the US?

It is impossible to get reliable statistics on the number of computer contractors at work in the United States. Large consulting firms do not make public the number of contractors working for them because they claim this information is a trade secret, nor do consulting organizations reveal their exact membership figures.

We can get some idea of the number of working contractors from the data computer magazines release about the number of "consultants" among their subscribers, though these magazine surveys may inflate this number because they include salaried consulting firm employees in their "consultant" category. For example, in 1992, *Computerworld* described 52,000 of its 600,000 subscribers as "providing contract services." In 1997, *Contract Professional*, a magazine specifically targeting computer contractors, claimed a paid circulation of some 60,000 contractors. Since these magazines only reach a fraction of the contracting population, it would not be unreasonable to estimate the total number of working contractors at 200,000 or more.

Moreover, this population is continually changing as employees turn into contractors and contractors return to the pool of salaried employees. Publishers tell us that the annual sales of successful "how to" books that target would-be computer contractors and consultants are in the 20,000 copy range, suggesting that at least another 20,000 people consider moving into contracting each year.

Are all computer contractors temps?

All contractors are hired on a temporary basis. But the statistics we've collected about the lengths of the thousands of computer contracts reported to our Real Rate Survey suggest the need for a flexible definition of "temporary," since many contracts last as long as salaried jobs.

As you can see from the chart below that graphs the frequency of various contract lengths found in our Real Rate Survey data, the most frequent length of contract reported for 1998 was six months, followed closely by one year. In addition, many of the three and six month contracts reported were actually extensions of previous contracts. Contracts lasting two years are common and significant numbers of contractors report working on contracts that last three, four, and five years—far longer than the job tenure of many a salaried employee. In fact, the longest W-2 contract in our records is reported as lasting for a whopping seven years.

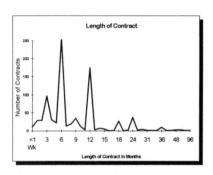

Indeed, because of the epidemic of downsizing that has swept through the corporate world during the past decade, it is not uncommon to find that the "old timer" in a department is not a loyal employee but is instead a contractor, one who has been working in the department on and off for longer than any of the company's current employees!

It is also not unusual for contractors to be offered full-time salaried jobs by clients after they have completed their contracts. Indeed, some companies that are looking for full-time employees bring in prospects as contractors so that they can evaluate the quality of their work before committing to a hiring decision.

What are working conditions like for contractors?

Most contractors work under the same conditions as employees. They report for work at the same hours, they take the same holidays, and, if necessary, they can call in sick.

If hired to fill contracts that involve supporting production systems, contractors may be asked to provide on-call support during weekends and late at night. If hired onto crunch-mode development projects, they may be expected to put in unlimited overtime.

However, unlike employees, contractors who are paid on an hourly rate basis can charge for these extra hours. And, because contractors can leave a project more easily than employees, managers interviewing contractors for a new project are more likely to tell them the truth about required overtime and being on call.

Contractors who get their contracts through consulting firms usually work for only one client at a time, 40 hours a week, though independents may apportion their time between several clients. Once the contract period begins, contractors are almost always paid whether or not there is work for them to do. Indeed, a common contractor complaint is that they get bored hanging around waiting for the client to come up with work for them to do. Very rarely, a client may save money by sending a contractor home when things are slow, but this is unusual.

What kind of status does a contractor have on the job?

Contractors must walk a fine line on the job. They must perform at a high level of competence while keeping a low profile and letting the glory go to others. Because contractors often earn considerably more than both client employees and hiring managers, they can, if not careful, make enemies out of regular employees who feel stuck in jobs they hate. As a result, many contractors have learned to downplay their status and behave humbly on the job.

Some companies treat contractors like second class citizens in order to discourage employee jealousy. They exclude contractors from morale building activities and deny them the status symbols, like a corner office, large desk, or credenza that are used to reward employees in lieu of better pay. However, this is not true in all companies. In those where many of the developers are contractors, management may encourage contractors to participate in morale building activities and other rituals of corporate life.

What percentage of contractors work through consulting firms?

Our 1998 Real Rate Survey data showed that 64% of all contracts reported were found through consulting firms and placement agencies. However, when we look at the details of these contracts, we find a great deal of variation in what types of contractors work for agencies and which work directly for clients. Contractors working for the large corporations with huge investments in computer technology that hire hundreds of contractors each year are most likely to work though consulting firms. That is because these kinds of companies often insist that *all* their contractors work through a small number of preferred vendor firms with whom they have negotiated blanket contracts. Contractors who serve a clientele of smaller, more flexible companies find it easier to work directly for clients without a middleman.

The charts on Page 9 analyze our Real Rate Survey data to see what percentage of contractors use brokers to find contracts, with that data broken down by the language, database, and package used. (The term "broker," when used by contractors, simply means a middleman like a consulting firm or placement agency.)

This data reinforces the point that contractors working for large corporate clients are likely to be brokered. Over three quarters of the contractors working with CICS, DB2, and COBOL, as well as those using IMS, SAP, and PeopleSoft, got their contracts through consulting firms while only a minority of programmers working in Access, FoxPro, and RPG, did.

Contractors working in certain industries are more likely to be brokered than those working in others. The chart on Page 11 shows that variation. As you can see, only 47% of the contractors working in the Health Care industry were brokered, while nearly 90% of those working in Aerospace and Marketing were. Though some brokered contractors are found working in all industries.

Geographical differences also exist in whether contractors find it easy to work directly for clients, as you can see in the charts on Page 11 and 13 which show the percentages of contracts brokered by city and by selected state.

Perhaps the most telling data is displayed by the chart on Page 13 which displays the relationship between being brokered and the length of the contract. It clearly shows that contractors working short contracts and those working extremely long contracts are most likely to find their own jobs, while two-thirds or more of those working contracts that last three months to two years get those contracts through brokers.

What are the advantages of contracting?

Contracting offers computer professionals the opportunity to earn the highest possible income in return for their labor without having to take the risk or make the effort it would take to build up a profitable entrepreneurial business. A contractor earning the $60 per hour median rate reported by contributors to our Real Rate Survey and working forty-seven weeks out of the year, which is also typical, would gross $112,800.

Contracting also offers computer professionals a greater degree of control over the direction in which their careers develop. This may be an even more significant benefit than high earnings. The reason for this is that the past decades have shown that the biggest threat to any computer professional's career is having their skills become obsolete. No matter what you may have achieved in the past, if you aren't able to work at a professional level using current languages, databases, and operating systems you will find it impossible to find any paid computer work.

Unfortunately, it is very easy to lose sight of this while you are working as an employee. Many companies have large investments in old and obsolescing systems and keep employees working on them for years, rewarding them with bonuses, raises, and promotions. When those systems are finally replaced by newer technologies, the staffers who built their careers on keeping them alive are often fired. Tragically, it is only then that these ex-employees discover how little value the work they have done over the years has for companies other than their old employer.

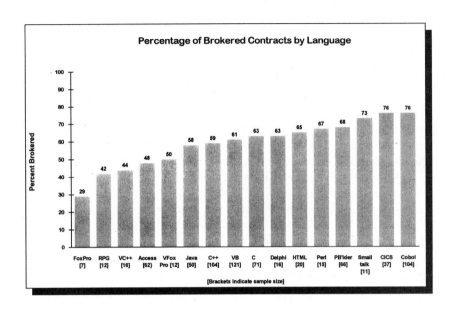

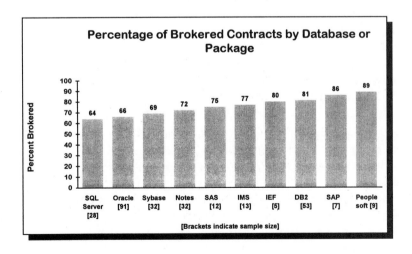

Because contractors must constantly stay in touch with the current requirements of the workplace, they are far less likely to fall into this kind of career blindness. Contractors can pick and choose every single assignment they take on. With some effort, they can make sure that each contract not only keeps their skills current but that it also exposes them to something new. Contractors can be picky about the role they play on projects and about the types of projects they get involved in. And because they work for a series of different companies, rather than for one company, contractors are less likely to get emotionally involved in the intramural dramas of any company or to overvalue the rewards that mastering its politics might bring.

The benefit of contracting that many contractors like the most is the freedom it gives them. Contractors can work when they want to and take time off when they want to. They can decide how much they want to earn and earn it, freeing themselves from a childish dependency on bosses and paternalistic corporations. If they find themselves in an unpleasant work situation they can leave in a few months, without worrying, as do employees, that by quitting they'll spoil their résumés. This freedom and the ability to control the direction of their careers often motivate contractors to stay in contracting even when their earnings are no better than what they could make as employees.

What are the drawbacks of contracting?

The biggest drawback of contracting is its unpredictability. You never know when you will be working or for how long. While you work the money may be very good, but contracts can end without warning and it may take longer to find a new contract than you expected. If your technical skills are highly specialized, you may have to travel around the country to keep busy or you may have to settle in a particular area, like Silicon Valley, where demand for your skills is strong.

Another drawback to consulting is that over time you may burn out on being a gypsy and begin to feel that in spite of all your labor you never build anything lasting. As you move from project to project you learn and forget the details of dozens of systems, while you form and break relationships with dozens of coworkers. This can be exciting for the first few years, particularly when coupled with high earnings. But after a while, many people find it hard to keep on living this way.

Yet another challenge of contracting is that contractors are almost always hired to do the kinds work they have done before. If you are a C++ programmer, you'll be offered C++ contracts. If you're a DB2 specialist you'll get jobs that involve DB2 databases. When recruiters offer you ever increasing rates for doing the same kinds of work over and over again, it is hard to turn them down and hunt for the rarer contracts that let you learn new things that enhance your skills. Because of this, over time it can become increasingly difficult to get paid experience using new technology. Eventually you may get stuck in a software ghetto, able to find work only in the handful of companies that still need people with your obsolescing skills.

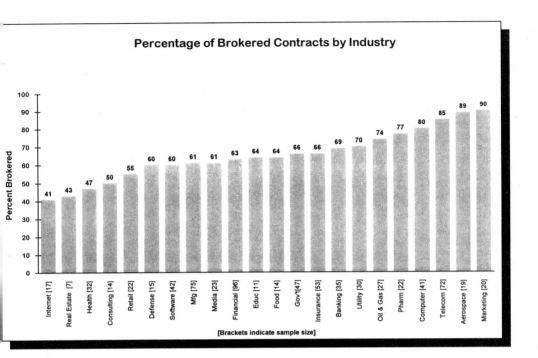

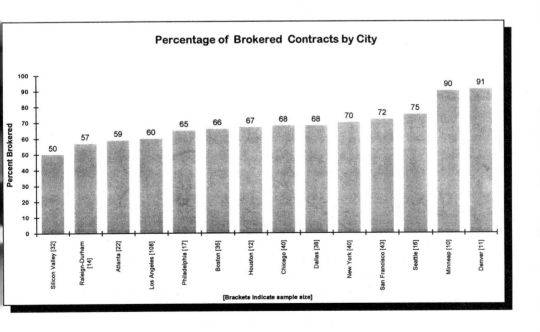

How many people make a long term career out of contracting?

Seventy-nine percent of the contractors reporting to our 1998 Real Rate Survey mentioned their years of experience. Of these, only 6% reported having more than twenty years of experience. Nine percent of them reported that they had been in the field for 16 to 20 years.

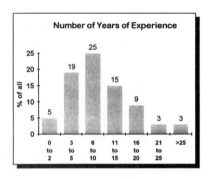

This group of old-timers may be small because fewer people made careers as programmers in the 1960s and 1970s when these old timers began their careers. Or there may be other reasons.

But is is clear that the prime years for contractors are the middle years of their careers. Sixty-nine percent of the contractors reporting years of experience to our survey reported that they had 3 to 15 years years of experience.

Where does contracting fit into long-term computer career planning?

Contracting can be a lucrative way to fill in a few months or it can be a prolonged stage in a long term career.

It may be the final form your computer career takes, as it is for many highly experienced professionals, and you may spend many happy decades s a contractor. But contracting can also serve as a useful step towards a different career path. If you prefer to be a permanent employee, contracting can provide a way to "tour" a variety of work environments until you find a company that is worth working for permanently. Working for any company as a contractor will give you a much better idea of what it would be like to be employed there.

Because contracting makes it possible to earn a lot of money in a short time, it can also be a way of amassing the cash stake you'll need to pursue entrepreneurial projects like starting your own software firm. Contracting may also be a good compromise for people who are not able to give 100% to a job but who need to earn a living. A contractor can earn the equivalent of an employee's salary in six or seven months, freeing up the rest of the year for the pursuit of hobbies, travel, and labors of love like playing music or raising children.

Alas, contracting may figure into your long-term career even if you don't choose it. That is because employers often fire older workers when they reach their forties and fifties. At that age their salaries have usually risen to high levels just as their increasing age pushes up the overall cost of the company's benefit plans. This makes them first in line when it comes time to cut staff. Because other firms are in no hurry to hire older workers, computer professionals who are laid off in their middle years may find that contracting is the only viable career option open to them.

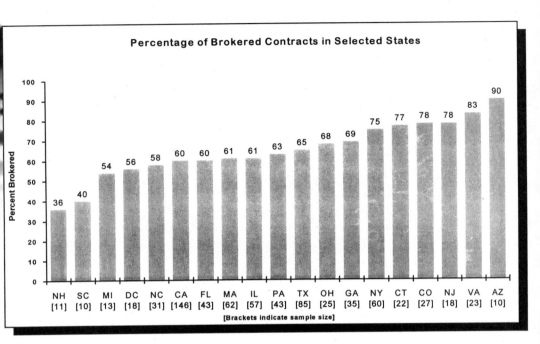

Percentage of Brokered Contracts in Selected States

[Brackets indicate sample size]

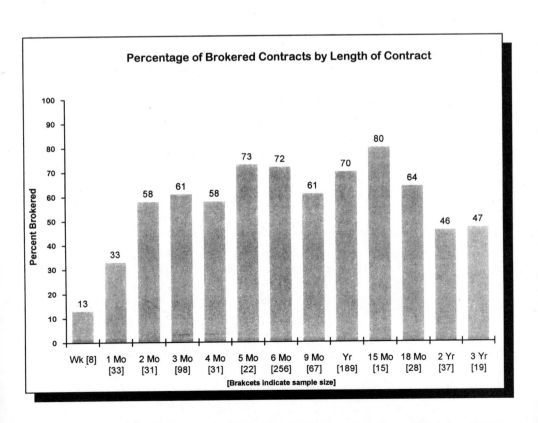

Percentage of Brokered Contracts by Length of Contract

[Brakcets indicate sample size]

FORCED INTO CONTRACTING

"I'm fifty-four and was just downsized by a company after nineteen years of employment with them. Had the company retained me for eighteen months more, the monthly retirement check I'll receive would've been more than doubled.

"So now I'm turning to consulting. I'm stunned by the rates being quoted to me—they represent more than doubling my salary—to do the very same things that company'd paid me to do. But I'm certainly not going to complain about it since I need to invest several years' of the difference to be able to afford pencils in my 'golden' years.'"

—Ginger Harold

Can I work part-time as a contractor?

Most contracts require you to work 40 hours a week, or more, on the client's site. So most agencies will not attempt to place contractors unless they are willing to work a full-time schedule. If you want part-time work you will have to find it yourself, which requires that you do some aggressive marketing.

But because part-time work usually pays poorly, you may do better to take a few short full-time contracts each a few weeks or months long and to use the time between contracts for other your pursuits. Most contractors avoid these short contracts, but they often pay well to compensate for the fact that they are so short. So you can earn as much in a few months of full-time contracting as you would in a year of working part-time. The only drawback here is that it can tough to schedule your life since you can't know in advance when you will be working and when you will be off.

Another way to find part-time work is to begin with full-time contracts and build strong relationships with your clients. When it comes time to extend a contract, you may be able to negotiate a part-time schedule because the client will prefer having you on any terms to losing you. You may also be able to pursuade past employers who recognize the value of your work to offer you part-time contracts.

Can I do contract work for remote clients from my home?

Though it is technically feasible to do excellent work for distant clients, it has traditionally been hard to find contract work that allows you to work off site, particularly if you work for large corporate IT shops. This is partly because many managers are not comfortable with being billed for your hours when they can't see you working and partly because of many development projects require that you be on site, interacting with other programmers and business users.

The growing acceptance of the Internet among business users not only makes it easier to work from your home or office, it also makes it easier to locate potential clients all over the world and sell them your services. But for the present, you shouldn't expect consulting firms or placement agencies find you off site work, unless you have a very rare and in-demand skill set.

But though off-site contracts are difficult to find, they exist. Our 1998 Real Rate Survey data showed that 18% of all contracts reported involved off site work. When we looked at contracts that were gotten through consulting firms, that percentage dropped to only 7%. Still that there were *any* shows that it is possible to find off site contracts through consulting firms.

If you are serious about working for clients off site, one strategy that often works is to move in stages towards working remotely. Build up a good relationship with local clients. Then, after they have learned to appreciate the quality of your work and to trust you, negotiate to do some of their work at your home office. Eventually, as some very talented contractors have done, you may be able to move somewhere like rural New Hampshire and bring some of these old clients "along" with you, providing you with enough steady work to keep you in business.

CONTRACTING IS CYCLICAL

"Back in 1989 through about 1993, the high tech hiring scene was just about entirely dead and salaries stunk. In my area, Ohio, employers were cackling gleefully and playing pinball with programmers' and engineers' egos as they played waiting games to get candidates to lower their price.

"I recall calling the post office to find out the name of a company placing a blind box ad, and being crabbed at by the post office worker that I was the eighth or tenth person calling to find out the same thing about the same box ad. I also remember a lot of managers at a lot of places I interviewed actually smirking.

"And, contracting back then? *Forget it!* Employers were so awash in résumés from get-a-lifer I-will-work-for-food types that they had their picks of desperate people with no dignity groveling for low paid jobs."

—Been Through the Wringer

What is the single most important thing to remember about contracting?

Contracting is cyclical! It goes through predictable boom and bust cycles that correlate to the overall economy. During the good times, like the early 1980s and the late 1990s, when industry is investing in new systems and skilled employees are scarce, contractors will be in great demand and can charge whatever the market will bear. At other times, like the period from 1989 through 1993, when clients are cutting back staff and controlling costs, layoffs will swell the pool of potential contractors and contract work will be scarce. In these periods of business recession contractors may be forced to take whatever work they can find at whatever rates are offered if they are to be able to work at all. Some contractors may even have to relocate to find contracts.

If you come into contracting during the boom times it is important to keep in mind that no boom continues forever. Save some money in an emergency fund and keep an eye on overall business conditions so that the inevitable slowdown doesn't take you by surprise.

Will contracting remain a viable career option for the next twenty or thirty years?

Computer contracting has been a viable way of earning a living with computer skills since the 1970s. But whether or not it will remain viable in the future is unknown.

The ascendancy of the Internet poses a threat to contractors in the United States and other countries that have a high standard of living, because it enables clients to locate and hire contractors from around the world, not just those in their local environment. The cost savings inherent in hiring teams of contractors who can work for $3 per hour rather than $55 per hour are compelling enough that many companies are now experimenting with moving their development work offshore.

In the worst case scenario, the only programming jobs that might remain in the United States would be those that involve strategic planning, high level design, and project coordination—precisely the jobs that our Real Salary Survey shows large corporations currently staff with *employees* rather than contractors!

But whether this shift of jobs away from the United States will actually occur is a topic of hot debate within the contractor community. Most people agree that contractors who work for smaller, local firms are more likely to remain viable if this shift occurs. It is also clear that the less generic your skills are, the more likely you are to survive.

Many contractors who work for corporations that are experimenting with offshore development feel protected from foreign competition because they believe that their skills are so unique that their clients will still need them. Others believe American companies will continue to hire English speakers who understand their businesses from an insider's perspective. But this chauvinistic attitude may dangerously underestimate the intelligence and technical skills of Irish, Russian, and Indian programmers who speak excellent English. Many of these programmers are getting significant project experience right now working for American companies that are already taking advantage of their extremely low rates.

So the wise contractor will keep an eye not only on the local business climate, but also on the state of the whole economy. They will also, wherever possible, choose to work for clients that hire locally rather than for companies that are already using low priced offshore labor.

Can you recommend any magazines I could subscribe to in order to learn more about contracting?

If you leaf through any magazine that purports to discuss "computer careers" you will immediately notice that most, if not all, of the advertising you see near career articles has been placed by consulting firms. The many thousands of dollars these firms pay these magazines, month in and month out, are what keep their publishers in business. It may even be true that it is the availability of rich consulting firms with fat advertising budgets rather than any desire to serve the computing community that motivates publishers to go into this niche.

But because these magazines are so financially dependent on consulting firms you are unlikely to read anything in them that might *offend* a consulting firm—particularly a large body shop with an equally large advertising budget. You won't find articles that explain how to negotiate a fair contract with a consulting firm or how to find clients without consulting firm help. Instead you'll read profiles of happy, well-paid agency contractors and news about the exciting new projects you will find when working through large consulting firms.

"REAL CONSULTING"

"Consulting, vs. simple contracting, is a very tough life and definitely not for most people. Consultants go where the clients are. They live in hotels and airplanes, rarely get home-cooked meals, and have to prove their value all over again with every new client. They REALLY like repeat engagements, since the clients already know what they can do for them.

"Top consultants also work under enormous pressures due to their high rates. No client wants to pay for more time than he really needs. Good niche consultancies (NEVER the big firms) recognize the difficulties their people face and provide considerable moral support along with the high incomes and benefits. Even so, the burnout rate is very high."

—William Redmond

My goal is to become a real consultant, the kind who sells advice. How does contracting fit into my plans?

Many people who call themselves consultants pay their bills by taking contract work, though you'll have to press them to discover this. Indeed, the line between "pure consulting" and contracting is a difficult one to locate or define.

Contracting can be a step towards entrepreneurial consulting. It gives you the opportunity to get to know a lot of managers and IT executives—and getting to know the people who buy consulting services is an important first step towards building a consulting career. But you may find that once you are thought of as a contractor, it will be hard to come back as an "expert" and command the kind of respect—as bogus as it may be—that an outside consultant may.

Another problem is that it takes a completely different mind-set to build a truly entrepreneurial consulting business, one that demands a continual immersion in the marketing activities that contract programmers can ignore. That is why, because it can be so easy to earn money as a contractor without marketing—and, indeed, without any sort of ongoing long term career planning—a stint of contracting is as likely to undermine your progress towards a more entrepreneurial consulting career as it is to enhance it.

WHAT DO YOU LOVE ABOUT CONTRACTING?

"1. My success depends more on how well I do my job, less on how well I can kiss butt. I'm good at the former, not very good at the latter! Contracting works well for people like me!

"2. No glass ceiling for women.

"3. I'm not complainin' about the CA$H!

"4. Respect - Even though I made equal contributions as an employee, people who are paying me much more money seem more appreciative. Amazing how that works!

"5. The freedom of choosing projects that interest you, vs. ones that your consulting firm has already accepted and delegated to you.

"6. The time flexibility. (I never was a 8-5'er, More of a 9ish to past the bewitching hour person.) Once a client realizes you can produce and they don't have to stand over your shoulder, they don't care *when* you do the work or where you do it, as long as you get it done.

"7. I have started taking more vacations. In spite of this, I still make more than twice what I did as an employee!"

—Tracy

CHAPTER 2

CAN I BE A CONTRACTOR?

What are the minimum qualifications you need to become a contractor?

To break into contracting you need to have *paid experience with in-demand technical skills*. These skills and these skills alone will open up contracting opportunities. When you set out to find a contract, your education and your previous work experience are irrelevant. To get in the door you need to have had paid experience using the specific software and hardware products that clients in your geographical area are looking for.

What do you mean by "in-demand technical skills?"

When we say someone has a "technical skill" we mean that that person is familiar with all the software—and possibly the hardware—used in a particular environment. This environment usually consists of a computer language or interpreter, along with the associated operating system or systems, databases, and development tools that support it. These development tools can include code libraries, debuggers, and compilers. To claim mastery of a skill set you may also have to show that you have had paid experience working in a specific applications area, for example, life insurance processing, embedded systems, or game development.

Consulting firm ads often refer to nothing more than a computer language. But to get an interview you will need to have the entire skill set. For example, to qualify for a contract advertised with a headline that says, "C++ IN SAN FRANCISCO," you may need experience not only with C++ programming but also with UNIX, CGI scripts, Javascript and dynamic HTML. Another "C++ in SAN FRANCISCO" contract might require that you know how to write hardware drivers for Window's NT. Each of these ads refers to a completely different skill set though the computer language involved is the same. You will only be able to get these contracts if your resume shows experience with both the language and the other factors that make up the client's software environment.

What kinds of skills are most valuable?

Generally the skill sets that are most in demand are those that you can learn only by working in large-scale production environments or in software product development shops. In fact, the easier a skill is to pick up at home, the less likely it is that you will be able to get a high-paying contract using it.

In fact, the most highly paid contractors are rarely those who work with the most difficult code. Instead, they are the contractors who work with expensive, high-end software packages like PeopleSoft's Human Resources software, SAP, or BAAN. These are expensive packages found only at huge corporations, and it is very difficult to get training in them unless you work for a company that has this software installed.

When only a few people have paid experience using a package that is the temporary darling of the business world, the rates these people can command can skyrocket. For example, in 1998, contractors with previous paid experience using PeopleSoft were routinely billing rates over $100 per hour. Their median rate, according to the 1998 Real Rate Survey, was $95 per hour. The median rate for SAP was $83 per hour, $23 per hour higher than the median rate for all contracts.

There is often strong demand for the development tools being hyped by the trade press, as was the case with Java in 1998. However, you are only likely to find a contract using this kind of new technology if you have already been paid to use it on a previous contract—which puts many programmers in a Catch-22 situation.

How important is it to have paid experience?

You must have some paid experience on your résumé if you hope to have a consulting firm place you on a contract. You don't have to have a lot but you need to have enough to establish yourself as a business professional rather than a hacker or hobbyist.

You may be able to find a client who will be willing to hire you without paid experience, but you will have to find that client yourself. Consulting firms won't place you since clients expect that the people they hire through consulting firms will be experienced pros and they define "experienced" as meaning, "having paid experience."

How much total experience do most contractors have?

As you can see from the chart below, the 1998 Real Rate Survey data for the 676 contractors who reported their years of experience showed that 56% had from 3-15 years of experience and 75% had between 3 and 20 years of experience. (Note that this figure may be slightly understated as some contractors report only the years of experience they have with a given software tool, not overall.)

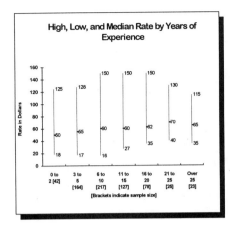

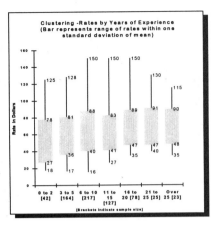

Only 6% of these contractors reported having less than 3 years of experience, and both their median rate and the range their rates clustered in were lower than that of more experienced contractors.

Both median rates and the range in which rates cluster increased gradually as the number of years of experience increased to the 20 year level, dropping off slightly after that. But the *number* of contractors decreased sharply as the years of experience increased.

This data reinforces the subjective observation that most contractors have from 3 to 15 years of experience. After that it becomes harder to keep skills current and maintain a contracting career, though the rising median rate for the highly experienced contractors in our sample suggests that those older contractors who do maintain their skills can do quite well.

What should I do if I have technical skills but no paid experience?

Take any entry level salaried position you can find that uses your existing skills and exposes you to the rest of the software you need to know to be able to claim experience with an entire skill set. If you are a college student, be sure to take advantage of college co-op employment programs. When you go out looking for your first job, don't worry about the salary. Just concentrate on getting yourself into an environment where you'll get good software experience.

If you can't find an entry level job, another approach is to volunteer and use your skills to help a nonprofit group. Design a website for your local Girl Scout troupe, crafts co-op, or church or help a local disaster relief effort. This kind of effort shows potential employers and clients that you are serious about using your computer skills and may give you an opportunity to demonstrate their quality. The connections you make with local businesspeople while doing volunteer work may also result in them recommending you for employment opportunities.

Once you land an entry level job—almost any entry level job—and put in a few months getting paid experience using your chosen software tools—even very poorly paid experience–you'll be amazed at how differently you'll be treated by consulting firm recruiters. As little as a year of paid experience may be enough to get recruiters excited if you have been using in-demand software at a company other companies have heard of. So while it may be daunting to look for that first, hard-to-find break-in position, keep in mind that you only need to find *one* and that once you have some paid experience, you can very quickly double or even triple your earnings.

Can I become a computer contractor by taking a mail order course?

I have never met a contractor who was able to build a career based on training received from a correspondence school. These schools have never had a good reputation among professionals and you will not impress anyone one with a certificate granted by one.

The problem is that while these schools can sell you a computer and a few compilers, their courses can't give you the kind of hands-on help you need to really master programming. Neither will working on the mediocre computer systems they sell you give you experience with the kinds of complex, networked business systems that most contractors are hired to work on. There is a lot more to being a programmer than writing and compiling a program or two.

If you want to teach yourself at home, invest in a high end computer, buy your own compilers and how-to books, and visit the online newsgroups and bulletin boards where programmers discuss your chosen languages, platforms, and databases. If you feel you need formal classes where you'll get a chance to ask questions and get guidance as to what to study next, check out local community colleges, professional development institutes, and college extension services, all of which give courses in popular computer software.

Some contractors have also found that a good approach to mastering new skills is to get a hold of the requirements for certification in the specialty they are interested in and then master the topics required for the certification exams. However, until you can put some paid experience on your résumé, no training, no matter how impressive the source, is going to open up contracting to you as a viable career path. Use your training to get an entry level job and plan to make your move into contracting a few years later, after you have honed your skills and accumulated a respectable amount of paid experience.

How do consulting firm recruiters evaluate skills?

Recruiters rarely have the ability to interpret what the experience described on your résumé really means. All too often, they simply do a "byte by byte" compare, looking for an exact match between the acronyms found on the résumés they receive and the ones on the open job orders they've gotten from clients.

For example, if a job order asks for someone who knows "CGI scripting" and your résumé lists "UNIX," "Perl," and "HTML" but makes no mention of CGI, few recruiters will know that Perl is commonly used to write CGI scripts, so you may never hear of the opening.

Because you can't count on recruiters to infer that you have technical skills other than those that are spelled out explicitly on your résumé, when you contact recruiters you must make sure to list the names of each and every piece of current software that you have ever worked with.

A CONTRACTOR EXPRESSES HIS FRUSTRATION WITH RECRUITERS

"None of them knows technical stuff. They're all after quick commissions—and the quicker the better, whatever the consequences for client and consultant.

"You've seen the advertisements: 'Unlike other agencies, we carefully match your skills and interests with our clients' needs to find only the best jobs for you!' Don't believe them. These people don't understand your skills, care little about your interests, and in most cases have no real idea of what their clients' needs are. Turnover is everything in the recruiting business, and agents try to maximize it however they can.

"Make the mistake of publishing your résumé (or even a list of buzzwords) on some Web site or faxing it to five recruiters, and you'll be swamped with useless telephone calls about inappropriate jobs you don't want, can't do, and won't get. Did you mention a three-month fling with VxWorks back in 1992? R-r-r-ring! Someone halfway across the country wants your VxWorks expertise! Never mind that you clearly stated that you're seeking C++ assignments on UNIX. If there's a 0.2% chance of making a sale, the recruiter will call you.

"I refuse to give out my résumé to new recruiters who don't call with details of real assignments that interest me. I don't want to be in anyone's database, and I don't want silly keyword-searching software to find me the perfect job."

—Irked

How technically savvy are the recruiters who read my résumé?

Most recruiters are hired for their sales skills and come to recruiting after working as salespeople in other fields. Though they work hard at hiding it, many have no idea what the terms on your résumé really refer to. They may know that the keywords they see there match those that their clients are asking for, but beyond that, expect nothing.

How important is the amount of experience I have with a skill?

This varies with how desperate the client is for a contractor, how aggressive a salesperson the recruiter may be, and how exact the requirements were on the client's requisition.

If the skill needed for a contract is in great demand and the client hasn't specified an experience level, you should be able to be considered for the position if you have had at least six months paid experience with the required skill. If the skill is more common, two or three years of paid experience may be required. Some clients specify the exact number of years of experience they want, either because they truly believe that the job calls for someone with that amount of experience or because their requisition form has a "number of years" field and they felt they had to fill in something. If the number of years is specified, recruiters may refuse to let you interview for a contract unless the years of experience listed on your résumé matches the number of years of experience the client requested.

However, because requisition forms are often filled out by non-technical managers and HR staff, don't be surprised if a recruiter tells you that the client needs someone with five years of Java experience or ten years of experience with Windows NT. You will often have to educate recruiters. If they still don't get it after you've explained why *no one* has that kind of experience, give up dealing with them, since entrenched idiocy of this sort is the mark of the kind of recruiter you don't want to deal with.

How do I determine if there is a market for my specific technical skills?

The simplest way to check out demand is to do keyword searches on several of the active headhunting boards found on the World Wide Web. While these boards do not list all available contracts, they list a representative sample and should quickly give you an idea of how much demand there is for your skills.

When you search one of these boards for a particular skill, pay attention to the other skills you see listed in association with the skill you're checking out. Because clients are almost always looking for people with complete sets of skills, if your skill is commonly found associated with other skills you won't be able to find contracts unless you have most or all of the constellation of skills cited.

For example, listed jobs requiring HTML may also ask for Javascript, Perl and Unix experience. If your only experience is with HTML alone, you may not be able to qualify for any of these contracts. Another common constellation of skills is the IBM "big iron" set that includes, COBOL, DB/2 and CICS. It is much harder to find work if your sole experience is in writing batch COBOL programs, than if you have experience with the entire big iron software suite.

WEB JOB BOARDS WHERE YOU CAN SEARCH FOR CONTRACTS BY KEYWORD

http://www.headhunter.com

http://www.computerjobs.com

http://www.dice.com

http://www.net-temps.com

http://www.computerwork.com

I see several ads in the local paper offering contracts that call for an obscure database I know. Does this mean I can contract with this specialty?

Not necessarily. It may only mean that a local company is looking for a single programmer for a short contract that calls for that skill. Because it *is* obscure, all the local consulting firms are advertising in hopes of finding one contractor with that experience. But if the skill is really obscure, it may be very hard to find any subsequent contracts that call for it.

Where can I find out more about conditions for contractors with skills like mine where I live?

Your best resource is the other contractors in your area who have skills and on-the-job experience similar to your own. If you haven't already met people like this on the job, you may be able to find them at meetings of local consultants' groups, like the ICCA (Independent Computer Consultants Association) or at an IEEE (Institute of Electrical and Electronic Engineers) Consultant's SIG (Special Interest Group). If you can't find a local branch of one of these organizations, check out other groups that attract computer professionals, such as users groups or chapters of national groups like the ACM (Association for Computing Machinery) or SIM (The Society for Information Management).

The other contractors you encounter at these meetings can warn you about unethical local consulting companies and clients. They can refer you to the better local consulting firms. They can point you towards projects that are just staffing up. Best of all, they can give you a better idea of what demand for contractors has been like in your market over the past few years.

I don't have "hot" skills but I do have a great deal of experience with the software development process. Is this worth anything?

Not much. Recruiters rarely understand broad-based experience or the software development process. Occasionally you will run into one who has an IT background and serves a clientele of intelligent managers that value a broad based technical background, but these recruiters are the exception, not the rule.

However, if you have a great deal of experience in software development but lack paid experience with the currently hot technical skills, all is not lost. You add new skills to your résumé through self education and then take the steps needed to get paid experience with those skills. We'll be discussing this further in Chapter 10, "How Can I Do Better?"

Furthermore, though your skills may not be the trendiest, searching the head-hunter job boards may reveal that there are companies that use the technologies you are familiar with who need contractors and are willing to pay you well for your skills. Though they were far from the cutting edge, there were still contractors earning a steady living in 1998 working with FORTRAN, ADA and IMS.

HOW TO FIND LOCAL CONSULTANTS ONLINE

Locate Chapters of Professional Organizations

http://www.icca.org

Look for local chapters and attend a meeting. Though the group's focus is independent consulting, many contractors are active in ICCA chapters.

http://www.ieee.org/usab/BUSINESS/network.aicn.html

This page features a list of local consultant's SIGS around the country.

http://www.acm.org

Search for a local consultants group. The ACM sponsors several.

http://www.simnet.org

Meet IT executives and other consultants at local SIM meetings.

Search for Local SIGS

Use the multi-engine search facility at **http://www.dogpile.com** to locate local Consultant's SIGS. Search on the keywords "Consultant," "SIG," and the name of your city.

Find Peers Through Newsgroups

You can often find local people with your skills online participating in one of the many language-, platform-, and database- specific newsgroups, which you can find through the newsgroup super-site, **http://www.dejanews.com**.

And don't forget to visit us at **http://www.realrates.com/bbs/**.

I used to be a programmer but I've been a manager for the last five years. Can I become a contractor?

Managers who have lost their technical skills are in a very difficult position when it comes time to look for contract work. Few contracts call for pure management skill, and out-of-date technical skills are the kiss of death in contracting.

However, managers who have managed to keep their skills current and who have managed projects that use state-of-the-art technology can find contracts where their role is to implement the new technology in a company that has no previous experience with it.

For example, Smalltalkers who have made their way through the development cycle in a team leader or management role report being hired as contractors to head up pilot projects in companies that are investigating the use of object oriented development strategies.

Managerial level technical people with experience in disciplines like capacity planning and network design also report finding contracts that require expert knowledge of their specialties. Both these types of contracts may pay extremely well—with rates of $100 per hour or more not unheard of. However, they are not common and it may take some research and networking with other professionals with similar backgrounds to find them—or to locate the types of specialized consulting firms that place people with these skills.

But bear in mind that the contractors who find these kinds of managerial contracts are almost always those who have maintained their technical skills and who have mastered complex technically oriented disciplines. The manager whose prime skill has been managing other people and maneuvering within the political context of a single company rarely has skills that transfer to another environment and may find it impossible to find any sort of contract work at all.

Can I be a contractor if I am not a programmer but have other computer-related skills?

You can find contract opportunities for help desk personnel, technical writers, people who do network installation and support, and repair technicians. The rates are usually not as high as those for programmers, but the work is there.

Is it a good idea to begin contracting straight out of college?

College students often have experience with up-to-date technology, especially if they have worked co-op jobs while attending school. So about-to-be new grads may find themselves offered tempting contracts by recruiters, ones that pay far better than the starting salaries they may be offered for salaried employment.

But it is rarely a good idea to start contracting at the beginning of your professional career. This is because your first "real" job tends to define the entire future course of your career. The work you do in your first job, the software libraries and developer's tools it exposes you to, as well as the industry it places you in and the phase of the development cycle that you experience on the job, all set the tone for the rest of your computer career.

For example, if your first job involved working as a developer at a software house that developed off-the-shelf PC software, you would learn a great deal not only about how to code and test that software in a marketing-driven production environment but also about how the off-the-shelf software business works. Contrast this with the experience you'd get if your first job was in a financial services company where computer systems center on IBM mainframes and where "development" projects involved shoehorning new function into systems designed fifteen years ago or slapping interactive front ends on ancient databases. After spending a year as a financial services programmer, you'd find it difficult to move into the product development shop, even if you had been writing software using the same languages used by the product developers, because the overall environments are so different. So taking a first job in a financial services firm could result in your spending decades writing financial services software!

That is why it is so important to choose a first job that puts you into a rich software environment in an industry that interests you. But when you sign on as a contractor, you give up your ability to choose what your first assignment will be. You will have to go wherever the consulting firm sends you. Even worse, because contract assignments tend to expose you only to the software environments you already know, as an entry-level contractor you are likely to use only the software you already mastered as a college student and never receive additional training. Because there is little on your résumé, the only contracts you may be able to fill are those where you code off someone else's specs or do maintenance on some dead-end system that no contractor with better skills would touch. These kinds of contracts add nothing to your résumé and make it hard to get interesting work on your second and third assignments.

So the only time it makes sense to begin your career as a contractor is when you don't have other, more attractive, opportunities to choose from. For example, in a tough job market contract work may be all that is available, and your only chance to be considered for full-time employment may be to take a contract that, if you do well, might lead to a regular salaried job. But in a strong market, a salaried job with an employer who will give you training is *always* a better option.

When is the best time to start contracting?

The best time to begin contracting is after you have worked for a few years as a salaried employee. Three years of paid experience during which you have worked on two or three projects is the best preparation for a successful contracting career.

With a few years of salaried jobs under your belt you'll have a résumé packed with paid experience involving a variety of tools. You'll have learned about the business aspects of an industry and have developed a sense where you'd like your professional career to go. By then, too, you should have learned to discriminate between the kinds of contracts that will further enhance your ability to earn a living and the dead end time-sinks that will render your skills obsolete and decrease your long-term prospects.

However, since this is not an ideal world, many people find themselves starting contracting careers with less experience, often after the sudden loss of what they thought was a secure job. If this is your situation and if you feel a strong pull towards contracting, don't fret about beginning in less than ideal conditions. Many a contractor has begun contracting out of dire need only to discover that they enjoy the work—and the pay—far more than they did their old, salaried job. And if after giving contracting a trial, you find you don't have skills strong enough to support a contracting career now, you should have no trouble finding another salaried job, perhaps even one that pays a better salary than the one you left. Employers tend to look at your current salary when judging how much to offer you. So a few months of earning contracting rates may make you eligible for a higher salary if you do go back to being an employee.

Do some types of personalities do better than others as contractors?

The people who enjoy contracting and stick with it tend to be people who enjoy the actual work of programming and don't take the outer trappings of the business world too seriously. They get their satisfaction from doing a job well and from solving difficult problems, not from external motivators like awards or promotions.

People who enjoy contracting enjoy constant change and have a high tolerance for confusion. Projects that staff up with contractors are often—though by no means always—badly managed projects that are attempting to make deadlines by throwing manpower at systems crippled by poor planning and bad design. So contractors often find themselves thrown into the middle of a chaotic situation where they are expected to figure out what is going on with a minimum of guidance.

It helps to have a lot of confidence about your abilities but it is just as important to have the high level of ability that justifies that confidence. A second rate employee can get away with a lot that a contractor cannot. To succeed as a contractor you need to be the kind of person who always does a very good job with little supervision. When you come into a new contract, you'll have about two weeks to get up to speed, master the environment, and become productive. If you find this daunting, contracting is not for you.

To succeed as a contractor, you will also have to have a high tolerance for uncertainty. You will never know where your next job is coming from. Your current contract may last three years or end, unexpectedly, tomorrow. Demand for contractors waxes and wanes with the business cycle. Sometimes you'll have five clients all clamoring for your services at the same time. Other times it may take six months to find a single contract. If you like your life to be predictable, if you get ulcers worrying about how you're going to pay your bills, contracting, no matter how good your skills, will be a nightmare.

I have a lot of bills. Could I pay them off faster as a contractor?

While it might be tempting to take a high-paying contract to earn money quickly to pay off pressing bills, the fact that you *have* pressing bills may be a sign that you aren't good at managing your money. If this is the case, contracting could prove a disastrous choice. As a contractor you may earn high rates, but your contract can evaporate with two weeks notice–sometimes less. Once that contract is gone, it may take weeks or months to find a new one. If you are already living on the financial edge, one unexpected contract termination may be all it takes to drive you into bankruptcy.

Contracting provides further challenges to people who aren't disciplined about managing their money. If you are sloppy about money matters and do your contract work as independent contractor, (a topic we'll discuss in detail in Chapter 3, "W-2, 1099, or Corp.?") you may get yourself into serious trouble with the IRS. That's because when you work as an independent contractor the checks you receive from clients and agencies do not have taxes and social security payments withheld from them. It is your responsibility to pay those taxes on a quarterly basis.

If you have lots of bills and debts, it is all too easy to spend those client checks when they come in, telling yourself that you'll use future checks to pay off your taxes. If those future checks don't materialize or if they follow the path of earlier checks, at tax time you can easily find yourself owing the IRS tens of thousands of dollars–dollars you have already thoughtlessly spent.

Experienced contractors suggest that you should only start contracting when you have amassed a financial cushion that could take you through a couple months of unemployment–and that could cover six months of living expenses, including car payments and rent or mortgage payments.

By the same token, it's not a good idea to rush into contracting just because you lost your job and are hard up for a new one. If you don't have the kind of résumé that can sustain a rewarding contracting career, you would do better to look for a new salaried job that could give you training in new skills that could eventually make a successful contracting career possible.

Is taking a salaried job with a consulting firm a good way to break into contracting?

Not usually. As a salaried consultant you'll do the same kinds of work that contractors do but you'll do it for a lot less pay.

According to our 1998 Real Salary Survey data, *salaried* consultants earn a median salary of $70,000 per year. For a consultant who works all year long, this translates into an hourly rate of $35 per hour. Our Real Rate Survey Data shows that *brokered hourly rate* contractors earn a median hourly rate of $55 per hour. So you can see that even with three months of down time, the hourly rate contractor earns $86,000 which equals or surpasses what they'd earn working all year at a salary, even if they have to buy their own benefits. If they work eleven months, they earn $103,000!

But there is another factor to consider: consulting firms rarely hire people they can't keep busy year round. So the very fact that a consulting firm wants to hire you suggests that they believe they can keep you working for more than nine months. The only other thing it could suggest is that they are planning to lay you off at the end of this contract. If that is the case, you would still be a lot better off working the contract at a high hourly rate rather than on salary since with the high hourly rate you will earn more money and can buy yourself health and disability insurance that won't disappear when you are laid off!

There is another, less obvious, drawback to working as the salaried employee of a consulting firm. These firms may offer you job security, but to keep your job you will have to take any contract the company comes up with. In practice, this often means that you will be forced to take long contracts that involve a ninety-minute one-way commute, or that you'll be stuck in long-term projects that use fading technologies and contribute nothing to your own long term employability.

This lack of control over the projects to which you get assigned is the worst feature of consulting firm employment, since, as we have seen, the key to keeping a contracting career alive over time is to select each project with an eye to how it adds to your skills and keeps your career viable.

Won't I learn more about the consulting business working as an employee of a successful consulting firm?

While working for a large consulting firm, you may learn something about how large consulting firms do business. However, little of what you observe in a large firm will translate into techniques you can use when *you* set out to consult. As a small consulting outfit you will have to use very different marketing techniques than those used by large, national companies with their lock on corporate preferred vendor lists and their huge advertising budgets.

Nor is it likely that you will get a chance to observe how the big guys market if you sign on as a consulting firm salaried employee. Most large firms have their impressive senior staff sell projects and only bring in the young new hires who do the actual work after that client has signed on. As one of those new hires, you won't see how the firm sells its projects, since you won't be brought onto a project until after it is sold.

If you work for a small locally owned, company you might be able to learn more. But as is always the case when you work for any small company, whether this will happen depends on the personalities of the firm's principals. Some take pleasure in training talented newcomers and in helping them develop their own skills. Others treat employees as potential competitors and jealously guard any "trade secrets" from them.

My spouse isn't crazy about the idea of my giving up a steady job. Will they change their mind when the money starts rolling in?

They may. But don't count on it. The stress of not knowing whether the family breadwinner is going to be employed in a few months is very hard on some spouses. So is the stress of not knowing when, or if, there will be a family vacation. Having you constantly moving from workplace to workplace can also add to a spouse's insecurity, to say nothing of playing havoc with the way you've been dealing with daycare arrangements and school schedules. If contracting forces you to travel, it can put a heavy burden on the spouse suddenly forced to cope alone with kids and other family responsibilities. So a unilateral decision to start a contracting career can easily trigger a family crisis.

That's why it's never a good idea to spring your decision to try contracting on your spouse without warning. Discuss the issue in advance and make sure that your spouse is willing to share the risks that you will be taking on before you burn any bridges. If they aren't, don't force the issue. Some contractors say that having a supportive spouse—particularly one with a secure job of their own that provides family health insurance—has been the single most important factor in their being able to handle the stresses of contracting and to make it a success.

WHY I LOVE CONTRACTING

"To a large degree, whoever you work for runs your life. If you work for a regular company, that company runs your life. If you work for a large consulting firm, that consulting firm runs your life. But if you work for yourself, you (with God's help) run your life!

"This can be scary! You can go bankrupt if you're not careful! But you sink or swim based on your own performance and decisions—not on somebody else's! And there is a lot more variety in what you do, because when you are running a business you have to be sort of a jack of all trades.

"I still remember an experience I had while I was working on the first contract I landed after going independent. I didn't have my office set up yet, so I was sitting on the corner of my bed, with my TV going, typing away at a keyboard that was sitting on my lap, and staring at a computer monitor that was set up on a TV tray. It was past midnight, and all of a sudden I said to myself, 'Golly! I'd better get to bed or I won't be able to get up for work tomorrow.' And then I said, 'Wait a minute! This is work!' And then I remember thinking, 'This is cool!'"

—Bob McAdams

CHAPTER 3

W-2, 1099, OR CORP?

Do I have to establish my business in a particular legal form?

There are several different legal statuses under which you can perform your work as a computer contractor.

Many contractors work as the employee of a consulting firm. If you do this, you can work as either a regular benefited salaried employee, treated like any other regular employee, or you can choose to work as an unbenefited hourly employee who is paid an hourly rate for every hour worked. Many contractors prefer this latter kind of arrangement. The unbenefited employee contractor who is paid an hourly rate is usually called a "W-2" or "W-2 contractor."

Alternatively, if your business meets certain standards which we will discuss below, you may work as a self-employed businessperson or "independent contractor," abbreviated "IC." Some ICs are sole proprietors. These are often called "1099 ICs" or simply "1099s." Others form their own corporations and do their contracting work as the employee of that corporation. Yet another status with which contractors may work is as a partner in a limited liability company (LLC).

What is a W-2 Contractor?

A W-2 contractor, named after the tax form employers mail their employees at the end of the year, is an employee who is paid an hourly rate for actual hours worked rather than a fixed salary. W-2 contractors generally do not receive benefits such as health, life, or disability insurance, nor do they get paid sick days or holidays. They usually *do* get paid a lot more than salaried consultants, which is why many contractors who work through consulting firms prefer to work as W-2 contractors.

Because they are employees, the law requires that W-2 contractors be paid on a regular schedule and that the consulting firms who employ them withhold taxes from their paychecks. The employer firm must also pay the IRS for the employer's share of Social Security and Medicare taxes—an amount that matches what em-

33

ployees themselves pay, as well as any state-mandated payments such as contributions to the state unemployment compensation fund or premiums for required workers' compensation coverage.

Unlike the salaried consulting firm employee who is hired for an indefinite term, the W-2 contractor is hired on a per-project basis that is defined in a written contract. This contract usually sets out the length of the contract, the conditions under which it may be extended or terminated, and when payment is to occur. The W-2 contractor's contract is an *employment contract* regulated by employment law, not a business contract between two independent entities.

What are the advantages of working as an employee contractor?

Though many contractors prefer to work as independent businesspeople, there are some advantages to working as an employee contractor that you should consider before choosing your contracting status.

Not the least of these advantages is simplicity. As an employee you do not have to worry about keeping detailed business records, filing appropriate government forms, withholding your own taxes, or complying with local business ordinances.

Another benefit is that when you work as an employee, you are covered by labor laws that prescribe harsh penalties for the employer who does not pay employees on a regularly scheduled basis or who indulges in obvious racial or gender discrimination.

This legal protection vanishes when you become a self-employed businessperson. Independents often find it tough to collect money owed them. Clients or consulting firms may delay payment for months and the legal steps needed to extract payment from a balky client or consulting firm are more expensive and cumbersome for independents than they are for employees.

Another benefit of working as an employee contractor is that should your contract terminate without warning and leave you without a job, you may be able to file for state unemployment compensation which will provide enough weekly income to keep you going until you find another contract. Since unemployment compensation is only for employees, self-employed contractors have no such safety net.

What are the disadvantages of working as an employee contractor?

The biggest disadvantage of working as an employee contractor is that employees cannot set up robust *retirement plans*, such as SEP, SIMPLE or Keogh plans, that both shelter current income from taxes and let investments grow untaxed.

Though consulting firms may offer access to 401(k) plans and employer matching funds, few employee contractors remain employed by the same consulting firm long enough to qualify for the employer's matching funds, and 401(k) plans do not let them shelter as much income as do the plans available only to the self-employed.

Another huge disadvantage to being an unbenefited W-2 contractor is that W-2 contractors cannot buy the *group health insurance* available to the self-employed. This means that, unless there is a spouse in the family whose job provides family health insurance, the only health plans available to W-2 contractors may be *individual* health policies. Unfortunately, insurers who offer individual health policies, including John Alden, Golden Rule, and Mutual of Omaha, are still allowed to discriminate against people who have any history of illness in their family and to refuse them coverage. This means that unbenefited W-2 contractors may find themselves unable to buy any health insurance at all.

Another disadvantage that affects some W-2 contractors more than others is that as an employee the only business tax deductions they can claim are *employee* business deductions. This is rarely a problem for the contractor who works on the client's hardware with the client's software at the client's premises and whose business-related expenses are therefore low. In this case, the loss of tax deductions is balanced by the fact that the W-2 only pays *half* the social security tax that a self-employed IC pays. However, if you invest heavily in hardware, software and training, maintain an office, and do a kind of contracting that requires significant amounts of travel, your business expenses may be significant and being unable to deduct them because you are a W-2 contractor could cost you money.

What formal steps are required to work as an employee contractor?

If you work as the employee of a consulting firm, whether as a W-2 contractor or as a salaried employee, the only paperwork you will need to supply will be a W-4 form with your Social Security number on it and a birth certificate or naturalization papers to prove that you are an American citizen. If you are a legal immigrant, you will need to present your HB-1 visa or Green Card.

Is a sole proprietor the same thing as an independent contractor?

A sole proprietor is another name for an independent contractor or IC. If you are self-employed and have not taken any legal steps to set up a business entity like a corporation or Limited Liability Company (LLC), you are, by default, a sole proprietor. No formal action is needed to set up a sole proprietorship. As a sole proprietor you must keep detailed records of your income and expenses and then report them on Schedule C of the IRS 1040 tax package when you file your taxes. You will also have to pay quarterly tax withholding payments to the IRS and to state and local taxation authorities.

What is an 1099 Contractor?

The terms "1099" or "1099 contractor" come from the name of the form clients and consulting firms send to the IRS at the end of the year when reporting how much an independent contractor was paid. Technically, 1099 forms should only be sent to sole proprietors or people working through unincorporated legal partnerships, not to contractors working as employees of their own corporations.

However, in practice, many organizations send 1099s to one-person incorporated contractors too. So the term is sometimes used to refer to any type of non-employee contractor. In these pages, however, we will use the terms "1099" or "1099 IC" to refer *only* to sole proprietors and not to incorporated contractors working as employees of their own corporations.

What are the benefits of being a 1099 independent contractor?

1099 ICs may deduct all legitimate business expenses from their income and pay taxes only on the net income that remains. This is one reason that many contractors prefer to work as independents.

They may set up retirement plans designed for the self-employed, including Keogh Plans, SIMPLES and SEPs, which let them shelter up to 20% of each year's earnings from taxes and allow that money to be invested, untaxed, until they retire or become disabled. These 1099 ICs may also deduct a proportion of their payments for health insurance on their taxes.

Because they are self-employed, 1099 ICs can buy into the group health insurance plans open to small businesses that are available through professional associations and civic groups like the Chamber of Commerce.

What are the drawbacks of being a 1099 independent contractor?

1099 ICs have to keep far more detailed and accurate records than do employees. Since they do not have money withheld from their checks, they are personally responsible for paying quarterly withholding taxes to federal, state, city, and, sometimes, county tax authorities.

Unless contractors can document significant amounts of allowable business expenses, they may also end up paying more taxes than employees. This is because self-employed businesspeople pay federal Self-Employment taxes instead of Social Security taxes. This Self-employment tax is currently 15.3% of self-employment income after expenses are deducted, which is double what employees pay for their Social Security taxes.

Another disadvantage, mentioned earlier, is that 1099 ICs are not covered by labor law. So collecting money owed by clients and consulting firms may be far more difficult. When you are an IC, timely payment occurs only at the whim of the client, rather than at the behest of federal law.

What legal steps do I have to take to become a 1099 contractor?

There are no formal legal steps needed to become an independent contractor. Once you have found a client or consulting firm who will pay you on that basis, all you have to do is keep track of all your business-related income and expenses and report your business income on a Schedule C when you file your federal income tax return.

Once you are earning IC income, you must pay Federal and State quarterly income tax withholding payments every April 15, June 15, September 15 and January 15. As a self-employed person, you must withhold an amount equal to the amount of taxes you paid in the previous year or 90% of your final tax liability for the current year.

You can get a package of information and tax forms, including a form you can use to estimate your federal liability for the year by calling the IRS Forms Line 1-800-829-3676 and asking for forms 1040 ES/V and 1040 ES. Or you can download the forms from the IRS Web site which you'll find located at

`http://www.irs.ustreas.gov/plain/forms_pubs/index.html`.

Requirements for reporting independent contractor income to your state and local taxing authority vary widely from state to state. Contact your state taxation authority as soon as you start earning independent contractor income to find out what their requirements are.

Don't forget to withhold taxes from each and every check you receive! In January of each year, each company you work for as an IC will mail a 1099 form to the IRS and to your state taxing authority. This form will list the total amount they have paid you over the course of the year. They will also mail you a copy for your records. You should *not* send your copy to the IRS when you file your taxes as the client company has already done this.

If you move during the year, be sure to notify any company for which you have done independent contracting work of your new address so that they can mail you your copy of the 1099 form.

One of the biggest perils of contracting on a 1099 basis is that it is very easy to lose track of income and forget to withhold the hefty amount (30 - 45% of each check) that must be paid as federal, state, and local taxes.

What do I do if a company sends me a 1099 statement with an incorrect amount on it?

By law, companies must mail out 1099 statements for the previous year by the end of January. Because errors do occur, it is important that you keep good records of all checks you receive and when you received them so that you can double check your 1099 forms against your records.

Some discrepancies you find may result because your 1099 form includes checks that were issued in the last week of December though you didn't log them in as income until the beginning of the following year. The date the check was issued determines the year in which the income is reported. So you must include these payments when checking your 1099s against your income.

If you still find errors, immediately notify the accounting department of the company who made the error and fax or mail them any documentation necessary to support your claim. Ask them to file a corrected 1099 form with the correct amount. Usually this is all that is needed.

If the company still refuses to change the amount on your 1099 form, you will have to pay taxes on the incorrect amount listed on the 1099. At that point if you have rock solid documentation to show that the company is fraudulently claiming to have paid you money you did not receive, you may consider turning the matter over to the IRS's Criminal Investigation Division along with your supporting documentation. A company who issues fraudulent 1099s is committing a crime.

What is involved in incorporating?

When you incorporate you create a legal entity that is governed by state and federal corporate law. This entity is created by filing various forms in the state that will be the corporation's legal home. If this is not the state or states in which you will you will be doing business, you will also have to file forms to establish your corporation as a "foreign corporation" in those states.

Once you have set up your corporation, you'll have to pay state and federal corporate taxes on the money your corporation earns. Some of these earnings will be passed on to you as your salary an employee of the corporation. Then, like any employee, you will have to pay taxes on that salary. Other income taken in by your corporation will be distributed to shareholders at set times as dividends. You can set up corporate benefit programs and pay benefits to your employees—which in a one-person corporation will be yourself.

Isn't it true that Incorporation is a great way to avoid paying taxes?

Many newcomers believe that incorporating is a great way to shelter earnings from taxes and quite a few books published in the past have reinforced this impression. But state and federal tax law changes have done much to decrease the attractiveness of incorporation as a tax shelter alone. For example, you may run into trouble if, in order to avoid paying Income and Social Security taxes, you don't pay yourself a reasonable salary as the corporation's employee. In some cases, incorporation may even be more expensive than working as a sole proprietor.

The act of incorporating your business can also be expensive. For example, it cost $900 to incorporate in California in 1998. Then there are ongoing maintenance costs. For example, some states, including Massachusetts, will make you pay a minimum corporate tax even if your corporation has no earnings in a given year. Others, including California, assess franchise fees on corporations whether or not they are profitable.

Once you incorporate, you must comply with legal regulations that vary from state to state. These often require that you file forms with the state at a given time. You must also comply with federal and state regulations that apply to employers, even if your corporation's only employee is yourself. Filing taxes becomes much more complicated, too, and you will probably have to pay a CPA to file your taxes properly.

Because incorporation is not trivial, it is well worth consulting a CPA or an attorney who specializes in business law before you make the decision to incorporate. They can tell you what the consequences of incorporation would be in your own unique situation and advise you on how to incorporate in a way that costs you the least over the long term.

What is the difference between a C-corporation and an S-corporation?

In a regular corporation, which is also called a Sub Chapter C-corporation, corporate earnings are taxed twice, once as corporate income and again when the stockholder receives those earnings as dividends or salary. Another form of corporation, the Sub Chapter S-corporation, was developed to prevent this double taxation in small, closely held corporations. In an S-corporation corporate earnings are passed through untaxed to the owners.

Since corporations are regulated by state law, there are differences in how each state treats, and taxes, corporations of all kinds. That is why it is a good idea to confer with an accountant or attorney before making the decision to incorporate and choosing a particular type of corporation.

Can I start out as a C-corporation and then change to an S-corporation later?

You may change your corporation from a C-corporation to an S-corporation within 75 days of the start of your fiscal year. You may change back to C-corporation status at any time but after making the switch back to C-corporation status, you must wait 5 years before you can switch back to S-corporation status again.

RECOMMENDED BOOKS ABOUT INCORPORATION

Contractors recommend the following books. Several of them are published by Nolo Press (http://www.nolo.com), long known as a leader in publishing books for the general reader on legal topics.

Tax Savvy for Small Business by Frederick W Daily, Nolo Press.

Legal Guide for Starting & Running a Small Business, 3rd Ed. by Fred S. Steingold, Nolo Press.

How To Form Your Own Corporation, 2nd Ed. by W. Kelsea Eckert, Arthur G. Sartorius III, and Mark Warda Attorneys at Law, Sourcebooks, Inc..

Incorporating in [Your State Goes Here] Without a Lawyer by W. Dean Brown, Consumer Publications.

WHAT IT TAKES TO BE A CORPORATION

"1. Once you create a corporation, you have created a separate legal entity in its own right that stands apart from you, even though you own all of the shares and control its operations. From here forward, contracts, checks, correspondence, etc. are in the corporation's name, with you as president, rather than you individually.

"2. If you haven't done so already, you must divorce the corporation's finances completely from your personal finances. Separate checkbook, ledger, bills in the corporate name, etc. If you commingle corporate funds with your own, expect to invite extremely negative IRS scrutiny.

"3. You are now an employee of your corporation and must pay yourself like one, with withholding taxes taken out and paid over at regular intervals. You cannot draw all of your compensation from the corporation as distributions. You invite very negative IRS scrutiny if you don't take some compensation as wages.

"4. Since you are an employee, your state will most likely want to see workman's comp. coverage and unemployment/state disability taxes paid. Depending on your state, you can exempt yourself from these coverages as a corporate officer/single-low-shareholder corporation. Otherwise, you have to pay up.

"5. Have a Board of Directors meeting (even if it's just you) with minutes taken and recorded, at least once per year. Fail to do this, and the corporate veil is easily pierced in a dispute because, simply put, you have to act like a corporation to get treated like one by the courts

"6. A CPA's time and expertise are well worth the money in the first year or two of the corporation's existence. You are now faced with filing myriad Federal and state forms for taxes, WC, etc. They can help you through this maze if you don't have the expertise or time.

"7. Buy an accounting program. I use QuickBooks, like it, and it works for me. There are other equally good programs on the market, and it beats pencils and ledger sheets by a mile. Only $100 or so, and well worth the money.

"8. Related to (7): if you don't have a rudimentary knowledge of basic bookkeeping, learn it via books, a short course, or pay someone to do it for you. You'll thank yourself come payroll, expense, and tax time."

—Bob McIlree

If I have to incorporate, should I use an online service that promises to incorporate me in my home state for $200?

This is a controversial question. Incorporation is a big step and may have ramifications of which you are not aware, so it seems obvious that you should not incorporate without first discussing your situation with an accountant or attorney familiar with the needs of businesses such as your own.

But over the years I've run into many contractors who have incorporated using do-it-yourself books and online incorporators who report that they have not run into difficulties. So if you intend to remain a small one-person firm that does nothing but contracting, it may be safe to go with a reputable do-it-yourself firm. However, if you do this, at least get referrals to do-it-yourself firms from other satisfied contractors working in your home state and run the final incorporation papers by a local attorney to be sure that in incorporating you haven't incurred any duties and responsibilities of which you aren't aware. If you have business plans that could involve hiring other employees, don't try to set up your corporation or corporate benefit plans without expert professional assistance.

OUT-OF-STATE INCORPORATION FOR CALIFORNIANS?

"It's rarely a good idea to incorporate in a state other than the one you're operating in. First, you'll still have to register in CA as a foreign corporation in order to legally conduct business there. Last I checked, the foreign corp. fee was identical to incorporating there in the first place.

"Next, you'll have to pay franchise taxes or something similar every year to the state in which you are chartered. These usually aren't steep, but are extra costs to maintain the corporate charter in that state. CA will also clip you for a similar fee to maintain foreign corp. status. So, you get to pay twice.

"Finally, you must maintain a registered agent in the state of incorporation. If you incorporate in the state you live in, you can act as your own registered agent, gratis. Incorporate in another state, and you must pay someone to do it for you - this runs as high as a couple of hundred bucks, per year."

—Bob McIlree

Is it a good idea to incorporate in another state where incorporation is cheaper than my home state?

Probably not. In the past there were some benefits to incorporating in Delaware. But once this loophole was recognized, states passed laws that ensure that any corporation practicing in their state must register as a "foreign corporation" and pay state taxes on any corporate income earned in the state. Hence in most states in-state incorporation is now cheaper and easier. Your accountant or tax attorney can tell you more.

What is a Limited Liability Company? Is it a better deal for me than incorporating?

The limited liability company (LLC) is a relatively new business form, just now coming into use in many states, which is intended to be an alternative to partnership for multi-owner companies. In some states LLCs can only be formed when several people are participating in the business, however, in others, individuals may form them, too.

The LLC offers protection from liability that the partnership does not while still passing through income untaxed like a partnership (or sole proprietorship). The requirements for setting up an LLC vary from state to state, as do the benefits. For most contractors, an S-corporation provides the same benefits as an LLC, though in states that are particularly hard on corporations, an LLC may be a better choice. Only an accountant can tell you if this is true for you in your own, unique situation.

LLCS ARE CONFUSING TO CLIENTS

"This question ['what's an LLC?'] illustrates the reason that I chose to incorporate as an S-Corp rather than an LLC (Limited Liability Corporation). Every potential employer knows what a corporation is and what it means to have 'Inc.' in your company name.

"Having to explain an LLC and convince someone that it is OK to do business with an LLC is a potentially damaging, or at least distracting, factor when trying to get someone's business. Concentrate on explaining how you can help your potential client rather than spending time explaining your business organization."

—Roy Rieman

I am planning to work with several friends who are all contractors. Would it make sense for us to form a partnership?

A legal partnership is a dangerous form of business because when you are involved in a partnership you are legally liable for debts your partners incur. If you plan to form a business with other people, it is always a better idea to form a corporation or a limited liability company.

Forming a multi-person corporation is a complex business full of potential problems. Do not attempt to do this without the help of an attorney experienced in such matters. Your incorporation papers will have to spell out exactly what will happen in a multitude of situations where conflict can arise. For example, what happens where one owner wishes to terminate their relationship to the corporation, and there is a disagreement about what assets they should be able to take with them and which clients belong to whom?

Conflict often arises in small corporations formed by contractors when one person is bringing in more money than the others, while another is spending their time on essential but nonbillable activities like bookkeeping and marketing.

Because it is so tricky to manage a multi-person firm, it is rarely a good idea to incorporate with others until you have a track record of working together and are sure that your business can actually sustain itself as a working partnership. In many cases it makes more sense to form separate one-person corporations and share work more informally.

A WARNING!

"I let my corporation lie dormant until New York State yanked my chain for back taxes, corporate franchise fees, and interest/penalties."

–Mike B

How do you decide which form of business to use?

In many cases, the decision is made for you by the consulting firms who find you contracts or by your clients. Many consulting firms will only work with W-2 contractors. Other firms and many clients require that contractors who work for them as independents incorporate. Still other firms will allow you to work as an unincorporated 1099 IC, as long as you sign papers assuring them that you carry various forms of business insurance and will take care of paying your taxes.

Outside the United States, virtually all computer contractors work as either sole proprietors or corporations, since, unlike the situation in the United States, no specific tax laws target computer programmers.

What other factors should you consider when choosing your status if you have a choice?

If you see contracting as only a short term phase in your work life there is nothing wrong with working as a W-2 hourly contractor employee. But if you intend to pursue contracting for the long term and wish to make the most of your high earnings during your contracting years, it is a much better idea to work as an independent, either incorporated or not.

That is because of the ability that being self-employed gives you to shelter earnings in robust retirement plans and to qualify for more inclusive group health insurance policies.

This ability to shelter income from taxes and to have it grow untaxed either through compounding or investment is particularly important to contractors, because they typically have a period of a few years where they are in high demand and can charge the very highest rates, followed by periods when it is tougher to get work. It is impossible to know what kind of business climate contractors will face over the next few decades. So the wise contractor will set aside significant portions of today's generous earnings towards a robust retirement fund that will provide something to live on should the technology boom end—or should technology take a direction that leaves them behind.

Health insurance considerations are important too. Many computer contractors are in their late 20s and early 30s. They are mobile young professionals who are single or childless and have therefore not yet reached the period in life where health insurance nightmares can emerge. Unfortunately, it is only after you or a family member have a serious accident or develop a chronic disease, or after you have a child with special needs, that you discover just how vital it is to have access to good insurance and how hard it can be to find.

The Kennedy-Kassebaum Health Insurance Portability Act of 1996 improved access to health insurance for benefited employees and for self-employed people who are employees of their own corporations. But it did nothing for unbenefited W-2 contractors who are still covered only by the individual health insurance plans which the Kennedy-Kassebaum Act did not cover.

If you have a spouse whose permanent job includes benefits, particularly health insurance, it may seem less crucial to do your contract work as an independent, particularly when you are starting out. However, it would be very foolish to rely on a spouse's benefits for the long term, given how few marriages last more than fifteen years. A spouse's benefit plan will also not allow you to set up an adequate retirement fund.

Why do firms vary so greatly in what employment status they demand?

The confusion that applies to contractor's employment status stems from of a paragraph in the federal tax code called Section 1706, which was part of the Tax Reform Act of 1986. Some, but not all, consulting firms and clients interpret this paragraph as making it dangerous, from a tax standpoint, for them to hire computer professionals as ICs.

Some background is needed to understand what Section 1706 does. Before the passage of this law, most computer contractors worked as 1099 ICs and there was no such status as the hourly rate W-2 contractor. The reason for this was that an older piece of tax law, Section 530, had exempted computer programmers and engineers from having to meet the IRS's usual tests for qualifying as an IC. This was because, back in the 1970s before the advent of microcomputers, all computer programmers, even self-employed ones, had to work on site using clients' mainframes and software and hence were unable to meet several important tests used by the IRS to distinguish between employees and self-employed businesspeople. For instance, they could not meet the conditions that ICs must provide their own tools and equipment and set their own hours.

Section 1706 did nothing but eliminate the exemption that had prevented computer programmers from having to meet the IRS's usual tests for independence. It was lobbied into law by a consortium of large consulting firms (a trade group that currently calls itself ITAA). These large firms hoped that shifting contractors to W-2 status would drive smaller consulting firms out of the market, since these smaller firms would have their slim financial resources stretched to the breaking point by the need to meet biweekly payrolls and pay social security taxes and other employee expenses.

Section 1706 passed into law with no public discussion. In fact, most contractors were unaware of its existence until it went into effect in January of 1987. Once it was in force, legal staffs at many large corporations interpreted it as meaning that their companies should no longer hire IC contractors but only use contractors who were the W-2 employees of other firms. This was true, even though Section 1706's wording appears to apply only to contractors in *third party situations*, i.e., those brought in by consulting firms.

What exactly does Section 1706 do?

Section 1706 removes the "safe harbor" provisions of the earlier section of tax law, Section 530, which exempted programmers, engineers, and systems analysts from meeting the IRS's usual criteria for determining which workers are independent contractors.

Section 1706 is usually interpreted to mean that you can only operate as an independent contractor if you can meet most of the conditions set forth in the IRS's document, *20 Factors for Establishing Independent Contractor Status*, summarized on Page 46. These factors include being able to set your own work hours, bring your own tools, work on your own premises, set your own work agenda, and conduct your business in such a way that you are open to possible financial loss.

Clearly many computer contractors who get their jobs through consulting firms do *not* meet these criteria and do, in fact, behave exactly like employees. They work forty hour weeks at the client's office, do what the client managers tell them to do, and get paid biweekly, whether or not the client pays the consulting firm.

However, because in practice there been very few audits and reclassifications of smaller consulting firms that allow contractors to work as ICs there are still many consulting firms willing to place contractors as 1099 ICs or as employees of their own corporations. Our Real Rate Survey data shows that of the 560 *brokered* rates contributed to the Survey during the first half of 1998, 21% (116 rates) were reported by contractors working through some third party firm as a 1099 IC. Another 13% of all brokered rates (73 rates) were reported by contractors working through brokers as employees of their own corporations. This was almost identical to what we saw in our 1997 Real Rate Survey data, where 21% of brokered contracts were worked by 1099 ICs and 14% by incorporated contractors.

IRS 20 FACTOR TEST FOR INDEPENDENCE

If you answer "yes" to any of the questions below, you are acting like an employee. However, the IRS is vague about how many of the test questions you have to flunk to be reclassified.

1. Does the client tell you what to do and how to do it?

2. Does the client provide training for you?

3. Are your services vital to your client staying in business?

4. Must you personally perform the work for the client?

5. Does the client hire and supervise workers who work as your assistants?

6. Is this a continuing relationship? Do you frequently work for this client over a long period of time?

7. Do you have to work hours set by the client?

8. Must you work full-time for this client?

9. Must you work on the client's premises?

10. Must you perform your work in a sequence set by the client?

11. Must you submit regular oral or written reports to the client?

12. Are you paid on a time and materials basis (i.e., using an hourly or daily rate plus expenses) rather than a fixed rate for the job?

13. Does the client pay your travel or business expenses?

14. Do you work on the client's equipment or using the client's tools?

15. Have you no significant investment in your own business facilities and equipment?

16. Is it impossible for you to suffer a business loss because of the way your contracts are structured?

17. Do you work for only one client at a time?

18. Are your services not advertised to the general public?

19. Can the client terminate your contract unilaterally, even if you have produced results that meet the original contract specifications?

20. Can you terminate your contract unilaterally, even if the client has met the original contract obligations?

Where do you find consulting firms that will work on a 1099 or corp-to-corp basis?

It is often a matter of geography whether or not you will be able to find firms that will let you for them as an independent. Our 1998 Real Rate Survey data found that most consultants who reported working on a brokered basis as 1099 ICs were located in Illinois, the New York City/New Jersey area, California, and Texas.

Anecdotal evidence from contractors who participate on our bulletin board reinforces the geographical nature of 1099 work. In a message posted in February of 1998, Bob McAdams wrote, "I did a survey of DICE [an online job board specializing in contracts] about 6 months ago, when legislation to repeal 1706 was being considered by Congress, and the percentage of brokers allowing 1099 work varied from about 25% to about 65% depending on where in the U.S. you were. The highest percentages willing to do 1099 were in the Northeast. The lowest were in the Mountain states and in the South Central and Southwestern U.S."

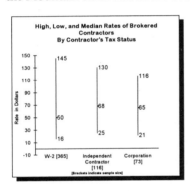 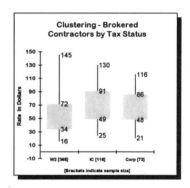

Does my employment status make a difference in how much I earn?

When we look at our Real Rate Survey data, we find that median rates of contractors working as 1099 ICs and corporations are, respectively, 36% and 30% higher than those of contractors working as W-2s. When we deduct the extra 8% that goes into the 1099 contractor's self-employment tax (or into the expenses of running a corporation), that still leaves a hefty increase. Independents' real take home earnings are higher still because they pay taxes on their income only after subtracting for legitimate tax deductions and they can also deduct a portion of what they pay for their health insurance from their taxable income.

But we should not hasten to assume that status alone explains this different between W-2 and independent rates. A large number of contractors working as independents work in California, Boston, and New York, where the standard of living, and hence all wages, are much higher than other parts of the US.

Another factor contributing to the independent's higher rates is that only more experienced contractors and those with in-demand skills that command higher rates are likely to have the clout to persuade an agency to let them work on an independent basis. So it may well be the ability of the contractor to earn the high rate that enables them to work as an independent, not the independent status that confers the high rate!

When we move away from taking a broad statistical view and look at the actual rates contractors report, we find that there are plenty of independents earning low rates. Our lowest reported brokered 1099 rate for 1997 was $25 per hour and the lowest reported brokered corp-to-corp rate was $21!

By the same token there are plenty of W-2 consultants earning very high rates. Fourteen W-2 rates reported to the Real Rate Survey in 1997 were above $100 per hour and half of these high rates were for long-term contracts lasting longer than a year! The highest brokered W-2 rate reported for the first half of 1998 was the $145 per hour paid to a contractor working a three-year long contract involving Verilog and ASIC verification on a long-term contract at a computer company in Silicon Valley. The next highest was the $130 per hour paid to a contractor working with JD Edwards software in Illinois for a manufacturer. So working as a W-2 by no means dooms you to low paid contracts, though it is true that *overall* W-2 rates are lower than those for independents.

Should I hold out for independent status?

If you are new to contracting or are planning to contract for the short term, it probably doesn't make all that much difference what status you work under. Far more important is how high the rate is that you negotiate with the consulting firm. We'll be discussing this at length in Chapter 4, "What Rate?"

If you work for clients 40 hours a week on their premises and use their equipment, you probably don't have all that many legitimate deductible business expenses. As an independent you'll have to pay much higher Self-Employment taxes and you'll have to pay a lot more attention to your bookkeeping and accounting. Incorporation may also increase your expenses, since it initially costs money to incorporate (the amount varies from state to state) and you will need to pay an accountant a hefty sum each year to file your taxes properly.

However, if you are planning to be a contractor for the long term, it is better to work as an independent if you can. As an independent you will be able to set up a generous retirement fund and can deduct your self-paid health care premiums. It is also helpful that as an independent, you can deduct the cost of expensive training programs and high-end hardware and software you might purchase to keep your skills current.

But keep in mind that this reasoning only makes sense if you have a choice of status. It would be foolish to refuse to take a long term W-2 contract paying $100 per hour simply because of the status involved if your only other options were independent contracts paying $30 per hour!

Will Section 1706 be repealed?

There have been several unsuccessful attempts to repeal Section 1706 since 1987. The National Association of Computer Consulting Businesses (NACCB) was spearheading yet another attempt in the Spring of 1998. Check our web site at: http://www.realrates.com for updates on the status of Section 1706.

Are there any situations in which it is critical that I maintain independent status?

The main situation in which it is critical that you reject all W-2 work is when you have already established an independent consulting practice where you work directly for a number of clients and have made a significant investment in building what is truly an ongoing business. In this case, working as a W-2 contractor doing the same kind of work you do for clients who pay you on a 1099 or corporate basis could raise questions in the minds of IRS auditors as to your true status for *all* contracts.

Can I change my status from W-2 to 1099 or become a corporation in the middle of an existing contract?

It is a very bad idea to switch to 1099 status while in the middle of a contract, as this means that the IRS will receive a W-2 and 1099 form with your name on it from the same company. This could trigger an audit.

In theory, if you incorporate your client should not send you a 1099 form, since this form is intended only for reporting money paid to independent contractors. However, in practice many companies do send out 1099 forms to incorporated contractors, so you may still have the same problem.

AUDITS DO HAPPEN!

"While it *is* possible to 1099 and W2 in the same year at the same company, it does attract both State and Federal audit attention.

"In my case, the state *did* audit, and was satisfied only after I demonstrated in several ways that I was an independent now (limited scope in a written contract with old employer, registration of business name, local business license, multiple clients, advertising in national and computer directories...)."

–Brad D.

A consulting firm told me that I have to incorporate if I don't want to work as a W-2. Is this true?

It may be, since incorporation makes it less likely that you will be subjected to an IRS audit and have to deal with meeting the IRS tests for independence.

While in the past incorporation was irrelevant to your actual status for IRS audits, changes in the 1997 budget bill now make it much less likely that the IRS will reclassify corporations that are correctly and legally incorporated. However, a corporation that does not behave like a corporation and fails to file the correct papers and meet the other obligations of a corporation under state law can still be stripped of its corporate status. Ideally, you should incorporate before you approach an agency for work, since incorporating the week before you take a contract raises questions about the legitimacy of your corporation.

What happens if you violate the IRS guidelines and work with the wrong status?

If the IRS decides that someone working for a client as an IC or as the employee of their own corporation should be reclassified as an employee, the *agency* or *client* that hired the contractor must pay back taxes on all moneys paid the contractor as well as interest and penalties on those back taxes. The reclassified contractor will also have to refile their taxes for the period in question, paying taxes as an employee rather an independent. But it is the agency or client, not the contractor who is subject to interest and penalties. This is why clients and consulting firms may be resistant to letting you work as an IC even if you make the case that the risk to them is small.

Have thousands of independent computer contractors been reclassified as employees, as an agency recruiter told me?

If they have been, they are keeping a very low profile, since not a single contractor I have ever spoken to in over a decade of following computer employment on a daily basis has ever reported having been reclassified this way.

I asked for hard statistics about reclassifications from the National Association of Computer Consulting Businesses (NACCB) a trade organization whose member firms frequently claim in the press and online that IRS audits limit the ability of computer professionals to work as Independent Contractors. The NACCB's spokesperson referred me to Harvey Shulman, their legal advisor, who was quoted in an article in the April 27, 1998 New York Times describing the chilling effect IRS audits are supposed to have had on computer contractors.

I contacted Mr. Shulman by email. When I asked him for some numbers that would back up the claim that thousands of contractors had been reclassified, he repeated the information already published in the Times article, saying that he has challenged 52 IRS audits and "prevailed in 50 cases and partially in another, but at a cost to clients of $50,000 or more." Shulman then said that he believes that the IRS has gone on to audit reclassified ICs, but says that because of IRS confidentiality policies no actual figures are available.

Given that the NACCB claims to have four hundred member firms, and that, by their own report, only one and a half of these firms were unable to withstand an audit, the actual prevalence of reclassifications seems to be very small. It is certainly not an issue you have to stay up all night worrying about.

What about the 1997 reclassification of Microsoft's contractors?

This high-profile case involved long term temporary workers working at Microsoft as 1099 contractors who themselves *requested* to be reclassified as employees. They argued that the company had used their contractor status as a way of avoiding having to give them the lucrative stock options that employees received during the same period.

Obviously this is a very different situation than that of contractors who do *not* want to treated be employees and are willing to go to the effort of incorporating to avoid it. It is also worth noting that none of these temporaries were programmers.

Why won't the agency pay me until a week after the client pays them if I work as an independent contractor?

One of the IRS's 20 factors for establishing that a person is an independent contractor is that the person *assume some financial risk* in the pursuit of his or her business. Many consulting firms (though not all) feel that they are safer dealing with 1099 contractors if they do not pay them before they are themselves paid by the client. This passes on the risk to the contractor, rather than treating them like an employee.

If you accept this condition, be aware that large corporate clients are notoriously slow to pay and that you may easily find yourself having to wait two or three months for payment if you wait until the client pays the consulting firm.

Why did the consulting firm tell me I need to buy expensive business insurance before they'll let me work as an independent?

It is not unusual for a consulting firm to require that a contractor carry significant amounts of business insurance before they will work with them on a corp-to-corp or 1099 basis. Commonly the coverages requested are Bodily Injury, Property Damage, and Comprehensive Auto Liability. These are standard types of business coverage. The rationale here is to make you behave as if you are, indeed, running a real business.

Consulting firm owner Dan Garland explains some other reasoning behind this request, saying, "Most of my major clients require our firm to have 1-2M in Injury and Property and 500K-1M in auto. The idea here is that once you are a corporation and start deducting for mileage, any accidents incurred while traveling 'on the job' can be targeted for a deep-pocket suit."

Sometimes agencies will demand that you carry insurance with very high limits, $2M or $3M of coverage. The idea here may be to weed out those who are not serious about working corp-to-corp and not willing to make an investment in their businesses. Sometimes demands of this nature are just a handy way of discouraging contractors from working as ICs at all. Demands for insurance may come from the agency or from a client's legal department. If you are faced with extremely high limits, see if you can negotiate them down to a more reasonable level.

I thought the whole idea of having a corporation was to protect me from liability claims?

This is a common belief, and, to some extent, incorporation does protect your personal assets should your corporation be sued. But it does not render you invulnerable should you as an individual harm someone while employed by your own one-person corporation, particularly if it appears that your sole reason for incorporating was to escape responsibility for your debts. Buying insurance for your corporation makes it clear that you are behaving like a legitimate, responsible corporation and that your reasons for incorporation are not merely to escape personal liability.

Unincorporated 1099 contractors may also be asked to buy business insurance as a sign of their commitment to running an ongoing business.

Even if the agency doesn't ask for it, shouldn't I have professional liability insurance?

There are two kinds of insurance that protect you against damages you might cause on the job. One, general liability insurance, covers you against property damage you might cause, for example, dropping a client's laptop. It does *not* protect you against damages you might cause through incompetence: for example, writing software that miscalculates the client's income taxes, resulting in IRS penalties. To protect yourself against claims arising from this latter kind of damage, you would need to buy a different kind of policy called an *Errors & Omissions* policy.

Premiums for Errors & Omissions coverage are much higher than those for general liability coverage, because unlike general liability coverage, which covers you only during the term of the insurance policy, E&O insurance covers all the work you may have done during your professional career. Premiums for this kind of coverage are usually calculated as a percentage of your company's annual income and may be $4,000 a year or more. Few contractors carry this insurance, though consulting firms often do.

Does my homeowner's policy cover my computer equipment at home?

If you run a business from your home, the business equipment in your home is generally *excluded* from the coverage your homeowner's policy provides. To protect your hardware and software from loss you'll need to buy separate business property insurance or EDP coverage. Safeware is one company offering this kind of insurance.

What is disability insurance?

Disability insurance is the one essential business coverage that most contractors neglect to buy. Unfortunately, neglecting to buy disability insurance while you are young and healthy can be the single biggest mistake of your professional life.

Disability insurance is insurance that pays you enough to live on should you have an accident or sickness that makes it impossible for you to work. Your disability premium and benefit are usually based on your three-year earning history at the time you buy the policy. Typical premiums for a person in their 30s might be in the $1,500 per year range. A typical policy would pay you somewhere around half of your annual earnings were you to become disabled.

This kind of coverage is impossible to get once you have any health problem listed in your records, so it is essential to buy it when you are young and healthy. By the time you develop the kinds of symptoms that might make you think about buying disability insurance, it is usually too late to buy it. Any symptom that makes you nervous will cause an insurer to reject your application on the grounds that you already have a preexisting condition.

This can be tragic! Though most 30-year-old contractors blithely assume that they will be able to continue working into their 70s, actuarial tables tell us that a hefty percentage of them will not. Some will get debilitating wasting diseases. Some will have accidents that impair their ability to think clearly. Some will suffer mental breakdowns. Without disability insurance these once- prosperous contractors will find themselves spending down their savings and then facing the prospect of twenty or thirty more years living on what welfare or relatives provide. Maybe you'll be one of the lucky ones who will work with undiminished vigor into your 90s, but why leave yourself open to what will happen if you can't?

Both independents and W-2 contractors can buy disability insurance through an independent insurance agent. The insurer will calculate your benefit based on your salary over the past three years if you are a W-2. Independents and newly in-corporated contractors may find it tougher to buy disability coverage until they can show a track record of three years of self-employment, though some insurers will write a policy sooner, basing benefits on past salaried earnings and current contracts. If you are incorporated, your corporate salary will be the basis for your disability benefit. So be sure to pay yourself a reasonable salary.

Where can I buy the business insurance I need?

Contact several local independent insurance agents and ask them for quotations. Professional groups like the ICCA and the IEEE also offer insurance packages to their members. Visit their web sites to find out how to get a quote from them. Other sources for business insurance may be your local Chamber of Commerce or other civic groups targeting local businesses. Online you can learn about the business insurance needs of computer contractors and agencies at

http://www.techinsurance.com.

Shop around and talk to several different agencies before you buy a policy, since terms and premiums can vary greatly. Carefully study the terms of any policy you are considering. Standard general liability policies may be cheap because they exclude coverage for computer-related claims, and some disability policies define disability more restrictively than others.

ONE CONTRACTOR'S DISABILITY INSURANCE

"I got a disability policy through State Farm, with whom I also have auto and home insurance. It's a reasonable policy, guaranteed renewable, with either a 90 or 180 day elimination period (I can't remember which right now).

"I decided it would be a good thing to have after reading Ric Edelman's *The Truth About Money* where he said that it is so expensive because of the likelihood of you becoming disabled sometime in your working career. And since I often change employers (I'm W-2), I wanted to have something I could take with me.

"It costs me about $65 per month with a $3000 per month benefit. I've recently learned also that since it's not paid for by my employer and since it's not deducted on my taxes, that any income paid out by it would be tax-free."

—Covered

Will I have problems getting health insurance if I'm working as a W-2 contractor?

You very well may. Indeed, it is a very good idea to thoroughly check out your access to health insurance before you leave any salaried job that currently includes health insurance benefits. The availability, quality and price of health insurance for people without permanent employment continue to deteriorate with each passing year. Unfortunately, because unemployed and self-employed people do not have powerful, well-funded lobbies while the insurance industry can afford the very best, the chances of things improving any time soon are not good.

You may have difficulty finding affordable health insurance (or any health insurance at all) if you or a family member have a medical history that reveals any past health problem. This includes obvious conditions like diabetes, cancer, and heart disease. But you'll also run into trouble if your record shows not- so-obvious disqualifying conditions like, asthma, depression, urinary tract infections, or attendance at marital counseling.

As a W-2 contractor, you will not be eligible for some of the better group plans. They are only open to people who can demonstrate that they are self-employed by showing a past year's Schedule C. These plans are usually available from the

Chamber of Commerce and give you access to group coverage from major HMOs and other business group insurers.

This leaves you with the option of buying individual (non-group) health insurance through an independent insurance agent. The problem with individual plans is that they are not covered by recent federal legislation that makes it illegal to refuse people insurance if they were covered by a previous plan, even if they have preexisting medical conditions. Companies providing individual health insurance plans can and do refuse to sell coverage to all but the healthiest people.

Where state law attempts to prevent insurers from rejecting all but the most profitable ultra-healthy customers, as is the case in states such as Massachusetts and New Jersey, individual health coverage may be even harder to find, since many health insurers, including the most predatory, leave the state.

If you apply for an individual health policy, you may be asked to give a blood sample to an insurance company representative for testing and forced to wait for the results of your blood test before you get coverage. You may also find that when you do file a legitimate claim, the company refuses to pay the complete claim, with the excuse that your charge is not "reasonable and customary" for your region.

It is important to do some research into the reputation of any insurer you are thinking of buying a policy from. Ask if they do business in a state that has consumer-friendly insurance regulators like Massachusetts or New Jersey and be suspicious if they do not. If possible, try to talk to someone who has experienced surgery or a major illness while being covered by the insurer in your home state to learn whether the insurer is balky about paying claims.

You can save a lot of money on individual health insurance by electing to buy a policy with a very high deductible ($1,000 to $5,000). If you have the money to cover this deductible amount, these policies are by far the best way to go. Just make sure that you are clear on the terms for meeting the deductible. Some sleazy insurers who do hard sell marketing to the public have been known to write policies where there is a "per incident" or "per illness" deductible not a general one. With these policies each new hospitalization may be defined as a new "illness" setting your deductible back to zero, and you may never get your claims paid.

It's also important to keep in mind that health insurance is regulated at the state level, so that the same insurer may offer very different policies with very different premiums in different states. This means that information you hear about insurers online from people living in states other than yours may not be useful.

Is it easier to buy insurance if I am incorporated?

Insurers classify businesses by the number of their employees not by their tax filing status. So a one-person corporation will only be able to buy the same insurance that is available to the unincorporated independent 1099 contractor.

What about continuing in my old employer's plan under COBRA?

A federal law called the Consolidated Omnibus Budget Reconciliation Act, or COBRA for short, mandates that you must be allowed to stay in your old employer's health insurance plan for 18 months as long as you pay the premiums yourself. Some states extend this period to several years or more.

Before the passage of the Kennedy-Kassebaum health insurance portability law in 1996 this law was useful to people who had lost company health insurance benefits when there was a history of bad health in the family. That was because, before this law was passed, group insurers were allowed to refuse coverage to people with anything in their health histories. The Kennedy-Kassebaum law now forbids this, though it still allows people with poor health histories to be charged higher premiums than others.

The problem with most COBRA coverage is that the company-paid employee health insurance plan often has an astronomical price tag. So you may face premiums of $1,000 or more each month to continue it. If you can buy a group insurance policy offered to self-employed people, you may be able to buy coverage more cheaply.

Can I get health insurance through a consulting firm if I am an hourly rate W-2 employee?

Some consulting firms offer W-2 contractors the option of buying insurance coverage through the consulting firm's employee insurance plans if the contractor pays the premium. This is particularly true in a tight market where consulting firms must compete to attract contractors. Sometimes in order to buy into the company's insurance plan you may have to pay for the complete insurance package including life insurance and disability insurance.

This may seem like a good idea, especially if you are embarking on a one or two year contract. But the cost of these plans may be a lot higher than what you could find on your own. So shop around before you commit. Also keep in mind that you are not likely to remain with the consulting firm for the year and a half that it will take for you to qualify for continued eligibility in a group plan under the Kennedy-Kassebaum Health Insurance Portability act. So you may no longer have access to group insurance plans when the current contract is done.

One advantage to buying insurance through a consulting firm is that you can sometimes pay the premiums for the company's benefit plan with pre-tax dollars.

Do I have to choose a business name to be a contractor?

You will only need to choose a formal business name if you incorporate your business. Otherwise, you can simply do business using your given name without taking any further legal steps. This is true whether you work as a W-2 contractor or as an IC.

If you work as an IC and decide to do business under a name that does not include your given name, you will probably have to file a form known as a "DBA," at your town or city hall. The term DBA stands for "doing business as." It connects your business name with your real name in the public record so that clients can find out the names of the person or persons behind your company. Contact your local municipality for details on what you must to do to file a DBA, since the specifics vary by locality.

If you plan to work as an IC, you may also have to file for a local business license. Whether this is required also varies from community to community. Your town or county clerk or other local authority can tell you what your local requirements are. Filing for a business license may bring you to the attention of local tax authorities who will assess local business property taxes on your business assets and equipment.

How can I ensure that my business name is unique?

Begin by doing an online search to make sure that no one is currently using the name you have chosen. This is important because if you begin doing business using a name that has already been claimed by another business, even one in a distant state, the other business can force you to give up your business name, resulting in confusion for your clients.

One way to check that a name is not in use already is to search Web-based phone directories like http://www.anywho.com for the name you are planning to use. However no free, publicly available resource lists all business names in use. So only a formal, expensive, legal trademark search performed by an attorney can guarantee that no one has already claimed the name you have chosen.

What business expenses can I treat as tax deductions as a W-2 contractor?

As a W-2 contractor you are technically an employee, so you can only deduct allowable *employee* business expenses. These expenses must be those that you were forced to incur by an employer, not those you chose to incur for reasons of your own. The amount of these business expenses that are deductible is the amount over 2% of your adjusted gross income. You can learn more about these deductions on the IRS's web site at:

http://www.irs.gov/tax_edu/teletax/tc514.html.

One important deduction you can take as either an employee or an independent contractor is the cost of duplicate living expenses you incur when you work for more than 60 miles from your tax home. This includes the cost of meals and lodging and travel expenses. To qualify for this deduction your assignment must be temporary—less than a year long—and more than 60 miles from your home. If you stay over a year on a "temporary" assignment, your tax home will become the place in which the assignment is located and you will lose your ability to deduct expenses related to food, lodging and travel for the *previous* year.

What business expenses can I claim as tax deductions as an independent contractor?

You can decrease your taxable income as an IC by the amounts you spend on all the items listed on Page 60. Be sure to keep all receipts.

Accountants recommend that you set up a separate business bank account for your business and that you use it for depositing all business income and paying all business-related expenses. This way you avoid mixing your business and personal funds. This makes life a lot easier for you should your business tax deductions be audited. If possible, you should also maintain a separate business credit card and charge all your business related expenses to it.

Can I deduct the cost of my health insurance?

As a W-2 employee you cannot deduct the premiums you pay for self-paid health insurance.

As a 1099 contractor filing a Schedule C, you can deduct a fraction of your premiums which rises each year. It will be 45% in 1998 and 1999, 50% in 2000 and 2001, 60% in 2002, 80% in 2003-2005, 90% in 2006 and 100% in 2007 and after. Legislation introduced in 1998 may change this. Consult the IRS Web site at: http://www.irs.ustreas.gov/plain/forms_pubs/index.html for the latest information on these deductions. This deduction should be taken on the 1040 form, not the Schedule C.

If you are incorporated, you may be able to deduct the complete premium you pay for your health insurance as a corporate benefit plan. However, you must consult with your accountant to make sure that you set up this or any other corporate benefit plan properly, ·especially since benefits you offer yourself may have to be offered to any other employees.

Can I deduct the expenses of maintaining a home office?

As a contractor who works for clients at their offices, probably not. The IRS allows taxpayers to deduct the expenses related to the maintenance of a home office only when it is their principal place of business, which means that they spend most of their working hours there and do not have another office. If you spend most of your working hours elsewhere, you can only claim a home office deduction if you regularly see clients at your home office or if your home office is in a separate building. The IRS guidelines for claiming a home office can be found on Page 59.

Would I save money by leasing a car for my business and then deducting the expense on my taxes?

This is the kind of question that only an accountant familiar with your specific situation can answer. However, if you treat a vehicle as business vehicle, you may have to register and insure it as a commercial vehicle which can be significantly more expensive than registering and insuring a regular passenger vehicle.

Will I have credit problems if I become a contractor?

If you work as a W-2 contractor, most banks will treat your current job as just another salaried job when qualifying you for a loan. This is not the case when you are self-employed. As a 1099 contractor or the owner of your own corporation you may be refused a car loan or a mortgage because you can't provide tax returns showing a history of three years of self-employment earnings.

This, however, is another one of those issues where you may find some local variation. Some banks may take into account your past earnings as an employee and the terms of your current contract and give you a loan even if you have only spent a short time as an IC. But others may not.

If credit is a concern, check out the situation before you change your employment status. Make an appointment with the lending officer of a local bank or two and ask them how they'd treat your loan application if you were to change your employment status. If you are in the process of getting a mortgage and are contemplating your first contract, it might be simpler to work as a W-2 contractor until your loan is approved.

IRS PUB. 587 — CLAIMING A HOME OFFICE

http://www.irs.gov/prod/forms_pubs/pubs/p58701.htm

1. Your use must be:

   a.   Exclusive (however, see Exceptions to Exclusive Use),

   b.   Regular,

   c.   For your trade or business,

   AND

2. The business part of your home must be one of the following:

   a.   Your principal place of business for your trade or business, or

   b.   A place of business where you meet or deal with patients, clients, or customers in the normal course of your trade or business, or

   c.   A separate structure (not attached to your home) that you use in connection with your trade or business.

Additional tests for employee use. If you are an employee and you use a part of your home for business, you may qualify for a deduction for its business use. You must meet the tests discussed above plus:

1. Your business use must be for the convenience of your employer,

   AND

2. You do not rent all or part of your home to your employer and use the rented portion to perform services as an employee.

DEDUCTIBLE BUSINESS EXPENSES FOR
INDEPENDENT CONTRACTORS

Accountant's fees

Admission fees for business events

Attorney's fees

Banking fees for business accounts

Business and professional books (including this one)

Business telephone line installation and monthly bill

Cell phone subscription and handset

Cost of courses and seminars you take to enhance your skills in your current line of work

Dues for joining professional organizations like the IEEE or your local Chamber of Commerce

Food and entertainment for clients (50%)

Hardware you buy for your business

Health Insurance Premiums

Insurance premiums for business insurance

Licenses and permit fees

Long distance calls itemized on your non-business phone line

Membership fees for professional groups excluding clubs

Miles driven in your personal car to the client's premises, as well as miles driven for any business purpose including looking for contracts, attending professional networking activities, trips to the post office, bank, library, and office supply store

Office supplies including paper, pens, letterhead, business cards, computer paper, toner, ink cartridges, file folders, staples, etc.

Online service and ISP charges for business website, email, and net access

Postage, Fedex, and UPS shipping charges for business related mailings

Software you buy for use in your business, including compilers, utilities, accounting software, and systems software

Subscriptions to business and professional publications

Can I get the benefits of independence working as an employee of an umbrella company

Umbrella companies emerged in response to contractors' desire to cut out agencies in the situation in which a client or agency refuses to work with independents. These companies "hire" the contractor who then performs their work for the client as an employee of the umbrella company.

The umbrella firm establishes each contractor as a separate "division" of the umbrella company. The contractor's billings become the division's income, which are passed through to the employee as salary after the umbrella firm deducts the business expenses the employee has incurred and the employer's share of Social Security tax and other mandated employers fees. The umbrella firm also charges the employee's division a service charge that goes towards the umbrella firm's profit. A typical fee is 4%. But remember this 4% is on top of the 7.65% employer's share of taxes and the costs of mandatory employee-related insurance that have already been charged to the employees division, so the total cost of working through an umbrella fee is 15-20% of the contractor's billing.

The umbrella firm may also offer employees access to employee benefits like group insurance and a pension plan (which are also paid for out of the division's—i.e., the contractor's—earnings). Because the contractor's expenses are passed through to the Umbrella firm's division as business expenses, the contractor can also decrease taxable income by the amount of business-related expenses.

Contractor's Resources at http://www.contractorsresources.com is the best known umbrella firm. P.A.C.E at http://www.pacepros.com is a new one that currently only serves contractors in California.

This kind of arrangement may make sense for the contractor testing the waters, who wants the benefits of incorporation without incurring the expense and long term commitment that incorporation requires. It may also be a very good solution for a contractor who would otherwise have difficulty buying health or disability insurance.

However, if it is likely you'll be in business for the long term, it makes more sense to incorporate. It's more professional, it costs less, and with your own corporation you don't face the risk of having an umbrella company go out of business causing you to lose your benefits.

Before you sign up with an umbrella company, be sure that the agencies and clients you will be working with go along with this arrangement. Though umbrella firms claim to have withstood years of audits, some clients and agencies may reject this arrangement as looking too much like a tax dodge.

AN EXPERIENCE WITH AN UMBRELLA FIRM

"I worked as an independent contractor for a large corporation and used the payroll and billing services of an umbrella corp. They processed all the paperwork and allowed pre-tax expenses along with other helpful things for a monthly fee of $185. This I felt was too much for the minimal amount of work that they did for me. In the end they got greedy and overcharged me by a couple of months, so I'm not going to recommend them to anyone else.

"It would cost only a couple thousand to retain the services of a good accountant to manage your own single person 1099 based consulting firm."

—Neeraj

CHAPTER 4

WHAT RATE?

How do I set my rate?

The rate you can charge for your work depends on a host of factors including the exact nature of your technical skill set, the geographical area where you work, the industry you're working for, and the length of the contract. If you are working through a consulting firm, you must also adjust your rate to account for the consulting firm's cut. So the first, and most important, step in setting any rate is to do some research.

Your goal is to find out what *range of rates* consultants with skills similar to your own are charging for contracts similar to the ones you could find in your local market. You'll begin doing this by talking to other contractors living in your area. Then you'll want to interview local recruiters and check out resources online like our Real Rate Survey and the newsgroups and bulletin boards that cater to people who share your skills. Only by doing this research can you get the information you need to set a high, but attainable, rate.

Can I believe what other people tell me about rates?

A certain amount of skepticism is in order when other contractors tell you their rates, especially if they do so unasked. The people mostly likely to tell you what they are earning are those who are earning rates at the high end of the scale. Since people don't like to advertise that they're losers, few contractors will share the information that they're only being paid a pittance. This tends to skew the numbers you hear when contractors discuss their rates. It may take a bit of digging to find out what the contractors earn who aren't bragging. But it can be done.

The reticence that used to keep workers from discussing their earnings has vanished in today's cutthroat, "hire 'em today, fire 'em tomorrow" corporate environment. Experienced contractors know that it is only by sharing rate information that they can keep abreast of market conditions and protect themselves from seriously underpricing their services. So if you ask about rates tactfully, most contractors will give you informative answers.

But the key word here is *tact*. Couch your questions about rates in "me" terms rather than "you" terms. For example, ask, "What do you think *I* could get for Java and CORBA here in Denver?" rather than, "What are *you* getting paid?" This approach keeps you from seeming pushy and obnoxious and gives the other person room to reply without having to reveal their own rate. If someone makes it clear that they don't want to share rate information, don't push. There are plenty of other contractors who will.

Because there are so many factors that influence rates, when you ask other contractors about their rates it's important to get as much information as you can about their precise skills, the types of clients they work for, the consulting firms they use, and how long they've been contracting.

Contractors who are on their third or fourth year of contracting are more likely to be earning rates at the upper end of the range than beginners. This is partly because they have proven that they are capable of doing contract works—which not all erstwhile employees can do. But it is also because after a few years they've networked with other contractors, become aware of the going rate, learned which agencies pay best, and gotten better at negotiating.

Can I believe what consulting firm recruiters tell me about rates?

Sometimes. Some recruiters will lie to you in order to maximize their cut of the billing. These recruiters thrive on hiring naive first time contractors and paying them far less than they could get elsewhere. These are the recruiters who tell you that you'd be lucky to get $30 per hour for your skills and then bill you out at two or three times that amount.

But there are also recruiters who will tell the truth. These are the ones who believe they can succeed in the placement business by building up a devoted core of contractors on whom they can call year in and year out. These recruiters treat their contractors ethically and take only enough out of the contractors' billings to cover the consulting firm's expenses and yield enough profit to make it worth staying in business. Ask one of these recruiters about rates and you may get a useful answer.

But the difficulty lies in knowing which type of recruiter you are talking to! There is no easy way to sort out the exploiters from those with ethics. That's why the more recruiters you talk to in the research phase of rate setting, the better off you will be. If you talk to ten or more recruiters, you'll probably hear a wide range of rates quoted for your skills, but some figures will repeat. These are likely to point to the real range contractors are charging for your skills.

How useful are surveys?

I originally set up my Real Rate Survey because I found the data from other better-known surveys to be almost useless. These surveys only show averages or medians for broad categories of workers. For example, they give rates for "Sr. Programmers in the Midwest." But since a Sr. Programmer in Minneapolis working with C++ might be making twice what a COBOL Senior Programmer earns in Des Moines, these figures are useless when you go to set your own rate.

When I established The Real Rate Survey in 1995, I took a different approach. We collect as many details as possible about each contract rate and post all our data in undigested form on our web site at http://www.realrates.com, so that visitors can draw their own conclusions from our data. You can view examples of what our raw rate reports look like on Page 66.

The data we display is full of significant detail: the location of the contract, its length, the contractor's level of responsibility, whether the contract was an extension of an existing contract, whether it involved off site work, whether it was brokered, what the billing rate was to the client, what the contractor's tax status was on the contract, what the contractor's level of experience might be, and what the contractor earned on their previous contract.

We publish statistical analyses of this data every six months in our *Real Rate Survey Report*. Like the charts you find in these pages, these reports describe our data in terms of medians and ranges. But we remind visitors to be careful about drawing too many conclusions from *summary* rate data, since it is the *details* of each contract that really explain why the rates vary as they do.

Over the years we have heard from many visitors who tell us that the rates posted on our survey look way too high. But we have also have heard from an equal number of visitors who tell us that the rates posted on our survey look way too low! This suggests to us that our data is just right and that it accurately reflects the range of actual contract rates found throughout the United States and the world.

When using Real Rate Survey data to help set your own rate, consider the data for your skill set, your region, and your industry, as well as the level of responsibility you take on, since it is these parameters that most closely define rates. Leading a team on Wall Street is going to pay better than coding on Main Street. Designing Java applets for a software company in Silicon Valley is going to pay better than writing batch COBOL for a Hartford insurer.

When you look at this survey data, bear in mind also that rates fluctuate over time. The data we give here is taken from our July 1998 Real Rate Survey Update. It draws on data collected between January 1, 1998 and June, 30 1998. We provide it here to illustrate general trends and to give you an idea of the kinds of rates contractors are charging. But these rates were posted during a time of extremely strong demand when rates were at an historic high. By the time you read this, conditions may have changed. So when you go to set your own rate you'll want to use the most up-to-date results. You will find the latest Real Rate Survey data posted on our web site at http://www.realrates.com.

One Week's Data from the Real Rate Survey

KEY

Off: Offsite Contract
Ext: Extension

Prev: Rate on Previous Contract
Bkr?: Brokered?
Cl't: Rate Paid by Client

Specialty	Location	Off?	Ext	Rate/hr	Date	Prev	Bkr?	Cl't	Stat	Length	Industry	Work Performed	Expertise
AS/400, RPG IV	San Francisco CA			$75	5/9/98	$55	No	$85	Corp	3 mos	Securities	Sr. Programmer/Analyst	17 years
AS/400-COBOL-Y2K	Dallas TX			$48	5/5/98		Yes		IC	3-6 mos	Real Estate Tax	Analysis & Remediation	4 years
AS400/BPCS	Sacramento CA			$95	5/6/98	$90	Yes	$130	IC	6 mos	Mfg/Dist	Analysis/Design/Program	23 yrs; 9yrs BPCS
ASP/MP/Technical Consultation	MA			$60	5/5/98	$50	Yes	$70	W-2	6 mos	Government	Oversee/Advise	4 year
C++/Java/NT/DCOM/Corba	San Jose CA			$75	5/10/98	$75	Yes	$96	W-2	6 mos	Manufacturing	Senior Ssoftware Engineer	Senior
C++/Solaris	Phoenix AZ		Ext	$68	5/6/98	$48	Yes		W-2	30 mos	Telecommunications	Design, Code & Test	12 years
C/C++/Unix	Northern VA			$51	5/8/98	$45	Yes	$92	W-2	6 mos	Design/Code	Design, Code & Test	Over 8 yrs in UNIX/C/C++
C/UNIX/Socket Programming	Chicago IL			$70	5/4/98	$60	Yes		Corp	12 mos	Product Development	Design, code & test	8 Years mainframe
COBOL, VSAM, DB2	Columbus OH			$45	5/7/98		Yes	$55	W-2	6 mos	Utility Company	Y2K Programmer Analyst	8 years
COBOL/CICS	Cincinnati OH			$33	5/5/98		Yes	$66	W-2	6 mos	Financial Services	System Maintenance	23 Years
COBOL/CICS/DB2	Texas TX			$45	5/5/98		Yes		W-2	14 mos	Retail	Design, Code, & Test	15+ Years
COBOL/CICS/Db2/Delphi	Westchester NY			$63	5/6/98	$50	Yes		W-2	5 mos	Y2K Etc.	Y2K Team Leader	
Cobol/Cobol II	Springfield MA			$42	5/5/98	new	Yes		Corp	open		Conversion: Cobol to Cobol II	3 yrs prog/ 6 analysis
COBOL/DB2/BPCS	St. Louis MO			$34	5/5/98	$35	No		W-2	3 mos	Health Care	Design, Code & Test	14 yrs
Delphi/Windows NT/HLLAPI	Israel IS			$40	5/5/98		No		IC	6 mos	Car rental	Systems Analyst	9 years
EasyTrieve, RPG II, VSAM, VSE	Milledgeville GA	off		$35	5/4/98	$21	Yes	$75	IC	1 yrs	Government	Level 2 troubleshooter	16 Years, one job
Frame Relay/NewBridge 36170	Dublin OH			$45	5/5/98		Yes	$65	W-2	3 mos	Telco/NOC	Sr. Programmer	9+years
Java Embedded	IA			$42	5/8/98		Yes	$80	W-2	6 mos	Avionics	Design & Code	10 years
Java/Solaris Win 95-NT MAC	Virginia VA	Off		$70	5/5/98	$70	Yes		W-2	6 mos	Telecom	Design, Code & Test	2 Yr.Java
Java/Windows95/Telecom	Dallas TX			$50	5/7/98		Yes		Corp	12 mos	Oil	Design, Code & Test	3 Yrs. Exp. CLP,MCSE
Lotus Notes	KS		Ext	$60	5/5/98	$70	No		W-2	6 mos	Diagonstics	Design, Code & Test	
Macintosh	CA			$40	5/5/98		Yes		Oth	hrs	Real Estate	Programmer	
MS Access	San Francisco CA		Ext	$49	5/10/98	$49	No		W-2	2 mos	Collections	Design, Code & Test	3 years Access/Office
Notes/Domino	Dallas TX		Ext	$65	5/6/98	$50	Yes	$50	W-2	6 mos	Manufacturing	Programmer	
NT Administration	GA	off		$32	5/8/98	$18	No	$50	W-2	1 yrs	Aircraft	NT Lead	MCP w/core MCSE courses
Oracle Applications	London UK			$27	5/10/98	$23.40	Yes		IC	11 mos	Manufacturing	Developer	5 years
OS/2, REXX, DB2	New York NY		Ext	$70	5/5/98		Yes	$80	W-2	6 mos	computer manufacturer	design, code, test	19 years
PeopleSoft/DB2	Santa Clara CA			$51	5/7/98	$53	Yes		W-2	14 mos		Technical support	
PeopleSoft/MVS/DB2	Bay area CA			$90	5/7/98		Yes	$120	IC	18 mos	commercial services	Sr. Programmer / Team Leader	3 years
Powerbuilder	Florida FL			$95	5/4/98	$38	Yes	$45	W-2	9 mos	Financial	Design, Code, & Test	
Powerbuilder 5.0/Sybase	Chicago IL			$36	5/7/98		Yes	$75	IC	12 mos	Financial	programmer	
SAS	San Francisco CA			$60	5/8/98		Yes		W-2	1 mos	Marketing	DBA	30 yrs
SQL Server 6.5	Renton WA			$50	5/4/98	$28.875	Yes		Oth	9 mos	Commercial Airplanes	Systems Administrator	4 Years SQL & Access
Sybase/Oracle/MS SQL Server	Denver CO			$48	5/6/98	$52	Yes	$80	W-2	9 mos	Satellite Entertainment	DBA/Architect	Specialize in Tuning
UNIX / AIX	Phoenix AZ			$64	5/10/98	$31	No		W-2	8 mos	Financial	Systems Administrator	10 Years
VB, SQL Server, Win 95/NT	MA	off		$38	5/4/98		No	$60	IC	2 mos	Healthcare	Design, Code & Test	1 yr. VB 5, 5 yrs. VC++
VB 5.0/Access, ASP	Los Angeles CA	off		$60	5/8/98		Yes		W-2	1.5 mos	Education	Project Manager	
VB/SQL	Los Angeles CA			$65	5/6/98	$27	Yes		IC	1 yrs	Healthcare	Team Leader/Programmer Analyst	8 years analyst/develop
VB5 / Win 95 / Oracle	Atlanta GA		Ext	$46	5/6/98	$45	Yes	$63	IC	6 mos	Healthcare	programmer	12 Yrs and MS Certified
Windows Development	SF Bay Area CA	Off		$75	5/6/98	$75	No		IC	3 mos	Computer	Developer	18yrs

What does your Real Rate Survey tell us about rates?

The charts on the next few pages analyze our 1998 Real Rate Survey data, breaking it down by various factors. Each set of charts includes one chart showing median rates and another showing the range of rates that represents one standard deviation from the mean. This second statistic is a measure of how tightly rates cluster around the mean. This gives you some idea of how rates are distributed throughout their range.

Most Common Rates

As you can see from the chart on Page 68 rates concentrated at amounts divisible by $5: $45 per hour, $50 per hour, etc.. Far fewer rates were reported between these points. The most popular rate reported was $50 per hour, which made up 8% of all rates reported. The next most popular was $60 also 8% and $65 at 7%.

Length

The charts on Page 69 show that when we sorted rates by the length of the assignment, rates for relatively short contracts clustered in a range that was higher than those for contracts as a whole. This may be because clients must pay a premium to induce good talent to take short contracts. But some of our lowest rates were also found in this group, because clients give beginners short contracts to see if they can do the work. Rates gradually declined as contracts became longer, except for long contracts lasting a year and a half and 3 years where clients may have to pay a premium to retain contractors. The lowest median rate ($50) was for contracts lasting fifteen months. The median rates for the most popular contract lengths, six months and a year, were among the lowest at $60 and $55 per hour.

Job Description

The charts on beginning on Page 70 display rates broken down by the contractor's job description. As you can see, contracts requiring higher levels of responsibility or skill paid better than those that required less.

Architects, database administrators, and network engineers/managers earned the highest rates, even more than managers, consultants and team leaders. Managers and people with the title, "consultant," earned more than programmers of all types. (The programmer categories here include people calling themselves "developer," "software engineer," and "programmer analyst.") Both Y2K work and Web development paid surprisingly badly compared to other specialties despite the hype that surrounded them in the media.

The charts on Page 71 and 72 split rates out by both job description and whether the contract was brokered. They show some interesting differences. In particular rates for nonbrokered architects and network administrators were far higher than rates for those who were brokered, but managers and team leadears who found work on their own earned rates similar to those of brokered ones. The data showed that software testing paid surprisingly well, often better than programming.

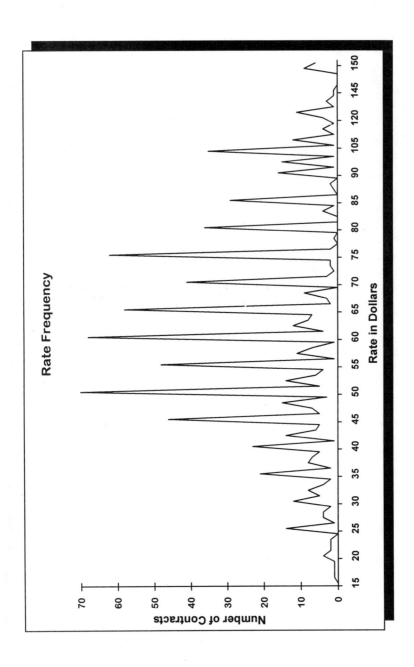

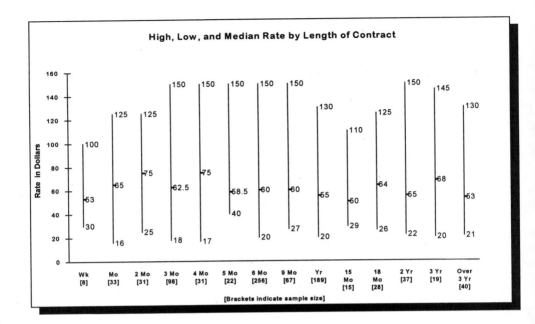

High, Low, and Median Rate by Length of Contract

[Brackets indicate sample size]

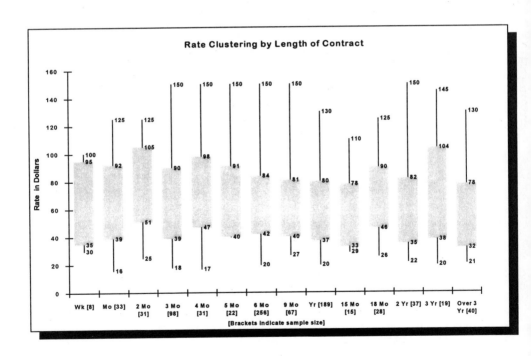

Rate Clustering by Length of Contract

[Brackets indicate sample size]

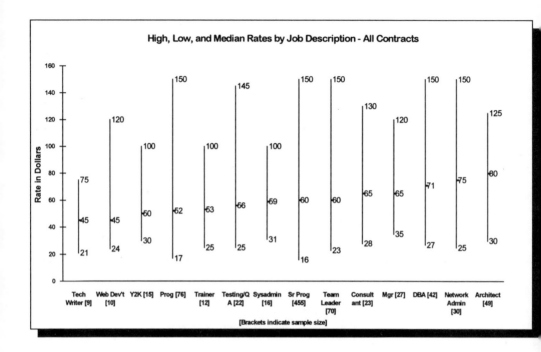

High, Low, and Median Rates by Job Description - All Contracts

[Brackets indicate sample size]

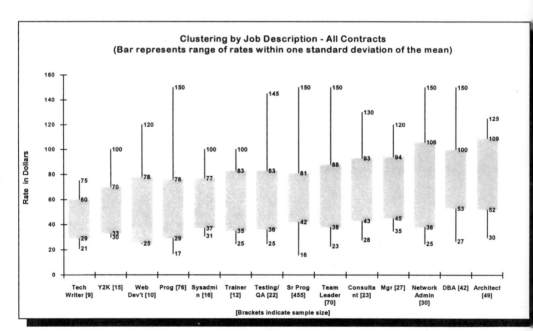

Clustering by Job Description - All Contracts
(Bar represents range of rates within one standard deviation of the mean)

[Brackets indicate sample size]

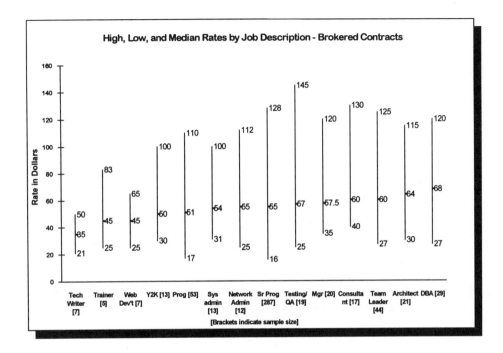

High, Low, and Median Rates by Job Description - Brokered Contracts

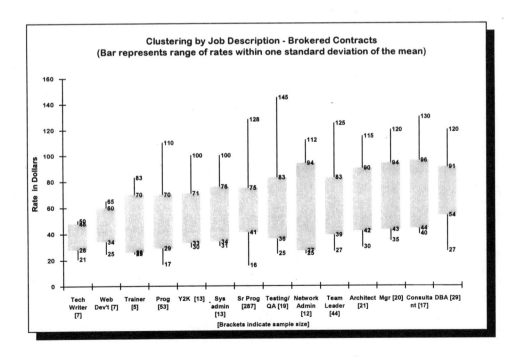

Clustering by Job Description - Brokered Contracts
(Bar represents range of rates within one standard deviation of the mean)

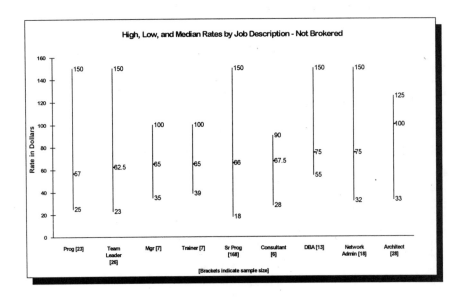

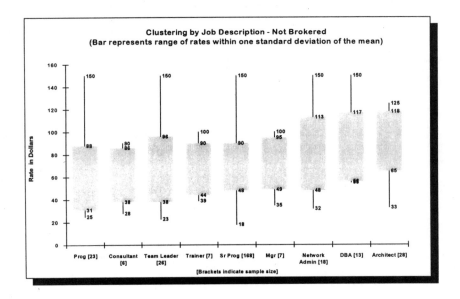

Language, database, package, and operating system

Rates also varied greatly depending on the specific language, database, package or operating system involved. The charts on Page 74 through 77 display the medians and ranges for specific languages, databases and operating systems. Where we had five or more rate reports in the same job category, we broke out that category and graphed it separately. So for example, in the Language chart on Page 74 you will find entries for "C++ ALL", which reflects the rates for all rate reports referring to C++, as well as separate entries for "C++ Prog" which refers to entry level C++ programmers, "C++ Sr Prog" which refers to all other programmers, developers and software engineers, as well as "C++ Architect" and "C++Team Leader."

Industry

Our data also explored the way that rates varied depending on the industry involved in a contract. The charts on Page 78 and 79 provide good examples of this. Median rates for all industries fell into the range between $48 per hour and $70 per hour. The lowest median rate for any industry was for work done in the Real Estate, Aerospace, and Utility industries, all with a median rate of $48 or $50 per hour.

The highest median rates were found in the Financial industry (i.e., Wall Street) with a median rate of $70 per hour, followed by the Pharmaceutical industry, ($67.50) and the Software industry ($65.) These are all very profitable industries, which highlights the fact that a client's willingness and ability to pay high contractor rates depends on how profitable the client is in general, as well as on how closely the contractor's work is tied to generating that profit.

When we look at how rates are spread throughout their range using our clustering charts, we find that rates paid to contractors in the Consulting industry and the Marketing industry concentrated in a range that extended higher than other industries. Rates were concentrated over the narrowest ranges in the Software, Banking, and Defense industries. However, the range in which rates concentrated in these latter three industries began at a level considerably higher than that of rates for other industries, suggesting that these three industries pay most of their contractors a higher than market rate.

Location

The charts on Page 80 and Page 81 show that when rates are broken down by state and by city, another important trend emerges. While rates cover a wide range in all regions, median rates track pretty closely to the costs of living in those regions, with the notable exception of the Washington, DC area where the cost of living is high but rates relatively low. Rates were the lowest in Arizona, where the quality of life is attractive and computer jobs relatively few. They were the highest in New York, where, as we have seen, Wall Street pays the highest rates and where the cost of living is also very high. It is interesting to note that rates in Chicago, a more moderately priced city, appear similar to those in Boston, San Francisco, and Silicon Valley where the cost of living is higher.

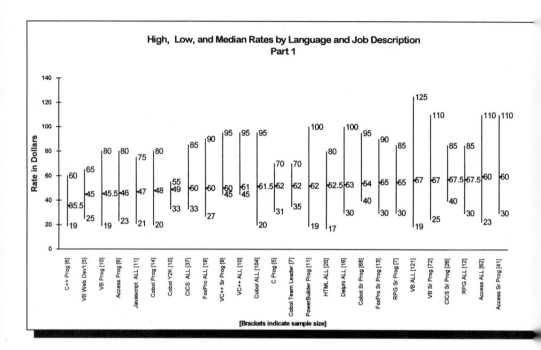

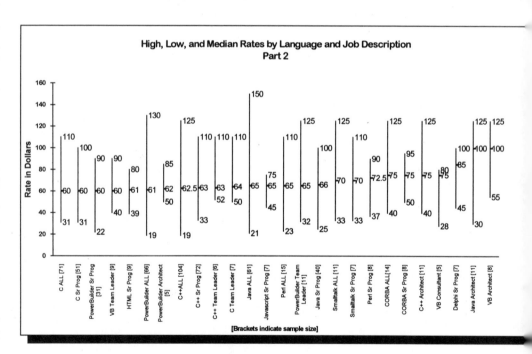

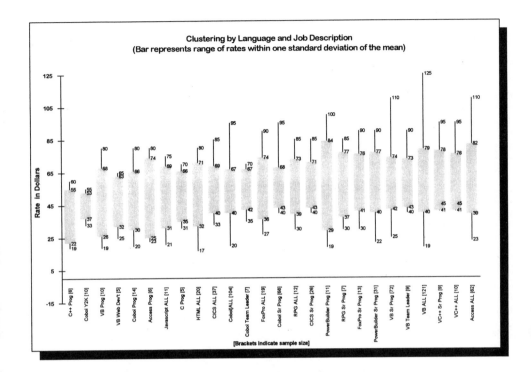

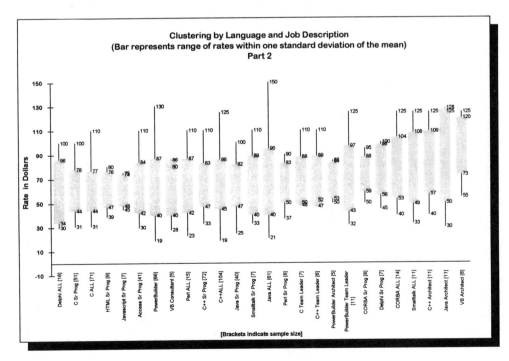

High, Low, and Median Rates by Database or Package and Job Description

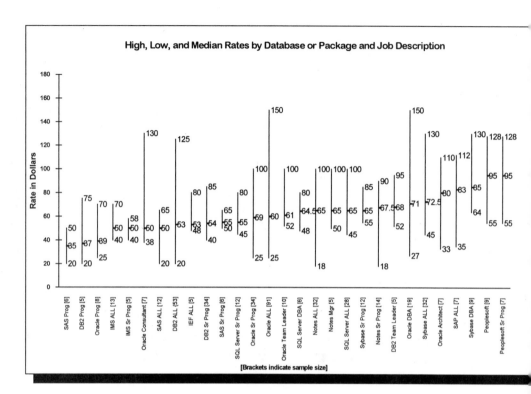

[Brackets indicate sample size]

High, Low, and Median Rates by Operating System Used and Job Description

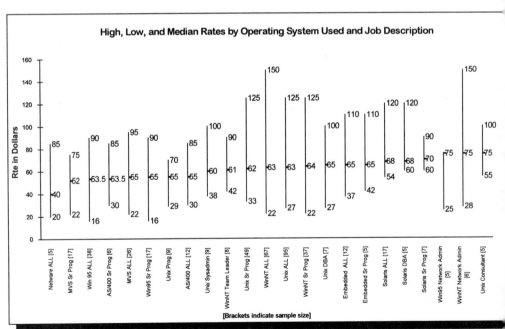

[Brackets indicate sample size]

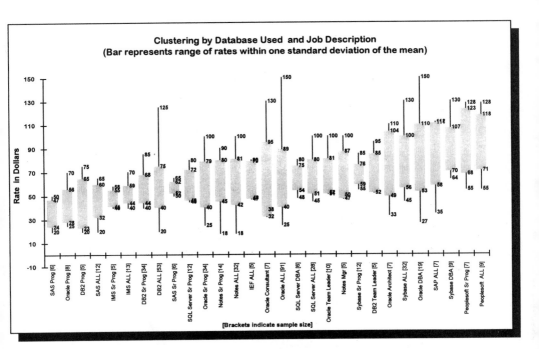

Clustering by Database Used and Job Description
(Bar represents range of rates within one standard deviation of the mean)

[Brackets indicate sample size]

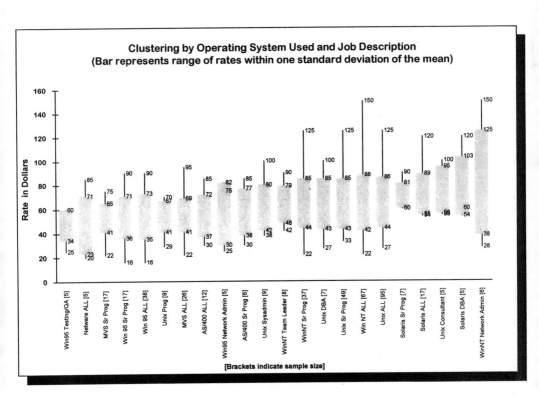

Clustering by Operating System Used and Job Description
(Bar represents range of rates within one standard deviation of the mean)

[Brackets indicate sample size]

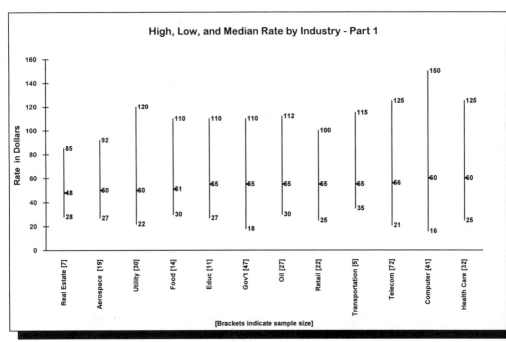

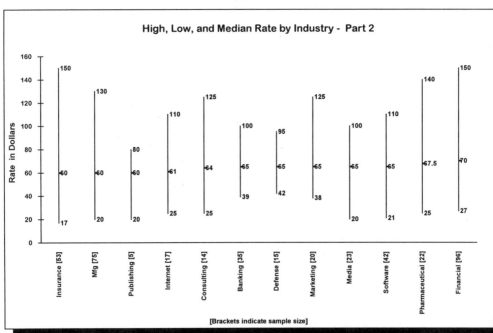

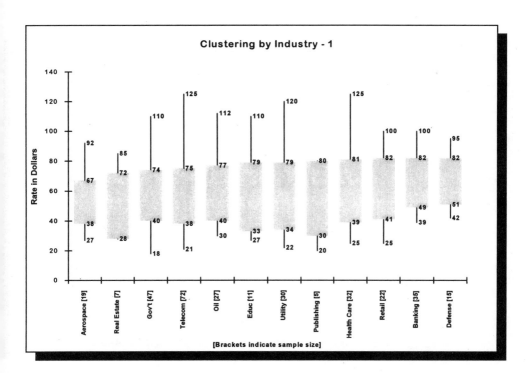

Clustering by Industry - 1

[Brackets indicate sample size]

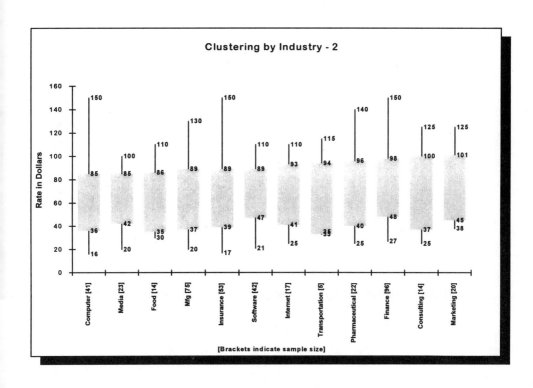

Clustering by Industry - 2

[Brackets indicate sample size]

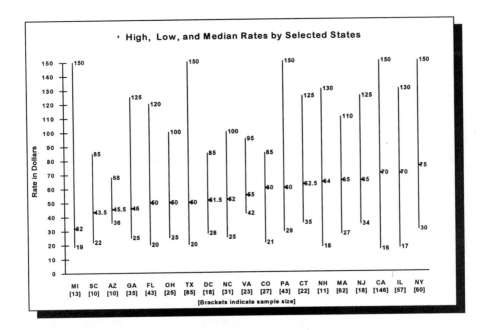

High, Low, and Median Rates by Selected States

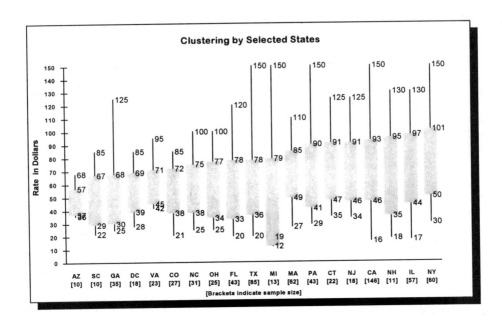

Clustering by Selected States

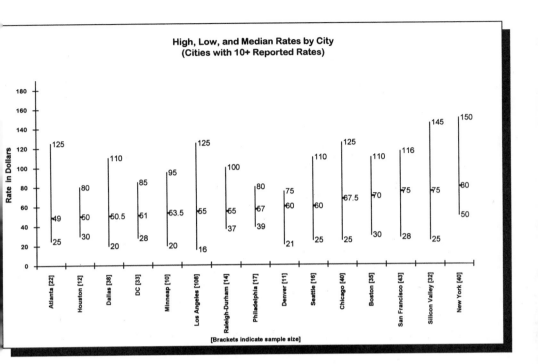

High, Low, and Median Rates by City
(Cities with 10+ Reported Rates)

[Brackets indicate sample size]

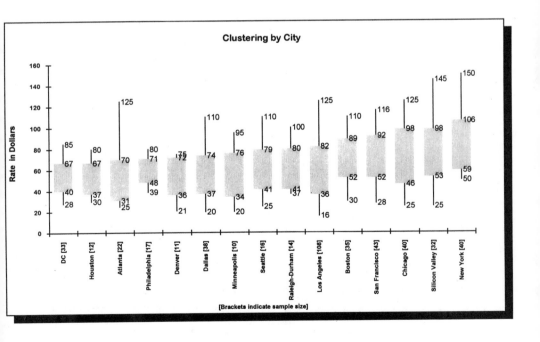

Clustering by City

[Brackets indicate sample size]

Tax Status

Rates varied too by the tax status of the contractor, with independents earning more than W-2s. The median rate for all consultants both brokered and non-brokered working as unbenefited, hourly rate W-2 contractors was roughly $15 per hour less than those for consultants working as 1099s or through their own corporations. (The unbrokered W-2s were those who found their own contracts but worked them as either a temporary employee of the client or as an employee of a pass-through agency or umbrella firm.)

When we looked at rate clustering we note the same phenomenon. The rates of W-2 contractors cluster more tightly than those of independents and fall into a range that is significantly lower than the range in which independents' rates fall.

The rates for both 1099s and incorporated contractors resembled each other, with incorporated contractors having rates that clustered in a very slightly higher range than that of unincorporated 1099 ICs. However, over the years some of the highest rates ever reported to our Survey have come from unincorporated 1099 ICs.

While low rates were reported by contractors working with all three statuses, the highest rates achieved by W-2 contractors were lower than those of independents. This is partly due to the fact that consulting firms paying W-2s must deduct 7.65% for their share of FICA.

However, keep in mind that incorporation in and of itself does not cause consultants to get higher rates They are more likely to incorporate because they are *already* earning those high rates and hence get tax benefits from incorporation at those income levels.

Nor does W-2 status with its lower rates necessarily imply lower overall *income.* Independents must pay that extra 7.65% of Self-Employment tax. And independent contracts paying the highest rates may only last for a few weeks with long periods between assignments, while a moderate W-2 contract may generate 2,000 hours of income.

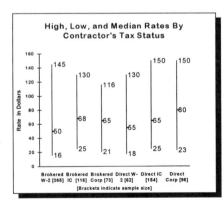

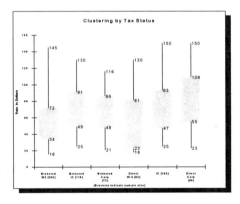

Is there a simpler way to come up with a rate?

The simplest way to come up with a rate is to apply the "rule of thumb" method. To do this, take the annual salary that you'd make as an employee using your current skill set and divide it by $1,000. For example, if you would be paid $65,000 as a salaried employee, you could safely set your consulting rate at $65 per hour.

As simpleminded as it appears, this formula works, even when rates and salaries fluctuate. That is why contractors have been using it for over a decade to get an accurate ballpark figure with which to set their rates.

What kind of income does a rate of $70 per hour translate into?

To estimate how much you'd earn at a given rate, figure that you'll work 9 months of the years or 39 weeks. This leaves room for bench time, holidays, sick days and personal days. If you are working as a 1099 contractor, be sure to deduct an additional 7.65% for the extra federal self-employment tax you must pay into the Social Security system.

Next subtract any additional expenses you'll be paying—expenses that would have been covered by your employer in the past. Examples are self-paid insurance costs, the costs of hardware and software you must buy to do the job, and the costs of training courses you buy for yourself.

The resulting figure should give you a good idea of what you can expect to earn. Though of course, you may earn more. Many contractors bill a full 48 weeks a year, and with overtime some bill even more.

What kind of cut does a consulting firm get when they place a contractor?

The issue of how much consulting firms should take as their cut of the contractor's billing is one that sparks hot debate among contractors. Consulting firms need to take something. How else would they pay their expenses and earn their profits?

But stories abound of unscrupulous agencies charging clients two or three times what they pay the contractor. And many firms feel justified in taking a third of the client billing, even in situations where contractors have brought them contracts they have found on their own. This contrasts very poorly with the practice in other industries where agents get a mere 10% to 15% of the money earned by the people they represent and earn it only when they find them clients! As a result many contractors cannot discuss consulting firm cuts without displaying rancor and paranoia.

It doesn't help that many consulting firms keep secret what cut of the contractor's billing they really take. Many refuse to discuss the subject at all. Others will purport to tell the contractor what percentage of the billing rate they take, but lie. Contractors often report seeing invoices for their services on their clients' desks that show that they are being billed out at a rate much higher than the one that the consulting firm told them they would be billed at.

Some experienced contractors argue that it shouldn't matter what the consulting firm bills the client as long as the contractor gets paid the rate they've asked for. They argue that consulting firms deserve to profit if they can persuade clients to pay rates higher than those their contractors demand.

But others disagree strongly with this argument, pointing out that the client who is paying a premium for consulting services is only going to get the kind of service he expects if the contractor is being paid a similar premium to provide it. They argue that the mismatch of an underpaid contractor with a client who is being gouged is guaranteed to generate bad feelings on both sides—bad feelings that may result in a confrontation that hurts the contractor's reputation.

What kinds of cuts are consulting firms actually taking?

To find out more about the size of the cuts consulting firms were actually taking we added a new field to our Real Rate Survey in 1998 that asked the contractor to report the rate charged to the client where it was known. Previously we had only collected the rate the contractor received.

When we analyzed the 299 Real Rate Survey rates for which we had information about the client rate in July of 1998, we found that the median percentage of the *client billing* kept by consulting firms for all contracts was 26%. For contracts that were extensions of existing contracts, where the rate to the client was known the median consulting firm cut was only minimally smaller at 25%.

When we looked at our data broken down by *language, database, and operating system* we found that the largest agency cuts were taken in Delphi contracts, with middlemen taking a median 62% of the client billing. The next largest were for

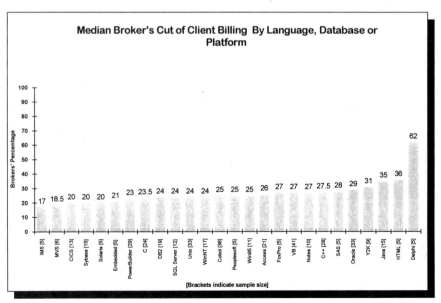

HTML and Java contracts, where the median broker cut was 36% and 35%. The lowest median cut was for IMS contracts, at 17%.

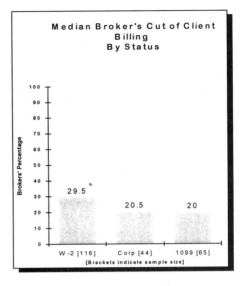

When we looked at our data broken down by the *status of the contractor*, we found that the median broker cut was 29.5% for W-2 employees, 20.5% for incorporated contractors, and 20% for 1099 independent contractors.

However, these charts show only median rates. When we look at our actual data we find brokers taking cuts ranging from 4% to a whopping 81% of the client billing! The explanation for very low markups is that consulting firms will sometimes place a contractor on an assignment where they do not earn profits simply to be able to get in the door with a client and make a placement. Consulting firms that place many contractors with a single client may also balance out a very low markup by placing another consultant on the project whose rate is marked up much higher.

Where does the consulting firm's cut go?

The agency's cut goes towards employee-related expenses, overhead and profit. Employee expenses are significant when hiring W-2 contractors. In that case, the consulting firm must pay the *employer's share of FICA* (Social Security tax). In 1998 this tax was 7.65% of all earnings up to $68,400, but this income limit rises each year. Even when the FICA income limit is reached, the consulting firm must continue to pay a 1.45% Medicare tax on the rest of what you earn. They must also pay state-mandated *Unemployment Compensation* insurance payments to provide unemployment benefits to laid-off workers, as well as *Workers' Compensation* premiums that protect employees who are injured on the job. These, plus the costs of processing a biweekly payroll should account for about 10%-15% of the W-2 contractor's earnings. Consulting firms do not incur these employee-related expenses for independents, which is why they receive a lower percentage of their billings.

Whatver the contractor's status, overhead eats up another 10-25% of their billing. Overhead includes fixed expenses like rent, salaries for secretarial staff, attorneys' and accountants' fees, phone and utility bills, office supplies, and office machinery like fax machines and computers. A chunk of the contractor's billing must also pay marketing expenses. These include recruiters' commissions and the cost of placing advertisements in magazines, newspapers, and online job boards.

The larger a consulting firm is and the more staff it supports, the higher its overhead is likely to be. This is one reason why you rarely get the best rates from the huge national firms that advertise heavily in expensive media like computer magazines.

And finally, the consulting firm must make a profit. Otherwise, why would they bother placing contractors? A consulting firm may take anywhere from 2% to 50% of a consultant's billing as profit.

EXAMPLES OF AGENCY CUTS

$$$

"The last consulting company I dealt with broke even on a 1099 at 19%."

—Bob Jamison (Contractor)

$$$

"The average overhead for billing, payroll, administration that most *end clients* have for W2ers is 22%. Those are costs that are there whether the end clients employs directly or an agency employs. There are further costs for marketing, fixed, and variable costs that any contract firm has that boost the 'break-even' to an average of 30% (again, W2ers). Anything above this is usually the profit depending on the company. This varies substantially depending on benefits, profit-sharing, perks, per diem, and about a gazillion other variables.

"The major reason why some of the ethical firms may have a markup of 70, 80, 90, even 200% on some people is that many people (again, we're talking W2—Subcorp is an entirely different issue) are marked up at a loss just so that we can keep the client staffed and the consultant compensated. I personally have a consultant I lose several hundred a month on, but she loves the environment and wants to be paid more than the labor category rates. In effect, I have two consultants at this client billing high so that the three average out to a margin the client deems 'acceptable' per the national contract."

—Dan Garland (Recruiter)

$$$

"I had the experience once where a broker told me that I could only expect $62 because the client was not willing to pay much for a certain position. A few days later another broker told me about the exact same position with the exact same client, but I was told that the client was anxious to fill the position and I could expect as high as $90."

—Wei-Han Chu

What percentage raise can I expect when I get a new contract?

Our Real Rate Survey data for the first half of 1998 showed that the median raise all contractors reported when getting a new contract was 11%. Brokered contractors got a median increase of 10%. Contractors working direct got a median 11.5 raise. The biggest median raises were for SAP (17%), IMS (18%), FoxPro (18.5%) and Solaris (20%). The smallest were for SAS (0%), Visual C++ (1%), and Access (5%).

What kind of raise can I expect when I extend a contract?

Our Real Rate Survey data showed that the median rate increase contractors got when they extended their contracts in the boom period of Spring of 1998 was 9%. It is worth nothing, however, that contractors active on our *Computer Consultant's Bulletin Board* during the same period reported several situations in which a consulting firm raised the rate to the client by a far larger percentage than the raise they gave to the contractor.

A CONSULTING FIRM EMPLOYEE'S RAISE

"I posted early this month asking how much more money I should expect from a new job assignment where my company would bill me at a 57% higher rate than they do today.

"The answer is, it ends up around 2% for me. Better position, more responsibility but most of the money will go to corporate. Sheesh!"

—Jake R.

Are there ever situations where I'd earn more as an employee?

From the standpoint of earnings, you almost always earn a lot more as an hourly rate contractor than as an employee, assuming your skills are good enough to keep you working nine months of the year. If they aren't, you'd do better to become the employee of a regular employer rather than of a consulting firm, as it is only as a regular employee that you will be able to get the training in technical skills and the hands-on experience that will improve your viability for the future. Low-skilled consulting firm employees are likely to be assigned only to contracts calling for those low skills where they are not likely to learn new and more marketable technologies.

The only situation in which you might have to choose salaried employment is when you or a family member has a preexisting health condition and you cannot find health insurance on your own. In that case, the advantages of working as a benefited employee covered by comprehensive health insurance may outweigh the higher earnings you'd make as an hourly rate contractor.

However, in hot markets, consulting firms may offer hourly rate contractors the option of joining their group insurance plans and paying the premiums themselves, so you may still do better as a contractor.

CONSULTING FIRM RATE ANALYSIS

"Our rates are made up as follows:

1. Direct cost for a 1099 usually includes the Hourly labor rate (e.g., $70) plus associated administration cost (usually 1-3%) of labor rate.

2. Overhead costs (%)of doing business. This may be applied for varies levels—Local, regional and national, e.g., local (usually 13%-19% of billing rate), regional(usually 8-12% of BR)and national/corporate (4-8% of BR). Overhead really is contingent on size of organization, number of branches, whether the cost is shared locally, regionally, nationally or across the board, etc.

3. Profit (12%-25%) - value placed on the risk of doing business/amount left over after all the bills are paid."

—Recruiter at a Big Consulting Firm

Another firm explains. . .

"My company uses only W2s. The company pays for all specialized training for the consultants. This can be a significant amount, averaging about $10K the first year and $4K yearly afterward. ALL W2s get 80% paid group health insurance and bench pay. The law in Texas also *requires* that unemployment insurance be paid by the company.

"With FICA, marketing costs and office overheads, the split in rates is as follows: 55% to the consultant, 30% to overhead, 15% profit. This is for niche consultants with billing rates of $100-$250 per hr. With our people making $55 per hr (1 yr. experience) to $120 per hr, no one is really hurting here."

—Principal of a Smaller Consulting Firm

Can I get a salaried job that pays what I'd make as an hourly rate contractor minus the cost of benefits?

It's not likely, though recruiters may claim that you can. The problem lies in how you figure the cost of benefits. Many HR departments use formulas that put the actual cost of employing an employee at as much as 50% of the employee's salary. Using this kind of formula, a recruiter may argue that a salary of $70,000 per year is the equivalent of a contract rate that earns you an unbenefited $105,000 per year.

But these HR formulas for estimating the cost of an employee almost always include *overhead expenses* in their calculations. For example, when calculating the cost of an employee, HR formulas are likely to include a prorated amount attributable to the cost of the employee's office space—including rent and utilities—and the costs of the hardware and software the employee uses. None of this employee-related cost goes into the pocket of the employee so it is irrelevant when calculating your real earnings as an employee. The value of the benefits you personally receive is all that matters when you figure your real earnings and that value is likely to be much less than 50% of your annual salary!

Even without accounting tricks, consulting firm estimates of what employee benefits are worth are usually inflated because they assume that you use all the possible benefits. For example, the estimate may assume that you take full advantage of tuition assistance, that you get full family health insurance coverage, that you attend two week-long vendor training classes each year, and that the company contributes the maximum amount possible to your 401(k) plan—which you are vested in, having worked for the consulting firm long enough to qualify. Few employees actually collect all these benefits.

If you add up the cash value of the benefits you would actually receive as a salaried employee, especially the ones you really need, the dollar equivalent is a whole lot lower. Term life insurance, disability insurance, and family health insurance, combined probably will not run higher than $10,000 and may be considerably less if you are under 40 years of age and single. Even if you have 3 months of bench time and only work 1,500 hours a year, a little calculation reveals that the cost of your benefits would work out to less than $7 per hour—a far cry from 50% of the median contracting rate of $55 per hour!

To really pay you a salary equal what you'd earn as an hourly rate contractor, a consulting firm would have to be willing to give you top-of-the-line benefits including a very generous employer contribution to your 401(k) plan, as well as perks like buying you state-of-the-art computers every year and sending you to several expensive vendor training classes. But why count on a consulting firm's promises that they will give you benefits like these—promises which many contractors have found go unfulfilled—when as an hourly rate contractor you will earn enough to *buy these benefits for yourself?*

To earn a good income as an hourly rate contractor I must work nine months of the year. Wouldn't I have more job security as an employee?

If a company didn't think they could keep you working for at least nine months of the year, they wouldn't be trying to talk you into working as a salaried employee. In fact, if a firm doesn't attempt to convert you to salary, it is may be because it figures it can only place you on one oddball contract that fits your qualifications. If that is the case, it may be all too happy to work with you on a 1099 basis since it means the firm won't have to worry about having you file for unemployment compensation if they cannot place you on a subsequent contract.

As an employee, won't I get paid for "bench time?"

"Bench time" is the phrase used for the time between contracts when you aren't working. Recruiters often cite paid bench time as one of the great advantages of working as a salaried employee. However, in reality, as a salaried employee you are much more likely to encounter unpaid overtime than paid bench time. While you may get paid while taking a week or two out from work, agencies can't afford to keep you on the payroll once it becomes obvious that your bench time will eat up the profits they've made off you in the past.

As a result, when you are an employee, the consulting firm is likely to force you to take any contract that comes along, no matter how boring or bad for your long term career development it might be or how distant it might be from your home.

That is why it usually makes more sense to work as an hourly rate contractor, earning a far greater amount for each hour worked and saving your money so you can pay for your own bench time.

How does salaried work as a contractor differ from salaried work elsewhere?

Contractors are almost always hired to do work that is identical to or at least very similar to the work they have done in the past. So as a salaried consulting firm employee, you will rarely if ever get significant exposure to new technology on the job. Nor will you get an opportunity to learn management or high level project design, which you might get if you took a good salaried job in a company that is not a consulting firm. As a consulting firm employee, you'll do the same work you'd do as a regular contractor. You'll just do it for a lot less money than you would have gotten if you'd taken the contract on an hourly rate basis.

PERMANENT W-2 CONSULTING FIRM POSITIONS

"Permanent work at consulting firms is a demoralizing rip-off. Not being on assignment is seldom a chance for a paid vacation: most firms will have you work on in-house projects of little interest and less significance. Some of them bill clients for your overtime but don't pay you extra.

"My one experience with permanent employment by a consulting company (which stated to me point blank that 'we are not a body-shop') was as follows: They paid me about 1/3 their billing rate to the client and kept me on-site (in another state) for 1 1/2 years. After milking me relentlessly, I returned to home base and was laid off after about a month, after no apparent attempt on their part to market me. I also clearly perceived on exit that they blamed me for being hard-to-place and didn't give one solid crap how much they had earned off of me in the past."

—Scott Horne

CHAPTER 5

WHICH CONSULTING FIRM?

What is a consulting firm?

The term "consulting firm" is a blanket term used to describe several different kinds of companies that are each in a slightly different business. It is used by Big Six consulting firms, vendor consulting firms, contractor placement agencies, and by small local firms that do entrepreneurial consulting work.

Some of these consulting firms do, in fact, offer consulting services to clients. Their partners are seasoned IT professionals adept at managing projects and implementing technology. But this kind of consulting firm is in the minority. Most firms that call themselves "consulting firms" are nothing more than temporary employment agencies that place computer professionals on long-term contract assignments.

What is a broker?

The term "broker" is often used by contractors to refer to any person or company that places contractors on a contract in return for a cut of their billing. Hence most companies that call themselves "consulting firms" are brokers. However, consulting firms rarely, if ever, use the term "broker" when referring to themselves.

What is an agency?

"Agency" is short for "placement agency." This is yet another term that contractors use when they are referring to the firms that find them contracts in return for a cut of the client billing.

What is a Big Six Consulting Firm?

The Big Six consulting firms those that are divisions or spin-offs of big Six accounting firms, like Ernst & Young, Coopers & Lybrand, or Andersen Consulting. These firms are run on principles very much like those of their parent accounting firms. They are staffed by two kinds of employees: partners who share in the firm's profits and regular salaried employee "consultants" who are usually hired straight out of good colleges or graduate business schools. These employee consultants take on an apprentice-like role. They work very hard for modest salaries. After a few years, most move on to work for other companies. A very few stay on and eventually are offered partnerships.

When business demand is strong the Big Six computer consulting firms also recruit IT professionals who already have one or two years of work experience. However, they rarely hire more experienced staff. An Andersen Consulting spokesperson was quoted in *Computerworld* in 1991 as saying that the average age of an Andersen consultant was twenty-five, which reinforces the impression that the majority of salaried Big Six consultants are still somewhat wet behind the ears.

CONTRACT FIRMS AND CONSULTING FIRMS

"I make a distinction between contract firms and consulting firms. Most contracting in our business is just providing so many warm bodies with the specified skills. The companies doing this are truly 'body shop' contract firms, regardless of the fact that they call themselves 'consultants'.

"The big firms usually have a small group of high-end people who are real consultants, but the bulk of their practices are body shops.

"They place people on board as W2s because they don't want any hassles. They may designate them as benefited and provide some meager benefits with a corporate level salary or as contract employees (unbenefited) and pay somewhat higher rates. They usually pay overtime at standard hourly rates, but may cut deals for 9 hr 'professional' day rates as well, where the employee is paid a fixed amount for the 9 hr day, with overtime only starting after that.

"These firms rarely have firm control on their own overheads and expect to make up for their own inefficiencies out of the billing rates. The employee rarely gets more than 60% of the billed rate, and the rates are usually fixed for a class of employee, rather than individually negotiated. You may make a little more than in your old corporate job, but probably no more than if you just made a good corporate job change."

—William Redmond

Big Six firms often bid on whole projects. Typical projects might be business process reengineering, major conversions, Y2K compliance work, and large-scale new system development. After experienced partners land the project, they usually send in a team of inexperienced, young salaried consultants to complete it If truly hard up for staff, the Big Six may hire hourly contractors, but they rarely work with independents and do not place individual contractors on contract assignments the way that placement agencies do.

What are vendor consulting firms?

A vendor consulting firm is the consulting arm of a software or hardware company. Originally set up to help clients use the company's product line, these firms often move into becoming full-fledged consulting firms themselves. Examples are IBM Consulting and GE Consulting.

These firms prefer to fill contracts with salaried employees, but if they have no other way of filling a client need they will also work with W-2 hourly rate contractors and incorporated contractors. Like the Big Six, they prefer to do whole projects, but they may also place individuals on contracts.

VENDOR CONSULTING COMPANIES

"As a far as we know all vendor consulting practices employ third party consultants and independent consultants. Our company has agreements in place with major hardware and software vendors and in our staff augmentation practice, we will 'sub' these people to vendors such as Sun, HP, AT&T Solutions, etc. and 'partner' with them if the project involves one of our specialties. While we have not done business with IBM lately, over the years I am aware that they have contracted with third parties and independents.

"Typically these vendors are looking for skill sets that address a need that they find difficult to fill with an employee. Examples include: ERP practices, Lawson, SAP, PeopleSoft, Oracle, Data Warehousing, Web enabling Technologies, Networking and NT, and Vertical Industry Software expertise. This is especially true for the big software vendors when the engagement or outsourcing job involves software other then their own.

"Of course it is easier for them to contract with companies rather than individuals but they do if they need to. Almost all the situations I am aware of involve contracting with a person who is a corporate entity. Very few companies out there will deal with an individual who is not incorporated."

—Tony Grace, Consulting firm principal

What about the consulting firms I see in the magazines and on-line?

The consulting firms you are most likely to encounter as a contractor—the ones that place large display ads in programming magazines and fill Internet job boards with listings—are large national placement firms that have branch offices in many cities. These firms generally place individuals, not teams. When they deal with contractors they behave exactly like temporary employment agencies. These are the companies contractors dismissively call "body shops" because their only function is to place warm bodies into open slots and they have no further involvement in "consulting" of any kind.

These firms prefer to hire contractors as salaried, benefited employees and to pay them employee salaries rather than hourly rates. However, because of the growing sophistication of the contractor work force and the very strong demand for contract services that prevailed in the late 1990s, many now place large numbers of individual contractors as unbenefited, hourly W-2 contractors, though they continue to be highly resistant to placing contractors on a 1099 or corp-to-corp basis.

The quality of these firms varies from excellent to scummy. Unfortunately for the neophyte contractor, it is very difficult to determine which kind you'll encounter when you respond to an ad or job posting. The size of the firm and the number of offices it maintains are no guide to the treatment it will dish out. In Chapter 6, "How Do I Work With Consulting Firms?" we'll discuss what you can do to screen these companies and find the ones that it is safe to work with.

What about the traditional temporary and employment agencies now placing technical contractors?

The potential for profit in the contractor placement business has attracted the attention many traditional employment firms. This has led to the establishment of computer consulting firms that are spin-offs of temporary placement agencies like Manpower and Kelly Girl that usually place secretaries and warehouse workers. Traditional DP employment agencies like Source EDP and Robert Half which used to only place employees have also expanded their businesses and now place contractors. Even many local employment agencies advertise that they place contractors. This is especially true in smaller cities that don't have enough of a contracting market to sustain branches of large national body shops.

You may do all right with a contract agency that is a spin-off of an established DP employment agency because they are likely to be staffed with recruiters familiar with the industry. But regular temporary firms and local employment agencies may be staffed by people who have little or no background in IT and who are unlikely to have personal contacts in the IT shops that hire contractors.

They are where you are likely to encounter the truly clueless recruiter. One contractor who visited our *Computer Consultant's Message Board* reported that the recruiter he met at an old style employment agency told him she'd just moved into recruiting after being an airline stewardess.

Because they have little or no experience with IT contracting, these firms may not operate according to the standard procedures used by firms that specialize in placing computer contractors. Their staff may also not be aware of the ways in which highly skilled computer contractors differ from the blue collar temporary workers they are used to placing. For example, they may insist that you sign a pre-employment contract or even ask you to pay a placement fee!

There is no reason to work with one of these firms unless you are located in a small market where they are the only firms listing computer contracts. If you are forced to work with one, be prepared to put some time into educating their staff about how the computer contracting business works.

What about smaller, local placement firms?

A step down in size from body shops is the small local placement firm that specializes in placing contractors at a few local companies with which over the years it has developed a strong track record. Some of these placement firms have stayed in business for decades placing virtually all their contractors at a single company.

Some of these smaller consulting firms are "boutique firms" that specialize in placing contractors who are experts in specific, expert niches like Object Oriented Project Management or Database Design. Because they market themselves in a niche, these small local firms often place experts in jobs around the country or the world.

As was true with larger consulting firms, the quality of these smaller firms can vary. Some are just placement agencies run by people with HR backgrounds who know little about technology but want to cash in on the technology boom. But it is in this tier of consulting firms that you often find the companies that are the best to work for. Not having the advertising budgets and name brand recognition of larger companies, these companies must offer something extra to induce high quality contractors to turn to them. Often they do it by offering higher rates and by coming through on promises of training, in short, by being more aware of and responsive to the needs of their contractors.

It is easier to check out these smaller local firms than the larger national ones because their staff tends to be small, and their recruiters, unlike those in bigger firms, do not move around. So you can trust what fellow professionals in the workplace and at local networking events tell you about their experiences working with them. Local managers also can give you feedback about these smaller local firms.

These small local companies sometimes advertise in publications targeting programmers, but many do not, relying instead on local word-of-mouth and referrals to attract talented contractors. Some may offer their current contractors bonuses for recruiting new contractors. These smaller consulting firms may be much more flexible about working with 1099 and corp-to-corp contractors than larger ones.

Unfortunately, over the past few years, the large national body shops have been buying up these smaller local firms as a way of quickly expanding their operations. As a result of this continuing wave of consulting firm consolidations, it is getting harder to find a good local placement firm than it was only a few years ago.

GREAT LOCAL FIRMS

"There are some great small contract firms out there that don't rip off the tech doing the work. These operate on a shoe-string usually, have very small overheads, and only carve off a nominal amount of the rate because they have the coveted pre-ferred vendor status with certain companies.

"When I was in corporate management, I preferred using this type of contract firm because they gave the best deal to the techs I was hiring. They seemed to have the best people too.

"The problem with these are that they usually have only a few regular clients and they are sometimes very geographically bound."

—William Redmond

What about small consulting firms that really do consulting?

Small entrepreneurial consulting firms that have grown to where they need out-side help on larger contracts may very occasionally find you contract work. Often these are single entrepreneurial consultants or groups of consultants and software developers who have built up entrepreneurial practices. These firms may hire W-2 contractors, but many prefer to subcontract pieces of a project to another inde-pendent or incorporated contractors. You'll usually only encounter this kind of firm if you participate in professional activities, online or face-to-face, where you can meet the principals, get across your capabilities, and establish an ongoing per-sonal relationship that can result in their passing on some of their client overload to you.

I see ads from what look like temporary agencies run by large companies. What are these?

In an attempt to save money on consulting firm markups some corporations that use huge numbers of contractors have formed in-house "temporary agencies" that use advertisements almost indistinguishable from those of consulting firms to re-cruit contractors.

Theoretically, since the company has eliminated the consulting firm's cut by hiring contractors directly, you should be able to get a higher rate from one of these in-house temporary agencies. But this rarely happens. These agencies are usually run by the HR department and their focus may be primarily on hiring clerical workers cheaply. They can be very out of touch with the going rates for contract work and with the technical needs of their company's managers. Accept a contract from one only if they can provide you with a market rate.

Do consulting firms earn obscene profits?

Contrary to what you might hear from some contractors, earning money in the placement business is not like picking up money off the street. Placement firms operate in a highly competitive environment, made all the more competitive each year as huge national placement firms buy up small local firms and then use their clout to negotiate sweetheart deals with large corporations that drive other small local firms out of business.

Nor is there always a boom market for contractors, though placement firms must still pay for their offices and other overhead whether or not they have contractors working for them. Advertising expenses are another large overhead item for many firms which must also be paid for in good times and bad. A quarter-page display ad in a national computer magazine may easily cost $5,000 per month and many companies advertise in dozens of publications. Newspaper advertising is also expensive, as is the cost of maintaining booths at job fairs. Yet another serious expense may be interest payments on the loans consulting firms must take out to get cash to pay their salaried and W-2 contractors when their clients take two or three months to honor their invoices. These loan payments may linger long after the contractors have moved on.

How do consulting firms pay their recruiters?

Firms usually pay their recruiters some mix of a salary and a commission based on the number of placements they make. Some firms pay the recruiter a flat amount for each placement. Others pay the recruiter a few dollars for every hour the contractor works.

Whatever the details of these arrangements, which vary from firm to firm, what matters to you is that even though the money to pay the recruiter comes from your billing, because of the way most recruiters are paid they rarely have an incentive to get you the best rate. The "flat fee per placement" arrangement in particular motivates recruiters to get you working at *any* rate, instead of at the *best* rate, since recruiters don't earn more by getting you a high rate than they do from getting you a low one. This is very different from what happens in most other agency relationships like those found in the sports and entertainment world or in real estate sales. There agents get paid a percentage of the amount they negotiate for the person they represent. That motivates them to get them top dollar.

It is also important to realize that though the consulting *firm* is getting a hefty chunk of your billing—that median 26% we discussed in Chapter 4, "What Rate?"—the *recruiter* is only getting a small portion of that chunk. The rest goes to expenses and then to the firm's owners as profits.

Another important fact about how recruiters get paid is that most recruiter pay schemes reward the recruiter for getting a contractor to *extend* an existing contract.

This guarantees that most recruiters will pressure you to extend any contract a client is willing to extend. It is also why recruiters will never take you off an existing contract to find you one you like better.

But it's worth remembering, too, that the recruiters you deal with are probably not getting rich. Whatever profits their firms may be netting, most recruiters are employees themselves–commissioned employees–who make considerably less than the contractors they place.

Indeed, in the late 1990s conditions for recruiters appear to have degenerated while conditions for contractors have improved because consulting firms are caught in a squeeze. In a tight labor market like that of the late 1990s they must compete with each other to recruit contractors by offering those contractors the best rates. At the same time as they must also compete with each other in offering those contractors to managers who are looking for the cheapest possible rates. In many cases the simplest way for consulting firms to maintain their profits is to cut the *recruiter's* share, so that they can offer the higher rates that attract contractors and still keep their billings to clients low enough to keep them buying.

As a result, turnover among recruiters at consulting firms is high, particularly in those marginal firms that are not well established in local markets. Recruiters themselves are recruited with ads that say, "Our best recruiters earned over $100,000 last year!" Once on the job, they quickly learn that whatever the company's *best* recruiters earned, the other 95% were lucky to make $30,000–which is why the consulting firm is always running ads for recruiters.

The work recruiters do is no picnic either. It is probably not accidental that the recruiters most likely to stay in the business for any length of time are those with the thickest skins and the most brazen personalities. It takes a certain kind of person to cold call potential clients and wary contractors all day long, and sensitivity is not among the traits that kind of person is likely to have.

HOW ONE RECRUITER IS PAID

"As far as recruiting dollars, $1,600 is for a full-time employee or for individuals who are on a contract for more than 90 days. Less than 90 days and the commission drops to $400.

"If the contract is extended, the remainder of the commission ($1,200) is then paid out over a 6 week period (divided into 3 pay-periods)."

—Lisa the Recruiter

Are the most successful consulting firms those that best understand technology?

Not necessarily. There are two kinds of successful consulting firm: those that understand technology and those that understand marketing. The former tend to hire people with technical backgrounds to be their recruiters and then train them in sales. Sometimes these staffers have been programmers, but quite often the recruiters in these firms are drawn from the ranks of laid off corporate IT managers, especially higher-ranking managers who have built strong webs of contacts in the local or regional IT community.

The second kind of firm hires people who have a track record in sales and gives them just enough training in technical matters so that they know enough not to try to sell a Visual Basic programmer to the manager of a UNIX shop or to pitch a DB2 database administrator to a Silicon Valley software development start-up.

While recruiters with a technical background tend to get along a lot better with the contractors they place, they often lose placements to technical ignoramuses with sales backgrounds who are better at closing the sale.

Who keeps the consulting firm in business, the client or the contractor?

In the view of almost all consulting firm staff, it is the *repeat client* who keeps the consulting firm in business, not the contractor. Contractors come and go no matter how well they are treated, while a single good corporate client with a large IT shop and an ongoing need for contractors can keep a firm in business for 20 years or more.

In fact, veteran consulting firm staff are more likely to treat the contractor as a source of problems than of profits, a necessary evil that comes with running their type of business, and save the red carpet treatment for their client base.

What kinds of problems do contractors cause consulting firms?

Here is a series of randomly collected complaints expressed by consulting firm staffers:

- Contractors lie about their expertise and claim to have extensive experience with software they either don't know at all or have only minimal experience with

- Contractors say they'll take a job and then back out at the last moment, leaving the firm with a furious client

- Contractors quit in the middle of projects without warning

- Contractors will ditch a consulting firm for a couple more dollars an hour, even when they've been treated very well

- Contractors demand rates that are not possible in the local marketplace and get furious when offered reasonable ones

- Would-be contractors get nasty when told they don't have the necessary experience to qualify for an interview and sometimes harass recruiters

- Contractors pester recruiters, calling them daily when the recruiter has made it clear they'll call when they have something

- Contractors don't tell the recruiter when they've let another firm submit them for a job, resulting in a worthless double submission

- Contractors with poor skills get vindictive when the consulting firm fails to find them work and then go and badmouth the firm to everyone in the contracting community

- Contractors have the social skills of mollusks and alienate the people at client sites with their poor hygiene, lack of fashion sense, communications skills, interpersonal skills, etc.

SCREWED BY THE CONTRACTOR!

"What do you think of this?

"We offered $60 hr, all expenses paid, weekend trips home (Mainframe P/Manager), $400 a week for the 'little extras.' A pretty good deal I'd think, The contractor committed to this project and accepted the offer. The Client couldn't wait for him to start and then his wife changed his mind—3 days before start date!

"Didn't he think to ask what she thought before going through the whole damn process and wasting my time?!!! I can't even ask if he's married, it's an illegal question!

"Or this. . .

"Phone call from new consultant: Go ahead and tell the client I'll start on the 9th of March but if I decide I don't want to go there then don't worry about me, I'll just stay in the job I'm at until you can find me something else.

"This way we'll have the contract secured for me until the 9th and that will give me time to change my mind if I want to. But this way, you can pretend you didn't know I wasn't taking the job until the 9th if anything happens."

—Lisa the Recruiter

How do I find a good consulting firm?

The best way to find good consulting firms is to talk to other contractors in your local area, particularly people who have the same technical skills as yours. The more people you talk to, the more well-rounded the picture you will get of local firms.

In particular, try to find some "old-timers" who have been in the contracting business for a few years. They'll be able to fill you in on important information, like which companies a local consulting firm usually places contractors at or the industries it concentrates on. This is important because some firms only place contractors with one or two large corporate clients or in a single industry, like defense or insurance. So if you don't want to work in the companies or industry they place people in, it is not worth contacting them.

Old-timers may also be able to tell you something about the backgrounds of the recruiters who work for local consulting firms. This will help you screen out the worst of the pond scum. Years ago, networking within my local IT community revealed that the owner of one local consulting firm I had contacted was so litigious that it was rumored he'd sued his own mother!

CONSIDER TURNOVER

"Find out what the turnover rate is at the contracting house.

"Some have a turnover rate of over 200%. A good contracting house has a rate of 35% or less. This means contractors are staying on and getting new contracts with the same company.

"Also be sure to ask how long the *recruiter* has been with the consulting firm. If the recruiter has stayed with one firm for several years they are likely to be good at placing people and to have a solid network of contacts in the local business community.

—Another Recruiter

What about consulting firms that post jobs on Internet job boards?

If you can't find a good local firm, you may be tempted to respond to one of the thousands of job listings you'll find on the on-line job boards. It is very hard to resist this temptation, since there are so many contracts listed there and it costs you nothing to reply.

Many of these job board postings come from the large national firms whose ads you see in magazines—the ones with offices in major cities and the reputations of being body shops. Other postings may be from smaller local firms. If you recognize the name of the consulting firm, know something about it, and if the advertised contract is local, this can be a great way of finding work.

However, if the job is local and you *don't* recognize the name of the consulting firm some caution is in order—assuming you have done your homework and have learned something about local consulting firms. It costs relatively little to post Internet ads so you often run into fly-by-nighters on the Web. I have personally seen one company posting ads in which they claimed to be a large well-known firm in a market I knew very well, where in fact, they were not only not well known, they did not even have a permanent office!

So be sure to exercise caution with firms you have not heard of. If they claim a local presence, make sure that they are listed in the local phone book to ensure that they've been around for more than a few weeks. If you contact recruiters at firms you don't recognize that claim to place contractors in your market, don't be shy. Ask for the names of local companies where they have placed people in the recent past. Then verify that they really have made those placements by calling the HR departments in the companies they've cited. Just as a client has the right to ask you for references, you have a right to ask for references from a firm with whom you are considering doing business. You can also ask them to give you the names of contractors they have placed locally in the past year or two.

If you are considering working with a consulting firm, it is also a good idea to check them out with the Better Business Bureau. If the BBB reports that they have unresolved complaints on file, you probably don't want to do business with them. However, contractors often don't report agencies to the Better Business Bureau, so even if a company checks out with the BBB there may still be problems. Another way to check out a company is to do a credit check. You can do one online at the Experian Web site at http://www.experian.com. Be wary of any consulting firm that appears to have gotten behind in its payments to vendors.

You can also learn a lot about an agency by posting questions about it on newsgroups or bulletin boards frequented by contractors. Find out what you can about the experience level of the contractors who give you feedback on an agency before trusting too heavily in their reports. Inexperienced contractors who have just started working with a firm often praise it, only to later regret their recommendation while incompetents may denigrate a perfectly good consulting firm.

How do I find a good out-of-town consulting firm?

If you are looking on-line for contracts in distant cities, even more caution is in order. Contractors tell horror stories of accepting contracts in remote cities, renting apartments, and moving their stuff, only to discover that although the consulting signed a contract with them, they didn't sign one with the client, so that the newly relocated contractor has no job. It can be difficult to sue an out-of-state company or, for that matter, even to *find* them if they are operating out of a hotel room and a post office box. So if you are thinking of relocating, stick with companies you can get information about from other contractors. Be particularly cautious when considering any contract that obliges you to move to an area where you can't find other consulting firms listing three or four open contracts that call for your skills.

Are there problems with responding to online contract postings?

The main complaint of contractors who have answered online contract job postings is that they ended up getting swamped by email that offers inappropriate permanent jobs in ludicrous locations.

To protect yourself from this kind of hassle, some contractors suggest that you never give out your real email address to recruiters. Instead they recommend you use a free Web-based mailbox address for all your postings on job-related newsgroups and for replying to online recruiter job postings. You can sign up for a free email mailbox at http://www.hotmail.com or http://www.juno.com.

Should I avoid the consulting companies that other contractors slam?

Not necessarily. Back when we were running a "Rate the Agencies" feature on the Real Rate Survey web site, we found that it was not at all uncommon to get widely differing reports about the same company. One would state that the recruiters were rude and unprofessional, while another would rave about the great rates and interesting contracts that the same company placed them in.

There are several explanations for this. Sometimes it is a matter of chemistry. Some contractors and recruiters rub each other the wrong way. Sometimes the problem is that a contractor simply doesn't have the skills that would make them someone the consulting firm could place with their clientele, but because the contractor doesn't understand how the contracting market works, he responds to the consulting firm's rejection by bad mouthing them.

If a contractor tells you that a consulting firm is greedy or unethical, listen up. But then take a little time to find out how the contractor defines "unethical." For example, there is wide disagreement among contractors about whether it is legitimate for consulting firm recruiters to ask contractors for the names of the managers they've worked for in the past and then call those managers and try to sell them contract help. Some contractors consider this extremely unethical behavior while others consider it a sign the recruiter is an aggressive marketer and figure that they will benefit from working with a company that aggressively pursues new clients.

By the same token, some contractors consider an agency that takes a cut of over 30% of the client billing to be unacceptably greedy, while others don't care what the broker's cut is as long as they get the rate they have decided they want.

Likewise, some contractors will slam a firm because they were not given a chance to interview for a contract because their experience levels didn't match up to the client's stated requirements or they were missing some of the skills the client was asking for. Other, more experienced contractors might take this as a sign that the consulting firm was doing its job and properly screening candidates. These contractors would slam a firm that sent out unqualified contractors on interviews!

Where you stand on these issues is for you to decide. What is certain is that you are more likely to be happy with agencies that please other people who share your skills, your level of proficiency, and your idea of what constitutes good business ethics.

When you ask other contractors for their opinions about local firms, remember that contractors who have completed three or four contracts and have had experience with more than one consulting firm are more likely to give you a balanced view of local consulting firms than people who are just starting their first contracts. So if you run into conflicting reports, give the experienced contractors' reports more weight.

What kinds of problems should I be looking out for?

The following are the kinds of negative reports you should pay particular attention to because they point to serious problems that everyone agrees *are* problems:

- The consulting firm bounced checks

- The consulting firm checks were often seriously delayed

- The consulting firm told a consultant they'd have to take a lower rate after a contract was signed that specified a higher rate

- The consulting firm promised that a contract would be on a 1099 basis before the interview, but after the consultant accepted the offer said it was W-2 only

- The consulting firm promised specific training (usually in some high-demand software package) that never materialized

- The consulting firm has been banned from placing contractors at a large local employer because of ethical problems

- The consulting company illegally imports foreign workers promising them green cards or visas that never materialize

- The consulting firm's recruiter suggested that the contractor should lie about their previous work history or skill set to obtain a contract

- The consulting firm pretended to submit the contractor's résumé to keep the contractor from letting another firm submit him. This eliminated competition for the firm's less qualified salaried employee who *was* submitted

- The consulting firm fired the contractor when they asked for a reasonable raise at the end of the contract period and then lied to the client about why they were replacing the contractor

- The contractor saw the consulting company's invoice and found that the client was being billed an amount much higher than what the recruiter told the contractor the client was being billed

The reputable consulting firms in town won't interview me because I'm currently employed by a large local firm where they have placed contractors. What can I do?

When you are looking to move from being a regular employee and a contractor you may run into problems finding a local consulting firm that will interview you. This is because most client companies put clauses into their contracts with consulting firms that forbid the consulting firm from recruiting their employees. As a result, local consulting firms that have placed contractors with your current employer may be unable to interview you as long as you are employed there.

One solution to this problem is to find a firm that doesn't do business with your current employer. However, if your current employer is a large corporation that uses a lot of contractors you should be wary of local firms who don't do business with them at all. These may be firms with an unsavory local reputation or marginal firms that are not effective at placing contractors.

Another, more drastic, solution is to give notice and *then* look for a consulting firm. The problem here is that you may not be able to find a contract and then will face all the difficulties of looking for a job when you are currently unemployed.

Before quitting, if you have a very good relationship with your supervisor, before you give notice you might consider leveling with your supervisor about your plans and asking them for official permission to approach the consulting firm. Several contractors who have tried this report that it worked. It is a much better approach than quitting when you have nothing lined up, since you are more attractive to clients when you are working than when you are unemployed.

This problem will go away once you have found your first contract and are no longer a corporate employee. Consulting firms who refused to interview you as an employee will then be eager to see you.

Some people tell me all consulting firms are rip-offs. How paranoid do I have to be?

A healthy paranoia is an asset to any contracting career. There are all too many unethical firms out there, as well as some just plain stupid firms. If you tangle with either kind, you can get hurt.

To illustrate this, we've included excerpts from reports submitted by contributors to our 1997 "Rate the Agencies" survey. We've compiled them into a "Consulting Firm Hall of Shame" which you'll find on the next page.

Consulting Firm Hall of Shame

Bait and Switch

Offered a contract "in Hawaii," paying $60 per hour with free local housing, transportation, and monthly trips home to the mainland (extremely attractive terms, don't you think, considering the desirable location?). Recruiter "needed to check" which city the contract was in. I submitted my résumé, and never heard from them again about this or any other contract (1 year now). This may have been a new start-up's way of building a résumé data base.

This firm advertises signing bonuses but never pays them as well as exorbitant salaries that it never delivers.

Agent promised interview and requested my list of references. As I found later this promise was a lie and my list of references was used for marketing.

Sales representative pressured me to sign a non-compete agreement after I interviewed with the client stating verbally to me that an offer was on the table. I signed the agreement. The day after I signed the non-compete, the representative stated that the client withdrew the offer. My impression was that the offer of a position was an out and out fabrication to induce me to sign the non-compete agreement.

Although the recruiter and I had agreed to a rate before the interview, when I called her several hours after the interview (which had gone well, as I was rejoining my former project), she tried (and failed) to chisel me down, saying that "the client is reluctant to pay your rate." This might have been plausible, except that she had quoted me what she said was the billing rate, and it was below that of at least one other team member (I had checked). When I mentioned this, she quickly dropped "the client's" demand, and gave me the rate we had originally agreed on.

"That job was moved to Colorado. We're still running that ad because, uh, we have a client who is looking for, uh, more people with those skills."

Pestering

Called me several times after I told them to stop, and I had also told them to take my résumé off of their database. I stopped getting calls from them only after I changed phone numbers. Staff acted like used-car salespeople.

Marketing was done in so unacceptable a style that some of my references asked me not to use their names again. I met other contractors with the same experience.

Contract Shenanigans

Submitted a different contract than the one signed by me and therefore a lower rate showed up on my pay check. After checking and verifying the difference, they corrected it after 3 weeks of calling and demanding the change.

👎 Required that [I] sign a "contract before the contract" before being submitted to anyone. This contract ...would have required paying a lawyer twice. One of the provisions was that, if the client makes an offer, the consultant must "finalize all contractual matters" within one business day of the INTERVIEW (not the offer).

👎 Before the interview, told me that I had to accept the contract if the client offered it to me. When I balked, they seemed visibly upset.

👎 Real contract has Penalty clause ($1,500) for canceling + restrictive non-compete. Very vague about this at the interview.

Pressure to Go W-2

👎 They claimed to deal with contractors or incorporated people, but when I went to interview with them, they "suggested" that it wasn't "profitable for you to go as an IC or Corp unless you were making at least $45-50 per hour," and instead I should become one of their employees. I brushed them off, and they called again recently saying they had a position at Chevron, and that I only had to send them a non-compete agreement before they submitted me. I did so, and they COMPLETELY avoided talking to me or returning any of my msgs.

👎 Extremely aggressive Legal department. Every contract renewal is a fight! - with more demands surfacing every time. Wanted 2 yrs Corporate Tax returns and all kindsa information - on a renewal...

👎 Initially said I must incorporate to be independent. Then, after I went into them for an interview, said I could not be independent even if I were incorporated. They were advertising their positions on the DICE Bulletin Board as INDOK rather than W2ONLY. At the interview (before revealing their requirement for W-2 work) they pumped me for my company's confidential client list.

👎 They had gotten me a job, which, to my understanding, was to be 1099. At the last minute, they said it was W-2 only, and that if I were to do 1099/corp-to-corp, I'd have to have had a "relationship" with them for over 6 months before they considered it. After telling them to fly a kite, due to "ethical" reasons, they "deactivated" me from further work with [their firm]. The recruiter I worked with was EXTREMELY pressuring, and very hard to deal with.

Looking for Cobalt Programmers . . .

👎 They also had test questions in CICS and COBOL that they gave consultants over the phone, and some of their "right" answers were out of date by about 10 years!

👎 The recruiter...felt I didn't have enough experience in WinNT (I have 2.5 years NT experience), because their client requested the contractor have at least 5 years experience in Windows NT...the program didn't exist back then.

👎 Trying to make maintenance and QA sound like development: "It's a development job . . .for test code." "It's new code for an existing product."

Promises, Promises

One week paid vacation after working 1,500 hours. But. . . you have to wait until your one year anniversary to get it, which they don't bother to mention.

I was supposed to get a commission on some business I referred—never saw it. The excuses were: "We wait until the client pays its invoices," "We wait until the end of the quarter," "We wait until six months of invoices have been paid."

"You will get a raise after six months," only to find out later, the contract is for three months.

"I don't know why he told you that you qualified for the per-diem. He shouldn't have said that" —HR manager referring to my recruiter, on the day I came to sign the contract.

High Pressure Tactics

Were trying to make me promise that I will take the offer if the client decides to take me. Idiotic bargaining by increasing the rate by $1 or $2 while I was asking for about $10 more. Absolutely arrogant.

Pay? You Mean You Expected to Get Paid?

I know several people working for them who earn $30 per hour-$37 per hour and are billed out at $90 per hour.

Stiffed me for the last week of the assignment then refused to return phone calls and/or letters.

After signing a contract which specifically stated I was a hourly employee, they placed me at a client that only paid consultants on a "professional day." This meant I was expected to work up to 10 hours for the same daily fee as 8. Regardless of my contract, the agency would not pay me the additional hours.

Contract states that they pay in 30 days, but I was lucky to get 45-60.

After getting a raise from them, it took over 2 months and repeated phone calls to actually see it on my paycheck.

Out of Control!

Sent my résumé to a client where I was on a contract without informing me.

"Well, I guess we really dropped the ball on that one," after they let the client's contract expire. It took six weeks to get the paperwork through so I could continue working there.

Faxed résumés to my boss for a contract position to replace *me* by getting the company's name from my résumé.

CHAPTER 6

HOW DO I WORK WITH CONSULTING FIRMS?

When should I contact consulting firms?

The best time to contact a consulting firm is when you will be available for work in a few weeks or less. Most consulting firms operate with a very short time horizon. Their clients need help yesterday and are not willing to wait more than a few weeks for a contractor no matter how good a match that contractor might be to their needs.

There's no harm in introducing yourself to a contracting firm several months before you expect to be available. This lets them know that you are there and gives them some idea of your skills. But if you contact them way before the time when you will be available, don't expect to learn anything about how placeable you might be. Because clients give consulting firms such short notice, recruiters rarely have any idea what their requirements will be two or three months down the line.

How many consulting firms should I contact?

Each consulting firm usually has a couple of client companies with which it does the bulk of its business. So it makes sense to contact several firms when you set out to find a contract. Working with several competing firms makes it more likely you'll hear about open contracts at a variety of firms. Choose three or four well-recommended firms to start with and concentrate your efforts on them. It may take a while to determine which consulting firms get contracts that call for your skills and which are just stringing you along.

Once you start getting interviews, you will have a better idea of which firms can place you. At that point you can narrow down the number of firms you deal with, though it is never a good idea to work with just one consulting firm. Doing that eliminates your ability to negotiate from a position of strength, since you will only be able to hold out for the rate and type of project you want if you have your choice of several open contracts. But to have that choice, you need to have several firms attempting to place you. No consulting firm will ever show you more than one contract at a time. The last thing they want is for you to feel that you have a choice and are in a strong negotiating position!

When you work with several firms, it is very important that you make it clear to each one you deal with that you are working with other recruiters. You must make sure they understand that they are *not* to submit your résumé to any client without first calling you and getting your explicit permission to send your résumé to that client. Otherwise, two or three agencies may submit your résumé to the same client, which will result in the client throwing it out and refusing to interview you.

Never work with recruiters who tell you that you have to work exclusively with their firm. This type of behavior is characteristic of firms that prey on newcomers.

Should I first contact firms whose employees have suggested I call them?

You may run into contractors who urge you to first contact their consulting firms if you ever consider contracting. Sometimes they do this because they really like their consulting firms and want them to succeed. But all too frequently, the reason behind a contractor's enthusiasm is the hefty referral bonus that his firm pays for every contractor he recommends who ends up working a contract of three months or longer. These bonuses may be $1,000 or more per referral. So it's always wise to treat enthusiastic contractor referrals with caution and to ask the contractor, before you rush to the phone, whether they get a bonus for referring you.

Should I look for consulting firms that pay a sign-on bonus?

In boom times you may see firms offering a hefty sign-on bonus to contractors who work for them for six months or more. This may seem tempting. However, it's worth keeping in mind that all the money the consulting firm pays you comes from the same place—the client billing. So whether you get it back as a higher hourly rate or as a lump sum bonus paid after you work some set period of time you'll probably end up getting the same amount. That's why it is always wise to keep your eye on the hourly rate and the reputation of the consulting firm, rather than letting yourself be distracted by a one-time cash bonus.

It is also worth remembering that six month contracts have a way of turning into four month contracts—or even three week contracts—when projects get canceled or the client's needs change. So you have no guarantee that you'll work long enough to collect a sign-on bonus.

What is the best way to approach a consulting firm?

First do your homework! As we mentioned earlier, it is essential to find out which firms have good reputations and which place people with your skills. These are the firms most likely to respond to an initial contact with enthusiasm. It also helps to approach firms that you know are actively looking for contractors, either because you've heard from other contractors that they are staffing up particular projects or because you've seen an ad of theirs that asks for your skills.

Consulting firms cannot find work where it does not exist, nor is it their job to talk managers into hiring people they haven't realized they need. Consulting firms match you against their file of open client requisitions and will only be interested in you if you have qualifications that match some listing in that file.

Once you have come up with a list of several firms that have good reputations and appear to have contracts for people with your skills, give each one phone call. It might seem easier to use email, but there are several reasons why a phone approach is better. A phone call gives you a better sense for how the firm and its recruiters come across on the phone, which is important because it will be by phone that they will be selling you to clients. The other benefit of a phone call is that it is simple and doesn't tax the often rudimentary computer savvy of consulting firm staff who may still be getting the hang of using email and the Internet.

However, if you are extremely shy and tend to get tongue-tied on the phone, you may do better to make your first contact through email. This is also true if you have a thick foreign accent that is hard for some people to understand. In that case, making your first contact through email may make it easier for you to put across your qualifications and to motivate recruiters to deal with any real-time communication difficulties you might have.

What should be my goal in the initial contact?

Your goal in your initial contact is to inform the recruiter about your skills and experience, to sound out if they might have work for you, to determine what that work might pay, and to decide if the consulting firm's recruiter is someone you would want to have representing you to a client.

How should I initiate the contact?

If you have been given a recruiter's name by someone who referred you to the consulting firm, ask for that person by name when you call. If you don't have a name, when a receptionist answers your call, ask to speak to the recruiter who specializes in placing people with your particular software skills. For example, you might say, "Please put me through to the recruiter who specializes in placing people with Oracle database experience."

When you reach the recruiter, keep your initial statements brief. This is not the time to go into detail about anything. The recruiter may be in the middle of another phone call or interview or be frazzled from a long day of talking to people who have no marketable skills.

Ask if this is a good time to talk and, if it isn't, ask when would be a better time to call back. If you get the signal that the recruiter is open to hearing from you, explain that you are interested in finding out about contract opportunities and then briefly give a focused verbal summary of your résumé. If the recruiter hears something that interests them, they will ask you lots more questions.

What kinds of questions should I expect the recruiter to ask?

The recruiter will probably begin by asking you to describe your software experience. Briefly list the languages, development tools, databases, and operating systems you have been paid to work with. The recruiter may also ask you if you have experience with other software that is related to the products you mention. All that is needed here is a simple "yes," "a little bit," or "no." If you have significant amounts of experience with something, tell the recruiter how many years you have worked with it, but if your experience is just a few months deep, don't mention time. In all cases, keep your answers brief and to the point.

The recruiter will probably also ask you what companies you have worked for. Give the company name and, if it is a large company, the name of the division or department you worked in. If, at this point, the recruiter pushes you for the names of the managers you worked for, be careful. You aren't making this phone call to give the recruiter new leads! Instead, turn the tables and ask the recruiter what managers in that company *they* have placed people with in the past.

At this stage, a good recruiter should say something to show you that they know something about past projects in the companies you have worked at and who managed them. For example, if you mention that you did a project in the Defined Contribution Pensions Division at MegaCorp, the recruiter might say, "Oh, was that on one of Pat Richards' projects?" or, "Oh, yes, we just placed someone there to help with Bob Smith's Sybase conversion effort."

This kind of response tells you both that the recruiter is familiar with your local market and that they have experience placing people with your type of skills. It also shows that they are interested in you, since they wouldn't bother trying to impress you with their competence if they were not.

If recruiters are interested in you, they will ask when you can start work. If the answer is "immediately" or "in two weeks," the recruiter may interview you further on the phone, or suggest a face-to-face meeting. If your skills are a close match to an open contract, the recruiter may even ask you to interview with a client the next day.

If the only response you get is a tepid, "Send in your résumé," you can be pretty sure that the company is not likely to place you. Recruiters who think they can place you will ask you questions, respond to your questions, and then dangle a couple of open contracts before you in the hopes of motivating you to fax or email your résumé as soon as possible.

Should I discuss rates during the initial contact?

Always find out as much as you can on the phone, unless you enjoy wasting an afternoon driving downtown and hassling with parking so you can listen to some idiot explain how his wonderful company never works with anyone but salaried employees paid $35,000 per year. You can and should ask about rates, keeping your questions broad and generic, so that you can screen out consulting firms that would be an obvious waste of time.

As an example of what we mean by a "generic" question, you might ask the recruiter "What kind of rates are you getting for network administrators right now?" This allows the recruiter to give you a broad reply, like "Forty to $75 an hour, depending on experience."

If these rate ranges don't match your expectations—assuming that you have done your homework so that these expectations are realistic—tell the recruiter then and there. If the company doesn't place people at the rates you would like to earn, there isn't much point to pursuing the contact.

Should I tell them what rate I want?

Seasoned negotiators say that the person who mentions money first loses. They suggest that you always get the recruiter to state his or her figure before you mention yours. Unfortunately, for you, it is *recruiters* who tend to be the seasoned negotiators—a lot more seasoned than most computer contractors. So in practice it may be difficult to finesse them into revealing their rate before you mention yours.

When recruiters ask, "What rate have you been getting?" they may be looking to see if their rate range matches your expectations or whether you are a prima donna who expects more than their clients will pay.

Be careful here! Don't mention your *previous rate*. Instead, focus on the *rate you want*. Show that you've done your research by saying something like, "Based on what I'm hearing from other contractors with my skills in this region, I expect to get something in the $60 to $65 per hour range." Ideally, the range you cite should extend a good 10% higher than what you really need to come away with, to leave some room for negotiation.

Should I ask about tax status at this point?

If you detect strong interest on the part of the recruiter, it never hurts to ask whether they will work with independents. This will tell you a lot about the company. When you ask about tax status, don't come across as an authority on the subject. Instead, project a certain air of innocence, to see whether the recruiter gives you a reasonable explanation of the issues involved with your working status or whether they try to take advantage of your naiveté by snowing you with untruths such as, "The law only allows us to only work with W-2s," or "The IRS has reclassified thousands of independent contractors."

Be alert for signs that the company tries to get all contractors to work as benefited salaried employees rather than hourly rate contractors or that they refuse to work with any independents at all. Even if you intend to work as a W-2 hourly contractor, you can learn a lot about a consulting firm by the way they discuss the question of your working status with you.

What else should I look for?

You should evaluate every phase of the conversation you have with the recruiter for signs that they are someone you'd be comfortable having represent you to a client. A good recruiter should have excellent sales skills, and this means they should be engaging and persuasive on the phone. If the recruiter sounds like a dolt when talking to you, why would you want them calling up clients on your behalf?

Try also to get some information about the recruiter's own background. Ask them how long they've been placing IT contractors and how long they've been working for this particular consulting firm. This allows you to screen out newly hired beginners who probably don't have the contacts, industry knowledge, or sales skills to find you a good contract.

What should I do if the consulting firm wants a face-to-face interview?

There is some disagreement among contractors as to whether it is legitimate for a firm to demand a face-to-face interview. Contractors who argue against these interviews say that, all too often, the only reason recruiters wanted to interview them face-to- face was to get them to fill in an application form that asked for the names and phone numbers of five or more past supervisors—information that then fattened up the recruiter's "new prospects" file. There is no question that this does happen.

But a good case can also be made that a consulting firm should have the right to check you out before they send you to a client as their representative. Unfortunately, there are plenty of would-be contractors who don't have the skills or experience needed to fill contracts, who lie about their qualifications and waste the client's time. So it may be a mistake to blow off every recruiter who asks for a face-to-face meeting.

But it might be a good idea to agree to meet with recruiters only when they convince you that they have a contract available that you could interview for immediately. If the justification for the interview is supposed to be for the consulting firm to check out your credentials, ask the recruiter on the phone who will be doing the technical interview.

When you go to the consulting firm interview, use it to further size up the consulting firm and to establish a good personal connection with the recruiter. You will do a lot better over the long-term working with a recruiter you know and can get along with than one you know only from email. Indeed, your inability to meet recruiters face-to-face when dealing with people from the out-of-town firms you meet on the Internet is another reason why some contractors feel strongly that local firms are preferable.

DON'T GET EXPLOITED AT THE INTERVIEW!

"I deal with the 'getting to know you' bunch by asking them to have their technical interviewer call me first. The 'real' ones will do just that, and the trollers usually don't bother me for a while."

—Scott Horne

"Several years ago when I first started in consulting I did meet with every recruiter that requested an interview. Biggest waste of time of my life. In one instance I remember asking for a high rate on one C++ contract, so the client asked me to come in and take a test (TEKCHEK for those of you keeping score). Apparently they figured I would bomb on it, and they could justify offering me peanuts. Unfortunately for them, I scored in the 95% percentile. They told me they would get back with me. I never heard from them.

"I also agree on holding out on references. My references go to the client after we've agreed on a rate and scope. I can't tell you how many times I've had a broker tell me they had a hot job but needed references. They usually hang up after I tell them I only give references to clients."

—James V. Reagan

"These agencies are telling me that they need to check two references before sending out a résumé as the clients require this. But I found out they were lying, as they had already sent my résumé out to several firms without my references and also before even telling me that I was being submitted to a particular firm."

—Elizabeth P.

How should I dress for an interview?

When you go to the interview dress yourself in whatever is the appropriate business attire for your region. This is usually a business suit, and for men, a tie. Treat the interview just as you would any interview with any highly desirable client.

Many technical wizzes feel that by ignoring all standards of business dress they get across the message that they are so good that they don't have to relate to the bogus symbolism that prevails in the business world. There is a place for this attitude, but it is generally not in the office of a consulting firm recruiter. Recruiters are salespeople and salespeople tend to take outward signs and symbols extremely seriously. You may be as good as you think, and clients might even agree, but you may not have a chance to prove it if you wear your sandals and T-shirt to the consulting firm interview and never get sent to see the client.

Standards for business dress vary from region to region. So you may be able to treat a vendor T-shirt as "business attire" in California but not in Des Moines. Just remember that when you show up wearing clothing that says, "I'm a serious business person," you reinforce the message that you deserve top rates as well as making it more likely that you will get in to see the kinds of clients who can pay those rates.

How do I handle the consulting firm interview?

Use the interview to find out what kinds of people work for this consulting firm and what kind of image it presents. Don't be taken in by glitzy offices. Many good smaller consulting firms can't afford them while body shops can. Just concentrate on the quality of people you encounter. Keep in the forefront of your mind that your whole reason for dealing with this firm is their ability to make sales and use the visit to further evaluate their sales ability.

Before you go into detail about your technical experience and past projects, take time to feel out the technical background of the person interviewing you. Some consulting firms have separate recruiting and sales departments. Their recruiters are people with strong technical backgrounds who interview candidates and determine whether they really have the skills they say they do before passing them on to a salesperson whose job is to place them.

If you are dealing with this kind of interviewer, you may need to give the "secret handshake" and show that you can throw around the insider language that people in your niche use. There are lots of people claiming to have in-demand skills who don't have them. So when an interviewer grills you, it is sometimes a sign that the firm cares about maintaining a reputation for supplying technically competent people.

But many other firms have the same recruiter interviewing candidates and selling them to clients. In this case, the recruiter may have been hired solely for their sales skills and have no technical background at all. As a result, they may have only a thin grasp of what your skills mean. They may know that "Java" is in hot demand but have no idea what object oriented systems design might be. If you are talking to one of these, keep your explanations brief and respond simply to the recruiter's questions, rather than giving them more information than they can handle.

Sometimes this kind of interviewer will attempt to grill you by asking stupid questions obviously memorized from some manual on how to screen technical people. In the worst case, highly skilled contractors have reported being quizzed until they could not answer a question on some irrelevant piece of coding trivia and then told, "We'll have to offer you a lower rate since you don't have the skills to support the rate you are asking for."

The consulting firm asked me to fill out an application that asks me to give contact information for my previous employers and clients. Are they just using me?

They may be. One approach used by experienced contractors to counter this is to list only other *consulting firms* in the Previous Employer section of the application form.

Another approach is to simply write "to be discussed" on the part of the form that asks you to list references. If questioned about it, explain to the recruiter that you'll be happy to supply references to the *client* once an actual interview is lined up but that you don't want your references pestered unnecessarily. Firms that really have work for you will understand your reticence.

Rather than obsessing about the company using the references you supply to expand its client list, it's much better to use the discussion of references to find out what the recruiter already knows about your past projects and management. If they actually know something about placing people with your skills in your local market they should already know something about your past projects.

When asked for information about your previous jobs, the best approach is to mention the company and department without giving the managers' names and see what kind of response you get. If the recruiter asks you for the names of all your managers, say something like, "Well, since you don't seem to know anything about who is managing Java development at ABC Soft, where *do* you place Java contractors?"

In my own experience, the recruiters who found me the best contracts could tell me all about the politics and the histories of projects at companies I'd worked for and were quite willing to do this to demonstrate to me that they knew their stuff.

Should I deal with a recruiter who is a technical idiot?

If you find that the recruiter you are talking to is a technical ignoramus, you may be tempted to blow them off on the spot, but this may be a mistake. If the recruiter has been in the business for a while, say three or four years, the chances are that they have built up a good base of people who call them when they need technical help, so despite their lack of technical savvy they may be very good at finding you work.

This is particularly true if the recruiter is an old-timer with a background in MIS management, who moved into recruiting in the period of massive MIS downsizing that occurred in the late 1980s and early 1990s. These people may not know the language of object oriented design but they know who's who in local corporations and they often have a good sense for whether programmers are bullshitting or not, even if they don't know the latest technological bells and whistles.

It is one of life's little ironies, that the recruiters who most annoy technical people are often those who are the best at finding them work. This is because it takes a personality very different from that of the typical technical wizard to excel at salesmanship. Wizards tend to be rational, honest, and open. Salespeople... Well, they tend to be salespeople!

Another point worth considering is that the obnoxious salesperson who browbeats you into taking a job you didn't really want at a rate that was a few dollars less than you hoped for, is also capable of browbeating managers into interviewing candidates who may not have exactly the skills the manager asked for and of getting them to hire contractors at rates a few dollars higher than the manager meant to pay. When times are tough, or your skills are less than stellar, these people can keep you working, when other, more personable, salesfolk cannot.

So before you write off a recruiter, remember that their role is simply to find you work. Demand that they have familiarity with the local employment scene and a solid base of contacts. Look for signs that they have been successful enough to survive in the recruiting business for several years. Look for hints that they are ethical. Beyond that, if the recruiter is pleasant and knows something about software, that's a plus, but it may not be all that relevant to whether they can place you in the kinds of contracts you want.

The recruiter tried to talk me into working as a salaried employee rather than a contractor. Is this a bad sign?

You can't fault the recruiter for trying. After all, their company earns a whole lot more when they pay you as an employee than they do when you are an hourly contractor, and they are not in this business out of an altruistic desire to enrich contractors.

Discussions about salaried employment only become a sign warning of danger if the recruiter continues to pressure you to be an employee and will not take "no" for an answer after you have explained you only are interested in earning a high hourly rate.

The recruiter gave me a contract to sign at the preliminary interview. Should I sign it?

No! This is a well-known agency abuse. There is no reason for you to sign anything with a consulting firm until the firm finds a client willing to hire you.

The firm that pressures you to sign a pre-assignment contract is generally a firm that exploits inexperienced first time contractors. Such contracts may bind you to work for a set rate before you've had a chance to interview for a contract or they may bind you to accept any contract you interview for if the client wants to hire you. Some may limit your ability to work with other consulting firms during your job hunt. Others may prevent you from taking contracts through other agencies at any company where this agency has mailed your résumé or scheduled an interview, even if you don't get the contract. Whatever the recruiter tells you, none of these pre-employment contract clauses are standard in the industry, and you should never sign any of them.

The only contract you may need to sign before an interview is a *nondisclosure agreement*. Clients may ask you to sign one before revealing to you the details of a new software development project that they don't want their competitors to know about. You can safely sign a nondisclosure agreement that binds you to keeping trade secrets private, unless it also prevents you from interviewing with local competitors where you might otherwise find contracts in the near future. Because of this latter possibility, you should carefully read any nondisclosure contract before signing it, to make sure that it doesn't include wording that could overly limit your ability to find work elsewhere.

SLEAZE TACTICS

"Prior to interview with client—ten minutes beforehand—the recruiter shoved a contract in front of me and said that if I did not sign and agree to the rate stated that I could not interview with the client. Needless to say I mentioned this practice to the client and they got smacked."

—John D. Allen

Can I ask to see their regular contract now?

You can and should ask to see a copy of the consulting firm's boilerplate contract *now*, before you go out on an interview and get seduced into wanting a contract the firm finds you. This is the time to look for abusive clauses and to get some idea of what you will face should this company find a client who wants to hire you. We'll be discussing consulting firm contract clauses further in Chapter 7, "What's In My Consulting Firm Contract?"

ASK TO SEE THE CONTRACT FORM BEFORE THE INTERVIEW

"The usual ploy seems to go as follows: Agency submits your résumé to client and you have an interview, client makes an offer, you are interested in the position, agency gives you the contract agreement to sign on Friday and the client wants you to start on Monday.

"Do you have enough time to review the contract with your lawyer? You might feel pressured to take the contract so you sign under duress. Then later you discover some contract provisions are not to your liking.

"Make sure they will give you enough time to review the contract!"

—Ed Swartz

What kind of résumé should I send a consulting firm?

The résumé you send a consulting firm should be organized so that your technical skills are highlighted, since technical skills are what consulting firms care about. Many contractors like to include a separate "Technical Skills" section on their résumé where they simply list the skills with which they have paid experience.

When you list your previous jobs and contracts on the résumé, be sure to describe each one in terms of the software and hardware involved. Mention every piece of software you have ever had paid experience with no matter how slim. This will enhance your chances of getting called for contract opportunities, since, as we mentioned before, recruiters and clients often process résumés on the basis of a byte-by-byte compare. Don't focus on your level of responsibility the way you would when creating a résumé to be used for applying for a regular salaried job. A contracting résumé is about skills.

If you include an education section on your résumé be sure to list all vendor training and company-sponsored classes in vendor technologies that you have attended. Don't forget any certifications. These are more interesting to recruiters and clients than your college credentials once you are a few years away from college.

If possible, keep your résumé focused on the past three years. Age discrimination is rampant in the high tech world, so you are more likely to harm than help yourself by revealing that you have been in the field for decades. In a similar vein, there is no need to give your year of college graduation if it reveals that you are over 40.

And keep your résumé brief! Two pages is the most anyone can be expected to look at. Make sure that the information you want them to see leaps off the page. Recruiters and clients are busy, so you want your qualifications to get across to them even when they skim.

Recruiters may tell you that they'll redo your résumé to make it a better selling tool, but many contractors report that the only thing consulting firms have done with their résumés is photocopy them onto the consulting firm's letterhead after removing their names and phone numbers. So do as good a job as you can with your résumé, since it may be the one that goes to potential clients.

Any tips on sending out my résumé?

The biggest danger in sending out your résumé is that several firms will submit it to the same client. Naive first time contractors assume that if this happens, they can take the contract through whichever firm pays the best. But this is not what actually occurs. If you are double-submitted for a contract, the client will probably refuse to interview you since hiring you could set them up for legal disputes with the consulting firms who submitted you.

Many recruiters will tell you that because of the danger of double submissions you should only work with one firm—theirs. This is baloney! It is always a better idea to deal with several firms since each has strengths and contacts in certain areas the others do not. Working with several firms makes it more likely that you will hear about several contracts appropriate for your skills.

All you need to do to prevent a double submission from occurring is to make it clear to each recruiter you deal with that you already have circulated your résumé to several firms. When you mail or fax your résumé, make sure to include wording on it or on your cover letter that says that you do not give permission for your résumé to be distributed unless the recruiter calls and gets your explicit permission to send it out. Add that you will not go on any interview that results from the unsolicited distribution of your résumé.

If after you've done this, a company still submits your résumé without your prior approval, cross them off your list. Notify them by mail that you will take legal action if they continue to distribute your résumé. The firms you want to deal with will honor a request that you approve any submissions beforehand.

ONE RECRUITER'S ADVICE ON RÉSUMÉS

"As a recruiter, I don't really agree with the 'more is better' philosophy. Our clients want to see the right buzz words easily.

"My suggestion is to have a summary statement—it gives us the 1st clue about what you're interested in. You also need a skills summary section— break it down into OS, RDBMS, Languages, etc. This is SO helpful!! And of course, include relevant career experience.

"Also, include your education and dates diplomas were received. Lots of people are also impressed by any professional training or certifications you've received."

–Kelly Gratland

What comes after the first contact?

After your first contact with a recruiter and any interviews you have with people at the consulting firm, you won't hear anything from the firm until they have found a client who is ready to hire someone with exactly your skills.

Resist the temptation to call every week to find out if the firm has work for you. It is a waste of time. If the firm has a contract you could fill, you'll hear about it immediately. If they don't, pestering the recruiter will not make it appear out of nowhere.

The recruiter has an interview for me. What now?

When a recruiter phones you with a contract, it is very important to learn as much as you can about the assignment on the phone to save yourself the wasted time and aggravation of interviewing for a position you either don't want or aren't qualified for. Recruiters tend to paint an overly rosy picture of all assignments that come their way, which is part of their jobs as salespeople. But by asking a few probing questions when the recruiter calls, you can usually eliminate the interviews that would be a complete waste of your time.

Ask as many questions as you can about the skill set involved in the contract. Because recruiters are rarely technically knowledgeable they will often call you for contracts you don't have the skills needed to fill. For example, if your experience with programming in C extends only to working on small standalone programs that run under Windows, it is not likely that a client would hire you for a contract that requires extensive experience coding C under the UNIX Bourne Shell or writing C firmware. However, recruiters will see "C" under the list of languages on your résumé and call you for those types of contracts.

Make sure also that you find out where the contract is located. Recruiters tend to be weak at geography and are prone to call with wonderful opportunities at companies located two hours away from your home.

Ask what kind of work the contract entails. Screen out those that involve things you don't want to do, like being on call or testing software, as well as those development projects where managers are looking for people willing to put in more overtime than you are able to give.

Ask what rate the contract would pay, but take what you hear now with a grain of salt. At this stage recruiters often overstate the rate by a few dollars to get you to go to the interview. If the rate you hear now is *lower* than the minimum you'd be happy earning, there is no reason to go on the interview, since in all likelihood the actual rate will turn out to be lower still.

If you tell recruiters that the rate is too low and they offer to raise it, explain that if the interview is a success, you expect to get the newly quoted rate and will not take the contract for less. But even if you do this, you can expect many recruiters to still try to talk you into taking a lower rate once the client makes you a firm offer.

If the recruiter can't tell you anything abut what a contract involves, ask them to get back to you with more information before you agree to go on the interview unless you really don't mind wasting a few hours.

A recruiter called with a contract that doesn't interest me at all. They want to do the interview anyway. Should I do it?

This may just be an attempt to manipulate you into going to the interview in the hope that you'll like the job better after hearing more about it from the hiring manager. Firms wouldn't pull this maneuver if it didn't work, and, in fact, it often does. Make your decision with the knowledge that if you do go to the interview and the client makes an offer for you, you'll be the target of the recruiter's hardest sell.

What happens at the client interview?

A consulting firm representative may meet you at the client's site and introduce you to the client. They will usually leave after making the introduction, though very rarely they may remain in the room during the client interview.

The client's interviewer should begin by giving you a description of the project and telling you what they are looking for. They'll ask you about your background and may even ask you questions to test your technical knowledge. Sometimes these questions will seem absurd, for example, contractors report being quizzed on the meanings of specific CICS error return codes or being asked to describe 2s complement math techniques.

Interviewers may ask these dumb questions because they are mangers with no technical knowledge who have asked a colleague, "Give me a few good questions I can ask to see if this guy knows what he says he knows." Clients may also subject you to intense technical quizzing because they have had a bad experience in the past with a contractor who attempted to fake expertise they didn't have. In some cases, you may be asked to take an exam to prove you have mastered your technical specialty. Usually, if this is the case, the consulting firm representative will have warned you about the exam before sending you to the interview.

NO HOLDS BARRED!

"The only predictable thing about contract interviews is their unpredictability. Remember this, you are not usually interviewed as a prospective employee would be. An employee interview process is usually under the firm thumb of a Human Resources Department and is usually scripted with careful consideration to the legality of questions, personal chemistry, etc. The contractor interview has none of these boundaries and safeguards.

"Some of them will be a pretty straightforward tech-out—can you do the job or can't you. They don't really much care if you have six arms and drool in your soup.

"Others get really wild since there are no legal restraints on the type of questions they can ask of someone who will not be their employee. They sometimes ask things about your personal life that would get them slugged or sued if asked of a prospective employee."

—Dick Young

Who will be interviewing me?

It is very important to determine at the beginning of the interview what role the person who is interviewing you has on the project. You may be speaking to the manager to whom you will report, but it is just as likely that you will interview with someone you will never see again. They might be someone higher up in the management chain who has responsibility for staffing the whole project or a team leader from another part of the project who happened to have some free time and could talk with you while the manager you'd actually report to was dealing with some crisis.

This happens because projects that need contractors are often projects in crunch mode—projects where everyone who really knows what is going on is too busy doing real work to take off an hour to interview contractors. So you may find yourself interviewed by almost anyone in a leadership position who has a slight connection with the project and some open time on their schedule.

This may make it hard to find out what kind of work the contract really involves. Sometimes an upper level manager who sees the project from an organizational viewpoint will spend the whole interview describing exciting-sounding work that is taking place in a part of the project that is not where you will be placed. If a team leader does the interview, you may find out more nuts and bolts information about the project—but only if the team leader leads the team to which you'd be assigned, which is not always the case.

If you take the time to determine what role the person interviewing you plays, you'll also do a better job of selling yourself. If they're an upper level manager, avoid snowing them with technical displays they cannot follow. If the person interviewing you can't answer questions that you must get answered to decide if you want the job, it is legitimate to ask them to let you have a word with someone else who can answer those questions after this interview is over.

CUT TO THE CHASE

"If I find out I'm talking to a team leader or a business unit manager, I just sit there and talk about the projects I've participated on in the past. I prefer to do all the talking—as I speak, I start letting on a couple of technical details (as much as I think the person in front of me can handle).

"Usually, the next thing I hear is, 'When can you start?'"

—Greg Serabian

Should I discuss rates at the client interview?

Usually not. The consulting firm will be paying you, not the client, so most contractors believe it is inappropriate to discuss money with the client. You'll negotiate rates when the consulting firm representative calls you with a firm offer after the interview. Some contractors feel they can get a better deal if they ask the client what they are willing to pay and use this information in their negotiations with the consulting firm, but this is a risky technique. Grilling clients about how much they are willing to pay may make a negative impression.

Should I discuss the start date at the interview?

If the person interviewing you is seriously interested in hiring you, they will almost always ask you when you can start. Usually they will want you to start immediately or in two weeks. Give them an honest answer as there is no point in having them make an offer for you to the consulting firm if you can't report when they need you.

How much can I find out about the contract at the interview?

In many cases you'll get a clear description of exactly what it is the client expects you to do and how long the project is expected to last. Feel free to ask as many questions as you need to, in order to get enough of an idea of what the project is about to decide if you want to do it.

At a minimum you should find out what the hardware and software environments are, not only in the part of the project that you'll be working on, but also in related areas. This is because it is not uncommon for a contractor to be moved from team to team as a project develops, so you should check out the whole environment to see what software you might be able to learn on the job—or what technically deficient backwaters you could get stuck in.

You should also find out what the company's policy is about assigning overtime to contractors and make sure that it fits with your own plans. Some companies assign any extra work to salaried employees who work extra hours without extra pay and like their contractors to go home after their forty hours are done. But others will tell you at the interview that they are rushing to meet a tight deadline and do not want anyone on the project who isn't willing to work sixty hour weeks indefinitely.

Be wary if the person interviewing you tells you that the contract will start out with you doing boring work using obsolete tools but that "later" you'll move onto another part of the project where you will get training in cutting-edge technology. This is a common ploy used by managers to lure talent to otherwise unattractive projects. Most contractors who have fallen for it report that they ended up working with the dead-end software for the duration of the contract and never got the promised training.

If travel is involved in this contract, you might want to clarify with the client at the interview how frequently you'll be expected to travel and how the company will handle payment for travel and lodging expenses. If you feel strongly about flying business class and staying a certain type of hotel, this is the time to bring it up.

This is only a temporary position. So I don't need to give it the kind of thought I'd give a real job, right?

Our Real Rate Survey data show that the most common length for a contract is six months followed closely by one year and two years. Contracts are often extended two or three times. So it is not at impossible that the brief contract you accept after a twenty minute interview might completely fill up your next two years of work. If you aren't careful in selecting that contract, you may find yourself working those two years in a situation that does nothing to enhance your appeal to your next client.

If this is just a six week contract, why worry?

Companies often offer six week contracts to inexperienced contractors because they don't know whether they'll be able to handle the work. However, the contract the consulting firm gives you for this six week contract includes an *extension* clause which may oblige you to continue working for the client as long as they want to extend the contract. That is why a six week contract may easily turn into a two year contract and why you should never take any contract that you don't see as enhancing your career, unless you are truly desperate for any work at all.

The contract they've got for me is "temp-to-perm." What does that mean?

Temp-to-perm arrangements are a great deal—for the client. Under this arrangement you work for three months as a contractor. Then, if the client likes you, they convert you to a salaried employee. This gives the employer a chance to see if you can do the work, while they retain the freedom to fire you at any time.

Sometimes these arrangements start out by paying you a contractor's rate, with the understanding that if you are hired permanently, your pay will drop to an employee's salary. Sometimes temp-to-perm contracts start out only paying you an hourly rate based on an employee's salary rather than a true contract rate. This is an even worse deal for you, since you are getting a very low contract rate while working a short-term contract that gives you no assurance you'll be hired on permanently.

Even if you are looking for a permanent job, you should treat a temp-to-perm contract just like any other three-month contract and demand the same rate you'd ask for any short-term work. Experienced contractors warn that if you take a temp-to-perm contract, you'll put in a lot of unpaid overtime and you'll be treated like an employee. They also point out that some unscrupulous client companies use the lure of permanent employment to talk contractors into working contracts for lower than usual rates, while having no real intention of offering the contractor a permanent job.

If a salaried job is what you are really looking for, temp-to-perm arrangements are not your only hope for getting hired. If you do well on the job as a contractor many clients will invite you to become a permanent employee even if you haven't signed a temp-to-perm contract. Indeed, clients have *more* motivation to make you a job offer when you are earning a high contract rate since they save more money converting a highly paid contractor to an employee.

The only time a temp-to-perm arrangement might make sense is if you are at the beginning of your career with a lackluster résumé that doesn't leave you a lot of other options. But when demand for contractors is strong, there's little inducement for experienced professionals to accept this kind of offer.

How can I optimize my chances of getting the contract?

Be honest about your interest; this is not the place for coyness. If you want the contract, at the end of the interview tell the manager that you find the project very attractive and ask, "If I were to be hired, when would you like me to report?" The response should give you an idea of how successful you have been.

INTERVIEWING TIP

"There is one little trick that has worked well for me in the past. If the manager and I seem to be getting along well and it doesn't look like he/she is searching for a way to get me out the door in 30 seconds flat, I start looking for occasions to use the word 'we' in its various forms.

"'How long have we got to get this project in?' 'Have the user requirements been handed over to us yet?' You are trying to convey to the manager that you are interested in and identifying with his/her project/problem and are a team player.

"Don't beat him/her over the head with it, but try to convey a sincere interest in solving the problem."

–Dick Young

What should I do if I can't find out much at the interview?

Though you may want to find out as much as you can about the work you'd be doing on a contract, this is not always possible. In some cases, the people interviewing you may not know what tasks you'd be assigned. They are hiring a pool of contractors and will decide who does what when they know what their final collection of talent looks like.

In that case, you'll have to make a judgment based on intuition, on the caliber of the people you meet at the interview and on your overall reaction to what you see at the company while you are there. Is this company staffed by bright, technologically aware people? Do the projects you heard about use software and hardware that would add to your résumé? If the answer to these questions is "yes," consider the contract. If not, it may be a better idea to look for something else.

What if I only get to do a telephone interview with a remote client?

If a recruiter finds you a contract in a distant city, you may only get to do a telephone interview with a hiring manager or team leader. In that case, it will be much harder to determine what you are really getting into. You may ask the same questions you would at a face-to-face interview but you won't get to see the environment or meet the people you'll be working with. This makes it much harder to gauge what is going on. For that reason, remote contracts should be treated with great caution.

TELEPHONE INTERVIEWS

"Telephone interviewing is really fun and easy to get through. The employer will always start the conversation with your project background. Telling your exact skill set and how it will match their requirements is really important.

"Normally the telephone interview will be in two steps. First step, the employer will do initial screening/technical questions to find out potential candidates.

"The second step will be for them to find out: are you really interested in the project? Mostly, in the second call, they will confirm your contract with them.

"I was in Michigan state last year and got interviewed by a Pennsylvania-based employer. First phone call, they asked me about 50 technical questions (I know it was pre-prepared questions). Next day, they called me to confirm the contract."

—Sundar

I'd like to interview for more than one contract before I decide on one. Can I do this?

You can and you should. But the only way to do this is to deal with more than one consulting firm at a time, and that requires care on your part. Consulting firms typically let you interview for one contract and then, if that client wants you, put a lot of pressure on you to accept.

The only way a consulting firm could give you a choice of contracts would be by disappointing the clients whose contracts you didn't accept—and the last thing a consulting firm wants to do is disappoint clients. As you'll recall, consulting firms stay in business by pleasing clients, not contractors!

So to get a choice of contracts, you must line up interviews through several different agencies, doing your best to schedule them within a few days of each other. Since acceptances will dribble in over a period of a few days, you'll have to hold off some firms until you've heard from the others. Meanwhile, you can expect to be pestered mercilessly by recruiters using use every bit of their sales ability to get you to take contracts where the client has already expresssed a desire to hire you.

What should I do when I get an offer?

As soon as the client notifies the consulting firm that they want to hire you, the recruiter will contact you with an offer.

When the recruiter calls and says, "Congratulations! MegaCorp wants you to start on Monday. We'll put the contract in the mail today," your only reply should be

"What's the rate?" The response will tell you all. It is here, and only here, that you find out how ethical the consulting firm really is.

The rate you hear now may have no resemblance to the rates this same recruiter quoted you in the past. If you are dealing with an ethical firm, that rate should not be more than a few dollars off. But be prepared for anything. If you're dealing with the typical exploitative body shop, the recruiter may blame the low rate on the client's stinginess, or try to convince you that the rate offered is all you can expect to get in this market. Whatever the excuse, the recruiter will claim that the consulting firm is helpless to do anything about the rate and will try to persuade you to take the contract anyway.

What should I do if the recruiter tries to lowball me?

If the rate is too low to interest you, or if it differs significantly from what you were quoted when you went to the interview, simply explain that you have already made it clear what rate you will settle for and that you interviewed for the position only because you were told you'd get that rate. Conclude by telling the recruiter that you aren't interested in the contract unless it pays that rate. Then hang up.

The problem may be that the client refuses to pay enough to give you what you are asking and leave a commission for the consulting firm or it may be that the client is paying plenty but the consulting firm is taking a huge cut. You have no way of knowing. You may just have been the victim of a classic "bait and switch" play. Because many contractors are naive and unskilled in negotiation, consulting firms do very well with bait and switch maneuvers. Indeed, they pull them as often as they do because they work! Sometimes if you stand fast, like a used car dealer the recruiter will call back with a better offer. Sometimes they won't. The only way to find out is to stand firm and be prepared to walk away from the offer.

But be sure before you walk away, that you really know the market rate for your skills and that you aren't letting yourself be carried away with unrealistic hopes. It is also vital that you get clear with yourself what the *real* rock bottom figure is that you'll accept, so that you don't lose a contract that you really wanted through playing games over a last dollar or two per hour.

What if they demand that I work as a W-2?

Sometimes it is only when there is a firm offer that the recruiter announces, "The client won't hire you unless you work as a salaried consultant," or "We can only let you work this job as a W-2, not a 1099." If you were told before the interview that you were interviewing for an independent contractor contract, not a W-2 contract, then you have all the proof you need that you are dealing with an unethical firm. If you are really committed to working as an independent, you might just have to stand firm or to move on to other interviews with other, more flexible, consulting firms.

I can't make up my mind about this offer. How do I handle this?

Tell the recruiter you'll consider his offer but you need to think about it for a while before you get back to him with your answer. If the recruiter pressures you for an immediate response, tell them it simply isn't possible. Then hang up. Spend some time thinking the situation through. Do you want the contract? Could you live with the rate? What are your alternatives? If you can afford to keep looking, do so, though you may find that walking away from the contract inspires the recruiter to improve his offer the next time you hear from him.

But when you make your mind up about taking a contract, it's never a good idea to make your decision on the basis of the rate alone. Just as important are the kinds of work you'll be doing on the contract and how much you'll enjoy doing it. You must also consider what working this contract might do for your future career prospects.

How can I improve my negotiation skills?

You can learn a lot about negotiation from reading up on the subject, but nothing helps you increase your confidence and negotiating skill like negotiating over and over again. Don't expect to start out a star. You'll almost always make a few mistakes in your first attempts to negotiate with consulting firm representatives. But you will also learn from those mistakes and will do better as your career advances.

I hate negotiating. Do I have to negotiate?

Not necessarily. For contractors with strong résumés the best approach may be to avoid negotiation completely. This is particularly true for contractors who cave in too easily when subjected to the hard-sell tactics favored by consulting firm recruiters or for those who would rather spend time learning new software rather than negotiation techniques. If you decide not to negotiate, simply set your rate, decide what other conditions consulting firms must meet to satisfy you, and work only with companies willing to meet those terms as stated.

If a consulting firm representative attempts to negotiate with you, simply explain that these are your terms and that they are not up for discussion. You may walk away from some contracts that you might have enjoyed working but you may sleep better at night knowing that you haven't been exploited. Contractors who have tried this approach report that when using it you're more likely to end up working with consulting firms that respect and appreciate you, since you'll alienate those that make their money by taking advantage of unworldly techies.

Besides my rate and status, what else must I negotiate?

If you are considering a job that is located downtown where parking is scarce, be sure to ask the recruiter to guarantee that the company provide you with on-site parking. This can be worth an additional $50 per week in some cities. If the company won't give you on-site parking and you are working as a W-2, you may be able to negotiate to have the consulting firm pay your parking as an employee expense.

You should also nail down the start date at this point too, so that you don't inadvertently accept a contract you can't begin or one that doesn't start for many weeks. If you have already made plans for a vacation, tell the recruiter that the client will need to give you unpaid time off when the vacation is scheduled. This is also the time for W-2 hourly contractors to discuss whether they can buy into the consulting firm's health insurance plan and how much it will cost them.

BOOKS TO IMPROVE YOUR NEGOTIATING SKILLS

Albrecht, Karl and Steve Albrecht. *Added Value Negotiating.* Homewood, IL. Richard D. Irwin. 1993. ISBN 1-55623-967-X The breakthrough method for building balanced deals. Focuses on the whole deal, not on the tricks and tactics of negotiating.

Fisher, Roger, William Ury, and Bruce Patton. *Getting to Yes: Negotiating Agreement without Giving In. 2nd edition.* ISBN 0-14-015735-2. A classic and a bestseller.

Haden Elgin, Suzette, Ph. D. *Business Speak.* New York. McGraw Hill. 1995. ISBN 0-07-019999-X. Using the gentle art of verbal persuasion to get what you want at work. Also see her "Gentle Art of Verbal Self-Defense" series.

How do I accept the offer?

Tell the recruiter that you are excited about taking the contract, but make it clear that you can't give final approval until the company faxes you an actual contract for you to review. This should take place as soon as possible, so that you have time to examine all the contract terms before you finalize the agreement. Until you have it an agency contract in your hands, you never know what you'll find in it. So don't give a hard commitment until you've reviewed the whole package.

Once you've seen the contract and negotiated any clauses that might need to be changed, (for details on how to do this, see Chapter 7, "What's In My Consulting Firm Contract?"), you'll fax or mail the signed contract back to the consulting firm.

When should I give notice on my old job or contract?

Before you give notice, check with the consulting firm to find out whether the client has signed *their contract* with the consulting firm. If you are told anything but, "yes" be careful. Sometimes a consulting firm will make it sound as if the contract is in the bag when the client is still deciding between you and another consulting firm's candidate. Since your contract has wording that lets the consulting firm off the hook if the client doesn't want you, many consulting firms will sign you up before they have a firm commitment from the client.

Only when you are sure that the client has signed on should you give notice at your current job. It is only then, too, that you should inform recruiters at other firms that you've taken a contract so that they don't waste their time attempting to place you.

Should I start working for the client before I sign the contract?

It is a very bad move to start working for a client without first signing the consulting firm contract. Once you are on the job it's tough to negotiate abusive contract clauses. You have no leverage because you are already on the job. So your only recourse if you don't get what you want is to walk off the job and infuriate the client. Because you are trapped, the most abusive of clauses are most likely to show up in a contract you see only after starting work. If the written contract doesn't show up shortly after you agree orally to take a contract, don't be taken in by plausible excuses. Listen politely while the recruiter explains away the lack of a contract but respond that your attorney has recommended that you never begin work without a signed contract in hand and that you can't make any exceptions.

GLAD I DIDN'T LEAP!

"I'm glad I didn't quit my full time job without first signing papers. I had the consulting gig all lined up, both the agency and the end company had interviewed me and were thrilled with my experience and skill set. It seemed all was in line. Then, without warning, the entire department just went away.

"It is a real good thing that I didn't quit first. The broker was like 'you're gonna give notice today, right???' I laughed at him for thinking that I'd do anything without first seeing a contract and signing papers. This is probably the only time in my life when I haven't leapt without looking. I'm glad I looked first."

—Scott Harris

CHAPTER 7

WHAT'S IN MY CONSULTING FIRM CONTRACT?

Do all consulting firms use written contracts?

After you have orally accepted the terms of a consulting firm offer, almost all consulting firms will ask you to sign a written contract. This is true whether you will be working as a W-2 contractor or as an independent. If a consulting firm neglects to present you with a written contract, it is either a sign that it is inexperienced at placing computer contractors or, worse, that it doesn't intend to honor the terms you've orally agreed to. In either case, you will need to proceed with caution.

Because of the bad reputation some consulting firm contract clauses have earned within the contracting community, contractors may think that they are getting away with something when a firm lets them work without a contract. But this may be shortsighted. Firms are not likely to treat you better because you can't document their promises. Nor will you find it easier to convert a firm's clients to your own direct clients in the absence of a contract, since the consulting firm, whatever its relationship with you, *will* have a written contract with the client that prevents them from hiring you directly.

It is in your own best interest to have a written contract, even though the consulting firm might try to slip in abusive clauses, because that written contract defines how and when you will be *paid*. If you don't have that information in writing you may find it extremely hard to collect money owed to you if the consulting firm decides not to pay.

Moreover, if you never sign a written agreement with a consulting firm, the fact that you provide service to the consulting firm or its client *implies* that a contract exists between you and the consulting firm–and you may not like the terms that the law provides for an implied contract. Thus, a written contract is a good way to get the terms that you want in writing, rather than being saddled with terms you don't want through inaction.

Who supplies the contract?

After you orally accept an offer to work for a client through a consulting firm, the consulting firm will send you a version of their boilerplate contract with the details of your specific contract filled in.

This contract has been drafted by the consulting firm's attorneys and has been written to protect the consulting firm's interests, sometimes at the expense of yours. You will have to review this contract carefully and eliminate or change any terms that could harm you or limit your ability to earn a living.

If you sign a contract that contains damaging wording without eliminating that wording, you will have a hard time making the case in court that you did not know what it meant and should not be held to its terms. It is your legal responsibility to find out what contract clauses mean before you sign a contract containing them.

If you are working as a W-2 contractor, you are legally an employee. So any contract you sign as a W-2 contractor is an employment contract and the wording of that contract cannot take away from you the protection afforded by labor law. However, if you are working as a 1099 IC or the employee of your own corporation and are not the consulting firm's employee, the terms of your contract will be all that define the relationship between you and the consulting firm, so you must be very careful what you agree to.

What parties are bound by this contract?

It is very important that you understand that the contract a consulting firm sends you defines a legal relationship between you and the *consulting firm*, not one between you and the *client*. In fact, throughout your entire relationship with the consulting firm, you will never have a direct legal relationship with the client!

Because the contract you sign is only with the consulting firm and not with the client, should problems arise on the job, you will only be able to take legal action against the consulting firm. If you don't get paid for time you put in working for the client, you can only sue the consulting firm for payment, not the client, nor can you ❖ expect the client to help you get the consulting firm to pay you.

That is why, when you decide whether or not to accept a contract, you should only consider the reputation of the consulting firm, not that of the client. The reputation, prestige and ethics of the client are irrelevant when you work through a consulting firm. Only the ethics and integrity of the consulting firm affect you. The fact that a consulting firm places a lot of contractors at a well-respected local company tells you nothing about the treatment you'll receive from the consulting firm. Many well-regarded and supposedly ethical clients hire armies of contractors from consulting firms that are famous for exploiting their contractors.

Occasionally, if a consulting firm's behavior to its contractors becomes overwhelmingly abusive, some ethical clients will cross them off their preferred vendor lists. However, this is rare and happens only after ten or twenty contractors have sued the consulting firm for back payments. In most cases, otherwise ethical clients have no compunctions about hiring contractors from body shops that are notorious for lying about rates and forcing abusive terms on their contractors. These firms can offer lower rates to clients because they talk their contractors into taking less. For all too many clients the cost savings these abusive firms offer appear to outweigh any ethical concerns.

Since I'm not contracting with the client, what contract binds them?

The consulting firm signs a separate contract with the client, which you will never see and whose terms you will never learn. That contract defines how much the client will pay the consulting firm for your services, when payment will be made to the consulting firm, and what steps should be taken should disputes arise with the consulting firm.

There are several clauses in this contract between the client and the consulting firm that have an impact on you. The most important is one that bars the client from hiring you directly. It applies over a time period that begins when you begin the contract and ends as much as five years *after* you have finished serving the client.

Many contracts between consulting firms and clients also include a mechanism through which the client can pay off the consulting firm if they want to hire you as a full-time employee. Usually this requires that the client to pay a hefty fee, similar to the one they'd pay an employment agency for finding you. This fee may be 25% or more of the salary you would draw as the client's employee.

The contract with the client also contains the clause we discussed in Chapter 5, "Which Consulting Firm?," that prohibits the consulting firm from hiring the client's employees as contractors.

What should I do if the consulting firm doesn't send a contract?

If you don't receive a contract shortly after orally accepting an assignment, be wary! One ploy of unethical consulting firms is to delay sending you the contract until after you have reported for work at the client's site. When you finally get to see the written contract, you may find that it specifies a lower rate than what you agreed to or has other highly abusive terms written into it.

It is extremely difficult to negotiate contract terms once you are already on the job. If you refuse to accept the abusive terms or lower rate, you will have no option but to quit, leaving behind an infuriated client who may blame you for leaving them in the lurch rather than the silken-tongued consulting firm salesperson. This can make it impossible for you to find further contracts at the client's company no matter how blameless you might have been. So, if the consulting firm says that the contract has been delayed and asks you to begin work while the contract is being prepared, it is best, if you can afford it, not to begin work until the contract has been signed by *both* yourself and the consulting firm, and you have received a fully-signed copy of the agreement.

If the consulting firm tells you they don't use written contracts, you should be wary, too, as this is a sign they are not very experienced in the placement business. If you are sure you want to work for them anyway, either hire your own lawyer to draft a contract for you and send it to the consulting firm or, at a minimum, write up a Letter of Understanding that outlines the terms of your agreement with the consulting firm as you understand them. Be sure to define the length of time the agreement will be in force, how much you will be paid, when payment should occur, and how the relationship may be ended. Then mail this letter to the consulting firm by registered mail before you begin working for the client so that there is a formal record of your agreement should a dispute arise.

How negotiable is the consulting firm contract?

The contract you receive from the consulting firm may be beautifully typeset and look as changeless as the Ten Commandments but it is nothing more than a word processor document drafted by lawyers paid by the consulting firm to protect their interests. It is full of phrases that work to the firm's advantage and your disadvantage. Some of these phrases are intended to intimidate you though they may be of dubious legal standing. Consulting firms put them in anyway knowing that many beginning contractors are too naive to remove them.

You shouldn't be! You must read every clause carefully and assume that there is a good reason for every word you find there. Never ignore a troublesome clause because it seems to pertain to something that will never happen. If the lawyers have put a clause into the contract, you can be sure that it relates to something that occasionally *does* happen. So be sure that you can live with the consequences of what the contract says will happen when it does.

If the contract is a complex one, it may be worth having an attorney who has experience with computer contracts look it over. If you are too cheap to pay for a lawyer, at least ask a more experienced contractor to take a look at your contract to make sure that you haven't overlooked something important.

Do I have to accept everything in the contract to take the job?

Absolutely not! Consulting firms may hope that naive newbies will accept everything in their boilerplate contracts but, when pushed, they are prepared to negotiate many of the clauses. Indeed, some clauses, like noncompetition clauses, may have been drafted more broadly than necessary on purpose, to allow some room for negotiation.

If a consulting firm presents you with a complex contract full of terms they refuse to negotiate, it may be necessary to walk away from the deal. This kind of inflexibility is a good sign that they are highhanded and unethical in their treatment of contractors. This may one of the many firms that prefers to hire people new to contracting since they can earn the most off beginners who don't know enough to challenge their unfair terms.

How do I negotiate a clause?

If you see a clause that bothers you, first ask the consulting firm representative why that clause is in the contract. Their explanation may be all you need to under-stand and accept the clause. For example, the clause you find in most contracts that assigns rights to the software developed for a client to that client is there be-cause all corporate clients insist on it. Without this written assignment of rights, the rights to software you write on the job might legally default to the consulting firm (if you are an employee of the consulting firm), or to you (if you are an inde-pendent contractor), rather than to the client who paid to develop it.

But once you understand the clause, you may still want to change its wording. For example, one visitor to *The Computer Consultant's Message Board* was faced with an assignment clause that stated, "Any and all inventions become property of the Cli-ent even if they are unrelated to your work for the Client or the Client's business and developed independently or for another Client."

This clause is unacceptably wide in scope as it would transfer to the client rights to any software, songs, novels, or even patentable home brewing equipment you might develop on your own time during the contract. To accept this contract you'd have to rewrite the clause so that it clearly states that the only rights being transferred to the client are the rights to the software that you develop explicitly for the client during the term of the contract.

Once you have decided what wording you can accept, call the consulting firm rep-resentative and run that wording by them. You may have to go through a few itera-tions of this process until you arrive at wording that you both can accept.

How do I modify a contract clause?

Once you have oral approval for any changes, get out the written contract and cross out anything you are deleting or changing. Then write in any new wording in pen. Write your initials by each change. If the change is a long one, type it up on a separate piece of paper, initial it, and refer to it in the body of the contract as an addendum. Some consulting firms are willing to provide their contract in a word processor format if it appears that you need to make substantial changes to the contract. This is a good way to instill trust between the parties.

What clauses should I expect to find in a contract?

Standard clauses you should find in any consulting firm contract include a clause describing where you will be working and for how long, a clause defining your contractor or employee status, a clause describing payment terms, a noncompeti-tion clause limiting your ability to work directly for the client without the in-volvement of the consulting firm, a clause assigning rights to software you develop for a client to the client, a clause describing how the contract can be terminated, a clause protecting the client's business secrets, and a clause describing what will happen should a dispute arise between you and the consulting firm. It is also common to find a clause that prevents you from recruiting the client's or the consulting firm's employees or other contractors to work elsewhere.

How do W-2 contracts differ from 1099 and corp-to-corp contracts?

W-2 contracts begin by defining the contractor as an employee of the consulting firm and listing any benefits that the employee will receive (or waive). W-2 contracts usually include a termination clause granting the employee the option of terminating the contract with two weeks notice.

Contracts for 1099s often begin by defining the contractor's independent status and then supplement this with a number of other clauses that may be intended to fulfill the criteria set by the IRS 20 *Factors for Determining Independent Contractor Status* (discussed in Chapter 3, "W-2, 1099, or Corp?"). For example, clauses in a 1099 IC's contract may state that the contractor will bring his own software tools or have the right to bring in subcontractors. The contract may specify that the IC must carry certain insurance coverages. The termination clause in a 1099 contract usually requires that the contractor give a longer period of notice than an employee's two weeks.

Both types of contracts are likely to contain clauses assigning rights, defining a noncompetition period, and protecting the confidentiality of the client's business secrets, as well as clauses prohibiting you from recruiting the client's employees.

How does a corporation's contract differ from that of a 1099 IC?

When you work as an employee of your own corporation, the other party to the consulting firm contract will be your corporation, not you as an individual. If your corporation is incorporated or headquartered in a state other than the one where you are performing your work, the contract may specify which state's law prevails should a dispute arise. Otherwise, a corporation's contract should resemble a 1099 IC's contract.

Are computer consulting contracts covered by federal law?

Some federal labor laws apply to employees (for example, the Family Leave Act, anti-discrimination laws, and laws defining which workers are exempt and nonexempt). Federal law also covers ownership of the copyrights in software. But much of labor law is enacted at the state level. This includes laws mandating what benefits employers must give workers, how overtime is compensated, and acceptable terms for employee noncompetition agreements. To find out what employee law prescribes for employees in your state, contact the State Department of Labor, local labor unions, or the state or local Bar Association.

Independent contractors are not covered by labor law. They are covered by federal and state laws that regulate the way businesses interact with each other. In many cases these offer you much less protection against unfair treatment and discrimination. Contact your local Chamber of Commerce for pointers to where you can learn about laws affecting small businesses in your state.

If in the course of your contract work you hire *other* contractors as employees, whether as an IC or through your own corporation, you will have to familiarize yourself with all the stipulations of state and federal labor law. Your local Chamber of Commerce should be able to point you to resources to help you comply with these laws.

The consulting firm is located in a state other than the one I work in. What state's laws prevail?

In a situation like this your contract will probably have wording that defines which state's laws will apply should a legal dispute arise. Since the contract has been drafted by the consulting firm's lawyers, you can be sure that the state that is specified is the one in which the consulting firm and its lawyers are based.

The consulting firm representative says that theirs is the standard NACCB contract and that they cannot change it. Is this true?

The National Association of Computer Consulting Businesses (NACCB) is an organization of approximately 400 consulting firms. It provides a model contract for use by its member firms. Consulting firms have been known to draft up contracts containing extremely abusive clauses and to force them on naive contractors with the claim that these clauses are part of the "Official NACCB Contract." But this is stretching the truth.

According to Harvey Shulman, the NACCB's legal counsel, "There is no 'standard' NACCB contract in the sense that every NACCB member must use a specific contract. We do have certain 'model' contracts that staffing firms must fill in their own blanks or choose to delete or modify certain provisions. We strongly urge firms not to make certain deletions or additions unless they want to increase the risk of an adverse IRS audit result."

If confronted with something that purports to be a NACCB standard contract, keep in mind that although portions of this contract have been drafted by the NACCB's lawyers, it is just as negotiable as any other contract. There is no reason to accept any clause that puts you at a serious disadvantage or that might cause you harm.

NACCB firms frequently defend abusive clauses in their contracts by arguing that they are meant to protect them in case of IRS audits. But there are many ways of avoiding audits that do *not* require placing a heavy burden on the contractor alone. If a NACCB firm won't negotiate clauses that you find troublesome, find another firm who will.

For example, I contacted the NACCB to inquire about one 1099 contract that a naive contractor told me he had signed, which contained a clause obliging the contractor to pay a penalty of $100 for every day remaining on a contract if he terminated it prematurely for any reason. The consulting firm had told the contractor that this was the "Standard NACCB Contract" and I wanted to know if this, in fact, was true.

The NACCB's official spokesperson, Max Steiner, seemed to agree that this particular clause was abusive and wrote to me that attributing it to the NACCB was "misinformation." However, when I contacted Mr. Shulman, the NACCB's legal counsel, about this penalty clause, he defended it, explaining that a stiff penalty clause was one way to meet the IRS contention that indefinite contracts are typical of employees rather than independent contractors.

Mr. Shulman went on to say, "I want to emphasize, however, that NACCB does *not* recommend an particular sum for the early termination penalty; firms use different measurements, e..g., \$X per day, or Y% of the billings lost, or . . .. Although I appreciate your comment that this may seem unfair to some ICs, it is entirely consistent with the common law test. I should also point out that if the IC leaves because, for example, the staffing firm is in material breach of the contract, under well established court rulings this type of breach is typically a complete defense to the staffing firm's effort to collect an early termination fee."

Mr. Shulman is doing his job here: protecting the interests of his NACCB clients. But there are plenty of *other* ways to write a contract that satisfies the IRS criteria that an independent contract not be open ended—ways which do not impose a huge penalty on the contractor who terminates a contract prematurely while providing no penalty for the consulting firm that terminates the contractor without notice at the client's behest.

When faced with this kind of damaging penalty clause, strike it out and come up with some other mutually acceptable solution to deal with the perceived threat of IRS reclassification. For example, rather than simply impose penalties on the contractor who ends a contract prematurely, write a contract that applies to a set period of time and allows *either* the client or the contractor to terminate the contract early by giving 30 days notice or by negotiating some other terms acceptable to both the client and the contractor.

What if I can't figure out what a clause means?

If the contract you are presented with contains a clause whose meaning is not clear to you, don't guess or take the consulting firm representative's word for what it means. Ask if you can rewrite the clause so that it conforms to what the agency representative says it is supposed to mean or have a lawyer review it for you to ensure that it is not potentially dangerous.

In particular, never sign a contract that contains damaging clauses because a consulting firm representative tells you, "That's just legal gobbledygook, we never actually invoke that clause." If it's there, you can be sure they invoke it, and if you sign a contract containing it, it may very well hold up in court.

This is particularly true of clauses that oblige you to pay cash damages for anything. Both W-2 and independent contractors may encounter clauses stipulating penalty payments for early termination, to pay back company-paid relocation costs, for filing immigration papers, or for the cost of company paid training. These clauses may hold up in court even if they oblige you to pay $10,000 or more. Even if such clauses do not hold up, it may take many thousands of dollars of legal fees and many months of court action to dismiss claims made under such clauses. So it is a far better policy to simply eliminate them from a contract before you sign or, if that isn't possible, to walk away from the contract.

THE NACCB OFFICIAL LINE

"I urge you to keep in mind that a number of the provisions you have heard complaints about are probably unpopular with staffing firms themselves; they make it more difficult to sign up ICs, to close a deal; they increase paperwork for the staffing firm; they can create bad feelings. Yet staffing firms insist on these provisions so they do not get forced into bankruptcy or required to sign agreements with the IRS not to use ANY ICs, and not because the staffing firms like all these provisions.

"For every IC that the IRS reclassifies who has earned at least $70 K per year (most earn much more), the IRS will collect about $8,500 in taxes—even if the IC has paid the taxes in full itself! If a staffing firm has only 20 ICs per year who earn this amount, and the IRS audits 2 years (as is typical), the staffing firm will be assessed $340,000 in back taxes for 20 ICs reclassified over a 2 year period. Perhaps for the IC there is less concern, because it is only one person; but for the staffing firm, the results of reclassification—triggered by problematic contracts and difficult IRS agents—can be devastating. I have personally seen situations like that develop."

—Harvey Shulman, Legal Counsel to the NACCB

[Note however, that Mr. Shulman, by his own report, has only seen this occur in one and a half audits out of 52 that he participated in.]

Can you show me a sample of each clause I should expect to see?

There is so much variation in wording from firm to firm, that there is no point in looking at a generic clause. In addition, because of differences in state law, particularly where it refers to labor practices, you may see different versions of specific clauses in contracts drafted in differing states.

However, in the next few pages we'll look at the *types* of clauses that you are likely to encounter and what it is that they do.

Defining the Work to be Done

This clause should identify the client you will be working for, including, possibly, the corporate division or department and its location. It may briefly describe the work you will be doing. If you are an employee contractor, it may simply define the job in terms of the number of months you may work for the client. Sometimes an independent contractor's contract will define a specific task or tasks to be accomplished, rather than a time period.

If the contract defines a time span, a clause should describe the date when the work will begin and the date it is expected to end. This is the formal term of the contract. But don't assume that, because a term is described in this clause, the contract will actually last the length of the term. As you will see later in this chapter, most contracts include a *termination clause* that allows the client or consulting firm to terminate your contract at any time without regard to the term specified in this clause. Most contracts also include an *extension* clause, also discussed below, which lets the consulting firm extend the term of the contract for another time period if the client wants to extend it. So the contract length you see defined in this clause should be treated only as an estimate of how long the contract will last. It does not bind the consulting firm to keep you on for the full length of the term defined in it.

The Extension Clause

Most consulting firm contracts include wording either in the clause defining the contract term or in a separate *extension clause* which describes what will happen should the client want you to keep on working at the end of the period defined by the current contract. Typically these extension clauses bind you to continue work under the terms of the original contract through any subsequent periods when the client might want your services. They may also bind you to continue working extensions at the *same rate* you got for the original contract.

Be careful here! Extensions are very common and it is not unknown for contractors to work three or four six-month extensions of their original contract. You do not have to sign anything that prevents you from getting a raise should your contract be extended. Indeed, since a contract extension requires no marketing efforts on the part of your consulting firm and is due entirely to the great work you've been doing for the client, you should make sure that the contract provides you with the right to ask for a raise when the client asks you to extend!

The only time this might not be true is if your original contract was written for a very short term, six weeks or less, in order to let a wary client verify that you have the skills needed to do their job. In that case, it might be legitimate to extend the contract to six months without asking for a raise. But in a strong market it is common to get a raise on extending your contract. Our Real Rate Survey data showed that the typical raise contractors received when extending their contracts in 1998 was 9%.

You should also be wary of clauses that could force you to extend any contract that the client wants you to extend, even if you want to take another opportunity elsewhere, particularly clauses that apply penalties to you should you leave. If the wording of an extension clause appears muddy or confusing, refuse to sign it until you've run it by an attorney or experienced contractor who can tell you what it really means.

Defining the Contractor's Status

If you are a W-2 hourly employee, you'll usually find a clause here in which you waive the benefits received by the company's regular salaried employees such as health insurance and paid vacations. If you have negotiated to buy into the company's benefit plans by paying your own premiums, this should be written in here too.

If you are working as an unincorporated independent contractor, that status should be defined here. Some contracts will include wording here that correspond to the IRS tests for independence and attempt to establish that you assume risk and set your own hours, bring your own tools, and that you are not behaving like an employee of the consulting firm or client.

If you are incorporated, the contract will probably include wording that states that your company contracts to provide services to the client through its own employees.

Defining Payment

The payment clause should indicate what hourly rate you'll be paid and when you will receive payment. If you are a W-2 contractor, payment should be made on a regular payroll basis at least every two weeks and you should not accept any wording that makes your payment dependent on the consulting firm being paid by the client. As an employee you should be paid at regular intervals, whether or not the client pays. This is one of the great benefits of working as a W-2 contractor and one of the reasons you are willing to give the consulting firm its hefty cut of your hourly billing. So don't sign it away!

If you are working as an IC, the consulting firm is on firmer ground when insisting that you wait to get paid until they have been paid by the client. This establishes that you are behaving like an independent businessperson and accepting risk, rather than behaving like an employee. But the time of payment should be negotiable. If you are forced to accept a delay in payment, you should get a bigger cut of the client billing, since the consulting firm is not incurring the expense of paying you before they get paid. The payment clause may also state that you are responsible for invoicing the consulting firm for your hours at some stated interval.

Watch out here for clauses that oblige you to work unpaid overtime or to put in a "professional day." This latter term means that the client can have you work nine, ten, or even more hours in any given day while paying only for eight.

Travel Expenses

If your assignment will involve long distance travel on the client's behalf, it is very important to spell out exactly how and when that travel will be paid for. If you are working as a W-2 contractor, you may want to write into your contract that the client will pay your travel costs themselves, booking your trips through their corporate travel departments. However, remember that your contract is with the *consulting firm*, not the client, and they may not be able to get the client to pay. So get independent written confirmation from the client that they will in fact pay your expenses before you make any reservations.

If you are working as an independent and don't want to look like an employee, specify that the client will reimburse you as soon as you present them with an invoice and any necessary documentation such as tickets or hotel bills. Otherwise, you may find yourself paying hefty travel expenses out of your own pocket and then waiting weeks or even months for reimbursement. Again, you should also get written confirmation from the client that they will pay you this way.

If you will be working more than 60 miles away from your home for a period longer than a few days but less than a year, you may also negotiate with the consulting firm to pay you a *per diem* payment in addition to your regular rate. (This topic is discussed in more detail on Page 198.) The terms of that per diem should be spelled out here.

Payment Terms and Payment Problems

Because your only contract is with the consulting firm and not with the client, it is very important that you retain the right to sue the consulting firm if you don't receive the payments owed to you. If you are a W-2 contractor, you should strike out any wording that would keep you from being able to do this.

If you are working as an independent, your contract with the broker may state that they don't have to pay you until they are paid by the client—assigning risk to you and justifying your independent status. But if this is the case, it is very important that you include a clause that obligates the broker to collect from the client as soon as you have fulfilled the terms of your contract. It should also give you the right to collect directly from the client if the consulting firm does not do this. That way, if the consulting firm does not collect from the client, for whatever reason, they have breached their contract with you, and you can sue.

Bonuses and Perks

If a recruiter promised to give you a bonus after you have worked for the consulting firm for some period of time, that bonus and its terms of payment should be spelled out in your contract. So should any other perks that were promised to you during negotiations with the consulting firm. Without written proof it may be very hard to collect on those promises or even prove they were made, especially if the person who promised them to you has left the firm or been transferred to another office.

Assigning Rights

As noted above, federal copyright law is contrary to what common sense would suggest: the rights to software written by an independent contractor remain with the contractor until they are transferred to someone else via a written contract. So technically, independent contractors continue to own the code they write for clients unless they transfer their rights to them in a written agreement. This is why you will almost always find a clause in a consulting firm contract transferring these rights to the client.

In contrast, federal copyright law stipulates that the rights to software written by an employee while on the job belong to the employer in the absence of a written contract changing this default. This means that any software created by an employee will be owned by the employer if it is the type of software the employee writes for the employer on a regular basis, *even if the software is written on the employee's own time, or at the employee's home.* In an employment relationship, no written agreement is needed for the employer to own the copyright in the software, although many consulting firms and other employers ask their employees to sign written agreements to ensure that the employee knows the extent of the employer's rights.

You should take this very seriously if you intend to write and market your own software products while employed as a W-2 contractor, since your employer could have a legal claim to your product! Because W-2 employees work for the consulting firm, not the end-client, W-2 contracts usually include wording that transfers their software rights to the end-client. Be careful that you sign over the rights only to software or inventions that you create for the specific client as part of the work you've agreed to do for them, and not to *all* your software or inventions, even if you don't see yourself writing other software or inventing things during the course of the contract. You never know what will happen in the future. It would be a shame to be unable to make use of an idea or invention you came up with just because you signed an all-too-inclusive rights assignment clause. Also be careful that if you use your own code libraries or tools in preparing software for a client, and if the client is not buying those libraries and tools, that title to them is explicitly excluded from the transfer of rights. If you are developing your own software products or libraries with resale potential don't sign any clause assigning software rights until you consult an attorney who specializes in intellectual property law.

The Noncompetition Clause

It is legitimate for a consulting firm who fixes you up with a client to prevent you from working directly for that client for some period of time after the firms finds you the contract. Without this kind of protection, consulting firms could not stay in business. Clients would simply hire all their contractors directly once the match was made. So you should expect to find a clause in your contract that prevents you from working directly for the current client for some period that begins after your work through the consulting firm ends. A period of a year is customary. If you hope to work without agencies in the future, you will want to keep the noncompetition clause period as short as possible so that you can reconnect with satisfied clients in a year or two and work for them directly.

This clause also prevents you from working for the current client through another consulting firm during the period the noncompetition clause covers. When you contact a new consulting firm, they will often ask you what noncompetition clauses you are bound by–partly because they don't want to get embroiled in legal action with other consulting firms and partly because they want to have their *own* noncompetition clauses honored. So you have be aware of all the noncompetition clauses you sign and keep track of when they end.

Consulting firm boilerplate noncompetition clauses are frequently abusive. It is reasonable for the noncompetition period to extend for a year, but five years, a length found in many contracts, is much too long.

The term the noncompetition clause defines usually begins only *after* you complete all extensions to the original contract, not at the end of the original contract term. This is reasonable. But sometimes a consulting firm will write a noncompetition clause so that it prevents you from working for *all* clients for whom you did work through the consulting firm for a period that begins when you stop work for the consulting firm's *last* client. This is a much more onerous noncompetition clause and there is no reason for you to accept it. Instead, limit the scope of the noncompetition clause to the client covered by the contract under discussion and have the noncompetition period begin when you end the work for the client defined by this contract and its extensions. If the consulting firm finds you a new client, you can write a new noncompetition clause to cover that new client.

Another abusive form of the noncompetition clause is one that defines your "client" to include every department in the current client's entire company. This can pose a problem when the client is part of a huge corporation with many divisions. Often a consulting firm has contacts only in a single division of a multinational corporation and cannot find you work in other divisions. An overly broad noncompetition clause prevents other consulting firms from being able to place you in the multinational corporation's other divisions when the original firm cannot. Therefore it is common for experienced contractors to limit the scope of the noncompetition clause to extend only to the division and sometimes just to the department in which the consulting firm placed them.

An even more abusive form of this clause is one that prevents you not only from working directly for the clients with whom the firm placed you but also for clients to whom the consulting firm has *marketed* you. This means that if the firm did nothing more than mail your résumé to a client company, they might claim that their noncompetition clause bound you to work there only through them. Strike this clause out!

The Nondisclosure Clause

Clients have a right to protect their trade secrets. The nondisclosure clause prohibits you from disclosing the client's trade secrets to other parties. In some cases it may also prevent you from working for the client's competitors for a period of time after the contract ends.

Clauses like this may be legitimate when you are writing software for vendors. Obviously, a company like Netscape cannot afford to have contractors hiring into Microsoft as soon as their contracts are over, taking with them all the intimate details of a browser's next release. The problem here is that a clause may define "competing companies" so broadly that it limits your ability to work anywhere in the future. If this is the case, you will have to adjust the wording so that you narrow its scope or turn down the contract!

The Termination Clause

All consulting firm contracts have wording buried in them somewhere which allows the client to dump you without notice. This is one of the unpleasant realities of contracting. The flexibility this clause gives clients is one reason why firms hire contractors in the first place. There is very little you can do to eliminate this type of clause, as clients demand them.

What varies is the flexibility with which you, the contractor, can terminate the contract. Only accept contracts that allow you to leave after giving the client some reasonable amount of notice. You never know what events might come up in your personal life which would make it necessary to leave even the finest client. Nor, for that matter, do you know what you are getting into when you begin any new contract.

If you are working as a W-2, you should be able to terminate a contract with the usual two weeks notice that is characteristic of employees. If you are working as an independent, you may have to accept a longer warning period in order to distinguish yourself from an employee. Thirty days should be enough. Refuse to sign anything that would make you have to pay penalties if you left before the end of the contract.

HOW THE NACCB PASSES THE BUCK

"The model contract offered by NACCB contains a provision that does not permit the staffing firm to terminate the IC before the promised duration/project termination; ONLY the CLIENT can decide that the IC is no longer needed. Of course, if we get directions from the client that the IC is off the project, there is nothing we can do."

—Harvey Shulman, NACCB's Legal Advisor

The Dispute Clause

Dispute clauses usually stipulate which state's courts will have jurisdiction should a dispute arise. If the consulting firm is located out of state, it will usually specify the state where the firm is headquartered. If the firm is not in your home state, be aware that this can make it a lot more complex and expensive to pursue legal action on your part. The most common dispute likely to occur is when the consulting firm refuses to pay you. So take this clause seriously.

Strike out any wording that makes you pay for both side's costs in a dispute you lose or otherwise attempts to make it difficult for you to pursue a just claim against the company. Some contracts may include dispute clauses that require you to go to binding arbitration instead of trying your suit in court.

ARBITRATE OR LITIGATE?

"As a lawyer who advises consultants, consulting firms, and service recipients [clients], I tell my clients that arbitration is a good news - bad news joke. The good news is that arbitration is final. The bad news is that arbitration is final.

"Litigation tends to be more expensive than arbitration, especially since litigation allows for multiple levels of appeals. Any litigant who doesn't like the result, and can afford to do so, appeals to the next level. By contrast, once an arbitrator issues a decision, it's nearly impossible to overturn it. The inability to appeal is good if you win, but bad if you lose. Either way, the matter is then decided.

"In litigation, you usually get whichever judge is assigned to the case, which makes it more difficult for both parties if the judge doesn't know anything about software. If the parties agree to arbitration, then they can choose arbitrators who are experienced in software disputes.

"Once a dispute arises, if there is no arbitration agreement already in place, the parties can then agree to submit the dispute to arbitration. However, the parties can't be forced into arbitration unless they previously signed a written agreement that all disputes will be submitted to arbitration. Thus, I often recommend that consulting agreements contain binding arbitration provisions."

–Fred Wilf, Attorney-at-Law

Indemnification and Liability Clauses

These clauses absolve the consulting firm of responsibility should you get into a legal dispute with the client. If you are incorporated or working independently, these clauses may also distance the consulting firm from any difficulties you get into with your own employees or subs or from problems with the IRS should a dispute arise about your tax status. These clauses may also oblige you to pay for legal expenses that the consulting firm incurs because of disputes you get into. In his book, *Wage Slave No More* published by legal publisher, Nolo Press, Steve Fishman recommends that contractors be wary of indemnification clauses, especially those related to the IRS, because of the associated costs.

The liability clause protects the agency from any damage claims the client should lodge against you.

Both of these kinds of clauses should only appear in a contract when you are working as an independent and are covered by your own business insurance, not when you are an employee.

The No Recruiting Clause

Clients usually insist that your contract have some wording in it that prevents you from soliciting their employees to work for another firm—i.e., the consulting firm. The reasons for this are obvious. Don't talk your coworkers on the job into becoming contractors, simply tell them that you'll be happy to discuss the subject with them once they are no longer employees. If they want more information about contracting, suggest they buy this book!

Other Clauses

The clauses described above often appear in consulting firm contracts and hence can be called "standard." However, every firm sends out its own unique contract and in each new contract you're liable to encounter some new clause that you've never seen before. Rack that up to the ingenuity of lawyers and proceed with caution. Be sure you understand the meaning of each clause you sign and strike out anything that could cause you difficulties if it were to be invoked.

I've heard that overly broad clauses will get thrown out in court. Does this mean I can ignore the most abusive ones?

Wrong! While it is true that some overly broad noncompetition clauses have been thrown out in court, the court's definition of "overly broad" varies from state to state. Contractors report that in Michigan, a state with a history of strong labor unions and hence employee-friendly legislators, noncompetition clauses extending more than six months may be thrown out as indefensibly long. But in other states, like Connecticut, where corporate lobbyists influence the legislature, you may find that a one year noncompetition clause holds up very well.

But you have to ask yourself, do you really want to pay some lawyer $200 or more per hour to learn if the clause holds up? It could take a lot of hours to find out, and most attorneys won't take your case unless you pay them a hefty retainer fee up front. Consulting firms have much larger budgets for legal representation than you have and can afford to be aggressive in taking contractors to court, even if after years of hassle and expense, they lose.

That is why, rather than guessing about the legal status of something you find in your contract, it is always best to eliminate any wording you don't want to have to live by or to hire your own lawyer before you sign the contract, rather than attempt to litigate the wording away after the fact.

How frequent are lawsuits by consulting firms against contractors?

Judging from the messages that have flowed across the many consultant's bulletin boards I have frequented over the past decade, actual lawsuits against contractors brought by either consulting firms or clients are rare. Attorneys have written to me several times to point out that in the few cases they know of where large consulting firms do go after individuals—usually around the issue of violating non-compete clauses–juries and judges tend to give the benefit of the doubt to the individual.

Where nightmare lawsuits do seem to occur is in situations where the *contractor* sues a consulting firm that has abused them, only to get tangled up in appeal after appeal, even after winning.

What happens to my contract if another firm buys the firm I sign with?

The late 1990s have seen a wave of consolidations in the consulting firm industry as huge national companies buy up small local firms. As a result, many contractors who signed on with ethical local firms have seen their contracts taken over by large national body shops known for their cavalier and unethical behavior.

Because of this, it may be a good idea to put wording in your contract that survives the acquisition or sale of the agency. Be sure to specify that your contract cannot be assigned to another company without your consent or that if the agency assigns your contract to another company, the contract immediately terminates without an enforceable non-compete.

VICTIMS OF A TAKE-OVER

"One of my projects was staffed by a large number of subs, mostly ICs, from a local, reputable agency who treated them quite well–no complaints about rates or payment. The owner recently sold out to a much larger, national firm, one who, based on my past experience with them some years back, defines the term 'scumbag.'

"The subs got called into a meeting shortly after the deal closed by a new manager and were told that their contracts at the old agency were going to be immediately replaced with their 'standard' IC contract–lo' and behold, the NACCB model contract modified further with some of the most ridiculous garbage I'd ever seen. They were also told that they would be leaving if they didn't accept it. They were strongly pressured to sign the new contract right then and there in the meeting. Some who didn't know any better did so, although most refused until they had a chance to look it over and consult their attorney or CPA.

"Now, a number of them have fired attorney-generated letters at the acquiring agency about contract breach, survivability of old contract, etc. The laws are murky in this regard, and the outcome is up in the air and will take a long time and many $$ to settle."

—Bob McIlree

CHAPTER 8

HOW CAN I WORK DIRECT?

Do I have to be an entrepreneur to find contracts without agencies?

No, many of the contractors who work without brokers work on contracts that are identical to those of agency contractors. All that they do differently is market themselves, rather than depending on consulting firms to find them clients.

What is the easiest way to find direct clients?

The easiest way to find direct clients is to convert old employers and clients you work for through consulting firms into clients of your own. These people already know and appreciate the quality of your work, so when you contact them you have already gotten past the biggest hurdle in finding new clients which is convincing them that you are reliable and can do the job.

Another advantage of calling old employers and clients is that you know that they hire people with your skills. Since you have worked for them in the past, you should also have a pretty good idea of whether they hire direct contractors and how generously they pay them.

How can I get old employers to hire me?

When you decide to start contracting, contact everyone you used to work for or with, both bosses and co-workers, and inform them that you are now doing contract work. Make your calls when you are feeling relaxed, and, if possible, when you are already working. If you call when you don't need work you won't come across sounding hungry or desperate and you will give others a subtle message that you are already succeeding as a contractor.

Many contractors find that old employers are happy to hire them. But even if your old business associates don't have work for you, they may know of other people

151

who do. Don't be shy about asking whether they know of projects that are staffing up and looking for people with your skills. If they mention that they know of a project that is looking for contractors, ask them for the project manager's name and phone number and tell them that you would very much appreciate it if they would put in a word for you with the hiring manager.

When you call the manager whose project needs help, be sure to start out your call by making it clear that you are a contractor, not a consulting firm salesperson. Then mention the person who referred you. For example, you might say, "This is Cathy Berman. I'm a DB2 contractor with ten years of experience with Insurance systems. My old boss, Joe Tibbits at MegaCorp, told me you were looking for some help with your new Agency Systems project. Is this a good time to talk?"

If doing this makes you uncomfortable or feels to much like begging, remind yourself that it is hard for managers to find competent professionals. So your friends and business associates will be getting points of their own when they recommend someone like you who is an asset to the projects they join.

Your biggest problem when old employers want to hire you for a contract may be that they may expect to pay you a rate that is a prorated version of your old employee salary. If this is the case, you'll have to explain that as a contractor you now must buy your own benefits and pay for your down time, which means that you must charge a market rate for your services.

TURN OLD JOBS INTO NEW

"Try to call back on old clients that may allow you to come back as an independent. I have done this recently, and am tremendously happy with my new assignment. Great rate, decent work!

"One thing I have always done is to make friends with full-time employees of my clients. I keep in touch with them as often as possible. This allows me to scope out opportunities to go back as an independent after the non-compete expires."

—Anonymous COBOL Programmer

How can I work directly for clients I met through consulting firms?

The key to converting consulting firm clients to direct clients is to keep your consulting firm contracts as short as possible. Six months is ideal. Then use a different consulting firm to find you each new contract. This works because consulting firm noncompetition clauses don't kick in until you leave the client, so keeping contracts short starts the clock on your noncompetition clauses and makes it possible for them to expire. A year after you leave a client, if you have taken our advice and negotiated your noncompetition clauses to last for no longer than a year, you can approach old clients and offer them your services without violating your old consulting firm noncompetition clauses.

It is possible that client may have signed agreements with the consulting firms that bind them not to hire you for a longer time. Because of this, when you get friendly with supervisors while working on a contract, mention that you'd be interested in working for them directly in a few years and ask for how long a period their no-hire contracts with the consulting firm extend.

How can I make the most of my existing contacts?

It is much easier to use your existing network to find new work than to approach strangers, so put some time into keeping your lines of communication open with anyone who might be able to refer you work.

Sending email and letters to business acquaintances is an effective way to do this because they help people remember who you are and what you do. This makes them more likely to recommend you when they encounter someone who is looking for somebody with your skills.

When you keep in touch this way, your goal is to simply remind people of what you do and to let them know that you will be actively looking for contract work in *the future*. You want to avoid making people feel that your only reason for contacting them is to find work now. People who think you are trying to use them are not going to give you referrals.

A good way to strengthen your business friendships is to phone people every three to six months to keep in touch. Once a year send out brief letters letting them know what you've been up to. You might also include a handwritten message with a word or two about your latest projects on your Christmas card.

Keep your tone personal in these contacts, so that the person feels that you contacted them because you consider them a friend, not because they were listed in your Rolodex. If you see a news item about an old business acquaintance, a great way to keep in touch is to mail them a note congratulating them on their promotion or mentioning the article you just read about their successful project. Just remember to end it with the information that you're now contracting and will be looking for an interesting new project in a few months.

Some people forward interesting email to business acquaintances as a way of keeping in touch, but this can backfire. Most people are up to their ears in spam and may consider the joke file you send them to be more spam. If you really feel that an email is worth forwarding, include a personal note at the top of your message to make your mailing less spam-like. And never send large files to anyone who hasn't requested them of you, since they can clog up mail servers and make it impossible for the recipient to get the rest of their business mail!

How do I find new clients?

Once you have made the most of the people who make up your current business network, you will have to take steps to widen that network. There are several strategies you can use to do this. We will only touch briefly here on a few that are appropriate for contractors, since you can find the rest discussed thoroughly in my books, *The Computer Consultant's Workbook* and *The Computer Consultant's Guide*.

The best way for you, as a contractor, to find new clients is to build relationships with businesses that for reasons of their own might want to refer you work. This includes other contractors and consultants who are so busy they can refer you their overflow clients, local business professionals like accountants and attorneys whose clients may need help with software but not know where to find it, and software vendors who want to be able to refer their customers to competent developers familar with their products.

You are most likely to meet other busy contractors and consultants at meetings of the professional organizations that cater to IT professionals. (See Chapter 2, "Can I Be a Contractor?" for tips on how to find these organizations.) When you go to these meetings, don't act as if you showed up only to make contacts, as this will only alienate people. Instead, when you talk to the managers and consultants you meet there, do your best to give the impression that you are sincerely interested in hearing about them and *their* work. If you can help someone out with some technical advice, do so, since this establishes you as a giving, competent person. As the people you meet at these meetings get to know you over time, they will become friends and will naturally think of you when they run into people who could use your skills.

Another way of generating a stream of clients might be to sign up for a vendor referral program. After you prove that you are an expert in using their product, usually by taking an exam, the vendor will enter you into a database of approved developers which they provide to their customers. This approach works for contractors who are experts in niche software where experienced developers are hard to find, though it is not recommended for heavily advertised vendor programs that involve mass market products. Referral programs for mass market products attract so many participants that the chances of any developer getting more than a few referrals are low.

Visit the Web sites of the vendors that sell the software tools you use to see what kinds of referral programs are available. However, because many referral programs cost money to join and serve more as a profit center for the vendor than a source of clients for their partners, before you sign on, network online with others who have joined these programs to find out if the vendor actually provided the promised referrals.

If you serve a clientele of midsized businesses, you might also be able to get referrals from a locally owned computer store that sells hardware, repairs, and upgrades to business customers but does not offer programming services. They may be happy to find someone competent to whom they can refer customers who need help with software, and you, in return, can refer some of your clients to them for hardware upgrades and support.

But before you set out to find people with whom to set up synergistic relationships, do some research into which local companies will hire contractors directly.

Otherwise, you may end up wasting your marketing efforts on people who can connect you only to companies that only hire from large body shops.

YOU NEVER KNOW WHERE YOU'LL FIND A CLIENT!

"Over the weekend, I was showing my dog at a 2-day show. My dog wasn't scheduled to show until later in the afternoon. I was ringside watching the other competitors when a well-dressed man came up to me and began talking to me. He asked me to hold his dog. We got to talking and it turns out he was the CIO of a major major corp. near Chicago. I told him I was a consult-ant and he asked me for a card and I happened to have one "dog-eared" card in my bag.

"He called me early Monday morning and I faxed him my résumé. He called me back Monday night and asked me if I was inter-ested in a contract and then explained what his department was needing. He then asked me what my bill rate was. I was so flabbergasted since I have been working W-2 contracts for so long that I just blurted out $85 per hour. He said how about $82.50 and I said OK.

"Good thing I have a good working relationship with an attorney as he was able to get me a contract drawn up early Tuesday morning! So now I am now officially sans agency-broker and just "doing it on my own.

"BTW my dog won his class on both days of the show!"

—Elizabeth P.

What kinds of companies will hire contractors directly?

Dynamic, smaller, newer companies are most likely to hire contractors without a middleman. But many larger corporations have implemented company-wide poli-cies that make it all but impossible for managers to hire contractors directly. That is because these larger corporations force managers to hire contractors from a nar-row list of preapproved "preferred vendors." If they do, the only way you can work for them as a contractor as the employee of a firm on that preferred vendor list.

What is a preferred vendor? Can I become one?

Preferred vendor lists grew out of corporate attempts to streamline purchasing procedures and use the company's huge buying power to negotiate deeper dis-counts with vendors. By centralizing all purchasing decisions rather than letting each manager make his own, corporations could cut costs and get deals.

Unfortunately, when implementing these purchasing procedures, many companies did not distinguish between the vendors who supply pencils or laser toner and those that supply contractor flesh and applied the same standards to both. So to be admitted to the company's preferred vendor list, a vendor must be large, able to supply product quickly when needed, and willing to give the corporation the lowest possible prices. When these preferred vendor standards are applied to vendors supplying contract services, they often limit the company to hiring from a handful of large and predatory body shops.

The corporations notorious for implementing the most restrictive preferred vendor policies are in conservative industries like manufacturing and insurance. These often refuse to hire any individual as a contractor unless they come in as a body shop employee. The only way to get around this policy is to market yourself to these companies as a "true" consultant, i.e., a problem solver, not a contractor.

Less restrictive companies may let you onto their preferred vendor lists if a manager makes a strong case for needing your services. But even then, they may only add you to their vendor list if you have been conducting your business like a true business and not behaving like a temporary employee. For example, they may demand that you show proof that you have been incorporated for more than a year, have an excellent corporate credit rating, work for other clients, and carry several million dollars in insurance.

DEALING WITH PREFERRED VENDOR LISTS

"My experience has been that if a hiring manager wants your services, they can get you on a preferred vendor list.

"AFAIK, a preferred vendor is someone who has signed the company's standard contract and is willing to abide by their rules. I also know a consulting firm that was 137th on a preferred vendor waiting list yet was added within 3 months. And these are all really big companies."

—James V. Reagan

"To avoid the PVL, you must differentiate your services enough from those marketed by agencies so that you are not categorized as contract labor. You cannot simply present the hiring manager your résumé, have a good interview, and expect to avoid dealing with the PVL.

"You must market yourself as a solution provider, rather than as a contractor (in particular, a contract programmer or analyst, even if that's what you'll end up doing...). This may require brochures/white papers/proposals/fixed-bid pricing - whatever works along these lines to get you in front of the economic buyer (AKA check signer/PO cutter).

"You're not filling a job order, you're providing a solution to a business problem they have. Since you are providing a solution, and not a body, per se, you are not an agency and can, especially if the economic buyer has been convinced to close the deal, circumvent the PVL."

—Bob McIlree

What kinds of firms don't use these preferred vendor lists?

Medium sized companies that have significant investments in IT but have not yet grown huge and bureaucratic are your best bet for working direct, as are high-tech start-ups that are still at the phase where they need talented technical people but may have trouble attracting them in competition with larger, better known companies.

You can identify these companies via discussions with local contractors and managers you meet at meetings of business and professional organizations. Once you find them, research what kinds of technical skills they are looking for and do what you can to beef up your résumé with the kinds of skills these firms, rather than the body shops, are looking for.

Why do clients hire from body shops when they can get better talent hiring direct?

Some companies don't feel that it is worth paying for talent. It is among these that you will find the most stringent preferred vendor policies. Over the years these companies have gotten along just fine hiring low-grade talent and paying them poorly. These are the companies that treat their technical people like easily replaced commodities. They are the ones most likely to indulge in ill-thought-out layoffs and poorly planned projects.

Contractors often believe they can sell themselves to these companies by making a case for quality. But if a company's top management believes that the cheapskate approach works, and if, in fact, it is working for them, no individual contractor is going to be able to change their minds.

When you encounter companies that are driven entirely by cost and choose contractors strictly on price, leave them to the body shops. Concentrate your marketing efforts on companies whose management is already aware that they get a competitive advantage from hiring the best.

Why do so many companies prefer to hire from agencies and consulting firms, especially now, when they can find my résumé on the Internet?

Clients hire from agencies, because agencies make life easy for overburdened managers at several stages of the contracting process. For starters, they make it easy to *find* contractors with the skills the manager is looking for. Busy managers don't have the time or inclination to spend 8 hours surfing through vanity Web sites looking for the résumé of someone who could do the job they need done right away, especially when they know that even if they find a local résumé that looks like a good match, it's very likely that the contractor is already working. Consulting firms also sell themselves to managers by claiming to *screen* contractors, which saves the manager additional hassle.

Larger consulting firms that deploy dozens of contractors at once, also make life simpler for clients by *billing* them for the whole herd and saving the client from having to deal with a flurry of invoices from different individuals.

Finally, consulting firms make life easier for clients because, if things go wrong after the contractor is hired, it is the consulting firm that has to fire the contractor and become the target of the contractor's anger. It also is the consulting firm that has to worry about any violations of labor or equal opportunity law and the threat of IRS audits. For many clients, this *shift of responsibility* more than justifies the additional $10-15 per hour it costs to hire contractors from consulting firms.

AGGRESSIVE COLD CALLING

"Pick up the Yellow Pages. Go to the section(s) for Computer Consultants/System Developers. Pick a column or a page (too boring to go straight alpha). Call every one of them. Tell them 'My name is ... I am an experienced developer for ... I've done projects for ... I am wondering if from time to time you have requirements for help in this area ...' Polish your presentation as you go.

"This works and here's why: There are many, many small team shops. They don't have experts in all areas. They do have clients. Their clients have needs. The client will go first to the established relationship that they have with a vendor, such as a consultant or networking group. The consultant groups want to help their clients.

"Sometimes you will get direct handoffs. The consultant will simply put you in touch with the client and drop out of the loop. Sometimes the consultant may want you to work subcontract.

"Success is having a strong, focused skill. Then you must work the phone relentlessly. You can turn one good lead per day, if you work the phone for 2 hrs in the morning and 2 hrs in the afternoon. Be pleasant. Every new call is just that: a new call. Forget the rejection you just experienced. Start over every call.

"Don't let anyone tell you that you can't do it!"

—Working from Home

How do I find out which companies in my area will hire direct?

When it comes to finding out this kind of information, there is no substitute for talking with other experienced contractors and local managers. Only they can tell you which companies really hire direct, and which companies may *say* they hire direct but, in truth, hire only from agencies.

Is it worthwhile to send a mass mailing to area managers?

If you find yourself stymied in your search for clients, you may be tempted to use some traditional marketing techniques including mass mailings and cold calling. But these are not effective marketing strategies for contractors.

Mailing a letter announcing your availability that is addressed to "Manager of IT Services" is a waste of time and money. Many contractors do this, but I have yet to hear from anyone who has had it bring in work. Even if you know the manager's name, sending a mailing to a stranger is not likely to get you work. Using email may be cheaper than mailing letters, but don't let the cheap cost tempt you to spam potential employers. Spam is not an effective way to make new contacts.

If you feel compelled to indulge in some type of cold calling, try using the phone after boning up on how to telemarket by reading Bill Good's classic book, *Prospecting your Way to Sales Success*. But don't cold call if there are only a handful of managers in town who could use your services. Cold calling is only useful if you can get by with getting one positive response from of a hundred phone calls.

How can I present myself as an expert?

Another set of strategies not only help you find new clients, they move your business up a notch, so that you are perceived as the kind of consultant who is brought in to give high-level advice rather than a contractor doing day work. These strategies let you meet potential clients in a context where you can come across as an expert. Some proven ways of doing this are lecturing to professional groups on problem-solving topics, writing for the trade press, sending out press releases about your business, and teaching courses that attract your target client. These strategies are covered extensively in *The Computer Consultant's Workbook*.

I've found a manager who is interested in hiring me for a direct contract. What now?

Once you have found a manager who will hire you directly, you need to negotiate your rate and determine what procedures will be used for payment. You also should verify what status you will be working under. Finally, you'll need to put your agreement into the form of a written contract.

But before you can negotiate anything, you must determine if the manager who wants to hire you is the person who has the authority to negotiate your contract. Don't guess on this one. Ask! If managers don't have the authority to hire you or to negotiate your rate and other contract terms, there is no point in wasting time going through negotiations with them. Simply thank them for their interest in hiring you and ask them to introduce you to the person with whom you must negotiate your contract's terms.

What status should I work under?

The considerations here are very similar to those we discussed in Chapter 3, "W-2, 1099, or Corp?" though you are not as likely to get a fight from a client over working as an unincorporated 1099 contractor.

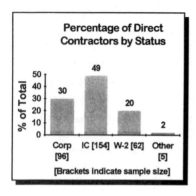

Percentage of Direct Contractors by Status

[Brackets indicate sample size]

In fact, our Real Rate Survey data suggests that the largest group of contractors working directly for clients work as unincorporated 1099 contractors. Of the 317 contractors who reported working on direct contracts in the first half of 1998, a good 49%, worked as unincorporated 1099 contractors. Another 30% worked as employees of their own corporations. Another 20% worked as temporary W-2 employees of the client or as employees of an umbrella company or pass-through agency.

The client insists that I work through a "pass-through agency," what's that?

Pass-through agencies are consulting firms that become the client of record for a W-2 or independent contractor when the client is afraid of hiring them directly. Pass-through agencies treat you just like a regular consulting firm would, however, since you are bringing the contract to them, they should take a smaller cut of your billing. Usually a client who insists that you work with a pass-through firm will tell you which firms to approach.

But pass-through agencies are not cheap. Typical pass-through commissions are 20% on a W-2 contract (which pays the social security tax and other required employee-related payments) and 5-7% on corp-to-corp or 1099 contracts. Because of the additional expense of working through a pass-through agency, the client who demands you work this way should be willing to pay you a little more than they would if you were truly working direct. If they don't, this sort of "direct" contract is nothing more than a consulting firm contract.

If you decide to go along with a client's request that you work through a pass-through agency, ask them for the names of agencies they've done business with in the past. Call several and make it clear you will work with the company that offers you the best deal. If you already have a good relationship with a consulting firm, contact them and ask them what kind of pass-through deal they could offer you. You should *never* let a pass-through agency put a noncompetition clause into their contract with you, since you, not the agency, found the client.

How do I negotiate my rate?

Negotiation is a three step process. First, you'll have to decide what rate you'd like to earn for the job, next you must decide how *low* a rate you will settle for, and, finally, you must determine at what point you would be willing to walk away from the deal because the rate is too low to interest you. Unless you are clear in your own mind what rate you will accept, you will not be able to negotiate effectively.

Ideally you should be asking for a rate that is somewhat higher than what you could get through an agency, though you should expect to settle for one that is a little less than what an agency would charge the client for your services. Like you, the client also wants to get a price break for cutting out the middleman. However, with consulting firms currently taking a median 20.5% of the client billing for placing corp-to-corp contractors and 20% for placing 1099 contractors, you can easily charge less than an agency and still come out better off than you would be working through a consulting firm.

Next add a little fat to your rate so that you can bring it down during negotiations and still get the rate you really want. Ten percent is a reasonable factor by which to inflate your rate.

How aggressive you want to be in actual negotiations is up to you. Some people enjoy the process and consider it one of the fun parts of working for themselves. However, many technical people hate negotiating and tend to accept whatever rate a manager offers just to avoid conflict.

Be careful here! Taking the rate that the manager offers when it is *not* the rate you want is behaving like an employee. As an independent self-employed contractor you should expect to arrive at a rate that pleases both you and the client. That means you may have to go through several stages of offer and counteroffer until you have arrived at a rate that you can both accept.

If the client's initial offer is less than what you want, come back with a counteroffer, one slightly lower than the rate the client rejected. The client may then tell you they have to confer with a boss and it may take a day or two for negotiations to continue.

Eventually the client will either come back and agree to the rate you've asked for or they may tell you that all they can pay is some lower amount. At that point you have several choices. You can accept the rate they've named, you can make another slightly lower counteroffer, or you can walk away from the deal.

What should I watch out for when negotiating directly with managers?

Most contractors are primed and downright paranoid when dealing with consulting firm recruiters. They expect to have to fight for their rates and they do. But when dealing directly with clients it's easy to lose your edge. You don't think of the client as an exploiter the way you do the recruiter, so you may, as a result, end up negotiating less effectively.

In particular, don't be manipulated by clients' "nice guy" tactics—where they behave so pleasantly that you feel like a heartless monster holding out for more money. Don't let yourself get sidetracked, either, by the fear that you are offending clients by asking for the rate you need. There's nothing offensive in going for the best deal you can possibly make. That's what being in business is about!

Another problem you may encounter is that managers who are used to dealing with employees may treat you like a recalcitrant employee during the negotiating process, subtly making you feel that you are being greedy and asking for an outrageous sum. That's their right, and it is often a very effective negotiating tactic—for them. But you must keep in mind that you are not an employee, and that because you are not an employee you will be paying your own health, life, and disability insurance, contributing to your own retirement fund, and paying out of savings for your own sick days, vacations, and holidays.

Some contractors find it useful to bring along a copy of our *Real Rate Survey Report*, which you can order from our Web site. They use it to show clients that the rates they are asking for fall well within the prevailing range for the kind of work they do. This can be an effective way of countering arguments that the rate you are asking is out of line.

If you really hate negotiating and know that you are bad at it, there is another approach that some successful contractors earning very high rates have found to work well. Simply inform the client of your rate and tell them that you don't negotiate it. $N per hour is what you charge and that is what they'll have to pay if they want you to work for them. Do this politely but firmly.

If you have enough work that you can afford to turn away clients, this may be the simplest way to approach rate negotiations. However, if you have just found your first client, it would be foolish to risk losing them by being too stubborn, particularly if they will pay you a direct rate that is better than what you can get from an agency. The problem with being inflexible in negotiations is that, just like you, the client also wants to come away feeling like a winner. So it's always a good idea, if possible, to leave a little room in your rate so that you can give the client that petty victory.

Who provides the contract when I work direct?

Many companies have a boilerplate contract they present to direct contractors. In that case, you negotiate their contract clauses the same way you would the consulting firm contracts discussed in the Chapter 7, "What's in my Consulting Firm Contract?."

In other cases, particularly when you work for a smaller company that doesn't use a lot of contract services, you will have to provide the contract. If that's the situation, once you've come to an oral agreement with the hiring manager, you'll need to prepare a simple contract appropriate to the status under which you will be working that states how you will be paid, when you will be paid, when you will start work, when the contract will end, and what the terms are for terminating the contract early for both parties.

In this situation, it is advisable to hire an attorney who has experience with computer consulting contracts to draft your contract, especially if the contract involves more than a few thousand dollars. Some contractors simply write up a clear summary of what has been agreed to and use it as a contract. Yet others mail their clients a letter of agreement which lists the terms to which they have agreed. In any case, be sure that you have a *written* contract that defines the terms of payment and the ownership of rights to software you develop on the job. Oral agreements are almost impossible to prove in court, and in the absence of a written contract the law prescribes defaults which may not be at all what you want.

What should my contract include?

An important clause in an independent's contract is the one that defines the contractor's status. This clause should state that you (or your corporation) are an independent contractor and that neither you nor your staff should be construed as being employees of the client. Other important clauses define how much you are to be paid, when payment should occur, and what recourse you, the contractor may have if payment does not occur in a timely fashion.

Be sure to state your hourly rate and list any special circumstances under which you would expect to be paid a different rate. Describe how you will bill for overtime or being on call or for time spent in travel on the client's behalf. The contract should also state when you will invoice the client and how soon after the client receives the invoice they must pay.

Some contractors put wording into their contracts to motivate the client to pay them on time. One approach is to offer a slight discount—for example 2% or 3%—for prompt payment. Another is to put in wording that says that if payments fall behind by more than two months, the client will be considered in breach of the contract and you may stop working for them. However, if you are contracting for a large corporate client, even putting in terms like these may not stop the company from paying you when it gets around to it which may be three or four months after your invoice is due, rather than when the contract says they must.

Your contract should also define the time period that the contract will cover. It should make clear who owns the copyright to any software you write for the client. If it is the client, title to the software should only pass to them after you are paid.

Finally, describe the mechanism by which either you or the client can terminate or alter the contract. You may also want to put in a clause that says that any disputes must be litigated in your home state.

WHY YOU SHOULD REGISTER SOFTWARE COPYRIGHTS

"If you are an independent contractor and you or your corporation owns the copyright in the software that you write, then you should register the copyrights in all of your software, or at least those portions of your software that is worth more than the $20 application fee.

"As the owner of the copyrights in your software, if the consulting firm or the client later fails to pay your invoices, then in addition to making a claim for breach of contract, you may then have the right to terminate the license to use the software, which means that any further use by the client of your software after termination of the license constitutes copyright infringement.

"To get blank copyright applications, call the Copyright Office at (202) 707-3000. You can also download the forms and instructions from the Copyright Office web site at http://lcweb.loc.gov/copyright.

"Fill in the blanks on the form, sign it, and send it with up to 50 pages of source code to the Copyright Office, along with a check to cover the filing fees The registration will be effective as of the date the Copyright Office receives the application. If you make a mistake on the application, you can later amend the registration.

"Under current law, if you file the application prior to the beginning of an infringement, or if you file within the first three months of publication of a published software work, then you would have the right to ask for attorney's fees, as well as an alternative form of damages known as statutory damages. Unfortunately, you do not get attorney's fees or statutory damages if you file late, and you will have no right to sue for copyright infringement unless you have the copyright registration."

— Fred Wilf, Attorney-at-Law

What do I do with the contract?

Once you've drafted up a contract, have an attorney review it, to make sure that you haven't inadvertently made a foolish mistake or used wording that has a different meaning in a legal setting than it does in daily life. It is not a good idea to simply copy a contract you find on a Web site or in books, since you cannot know whether the law has changed since it was drafted or under which state's law it was meant to be used.

Once you have the contract, present it to the person at the client company who has the authority to sign it and get their signature.

Can I work without a formal signed contract?

It is a very bad idea to work directly for a client without a formal signed contract. Without written proof that the client agreed to pay you for your work, it may be impossible to collect if a dispute should arise. You need to have all payment terms clearly set forth in writing to be able to call on the legal remedies available to you. Remember that it is a lot harder to compel payment when you are self-employed rather than an employee. So make sure that you always have a written contract that specifies whom you are working for, what work the rate is being paid for, what that rate is, and when the client is supposed to pay you.

It is also a very good idea to get periodic sign-offs on work you do. That way you have proof that you completed the work to the client's satisfaction. You should also document in memos any additional agreements you make with the client that change the scope or terms of your original agreement. If the change is a significant one, have the client sign an addendum to the original contract that clearly sets out the changes you have agreed to.

Do I need a contract when I know the managers I'm working for very well and trust them completely?

Yes! Managers may suddenly move to another department or get laid off. The people who replace them often begin by eliminating all traces of the previous managers' way of doing things. If you are part of that old way of doing things, you may find yourself kicked out the door with little chance to explain what you've been doing. If there is no written proof of your agreement with the previous manager, you may have difficulty in getting paid for work you've already done. Even if you are kept on, without written records you may have to renegotiate your contract with the new management from scratch.

What is an invoice?

As an independent contractor you must present an invoice to your client in order to get paid. The invoice should list your company name, address and contact information at the top. Include your payment terms, which should be "Due on Receipt" if you are to be paid immediately or "Net 30" if you have agreed to wait a month for payment.

Then provide a table that has columns for a description of the work you are billing for, the hours you are billing for, and the rate you are charging for those hours. Put the total amount owed at the bottom. You can view a sample invoice on Page 167. Make sure you send out your invoices as soon as possible as most companies will not begin to process your payment until they receive the invoice.

What should I do when I get paid?

If you are working as an independent contractor you will get paid the full amount you've billed the client, with nothing taken out of your taxes. That means it is very important that you estimate how much of each check will have to go towards paying your taxes and set that amount aside immediately so that you aren't tempted to spend it. Don't forget that you also have to set aside money for state and local taxes.

To be on the safe side, you might make a habit of setting aside 40% of each check until it is time to pay your first quarterly withholding payment. Then use the worksheets that come with the federal 1040 ES tax form and with your state tax quarterly withholding forms to estimate your taxes for the whole year based on your earnings for the quarter.

If you can't easily do this on your own, call on the services of an accountant. If you are earning rates of $50 per hour or more, you are earning enough that your tax liability will be significant. A good tax professional should be able to save you more than you spend on their fees.

What should I do if I don't get my check?

Large companies can be very slow to pay. Your first step should be to contact the person or department to whom you have been sending your invoices. Verify that they have received your invoices. If they have, ask them when you can expect payment. Some companies routinely delay payment to their vendors for as long as three months. This is one of the reasons some people prefer to work through agencies. If you still don't get paid, follow the steps for dealing with nonpayment described on Page 186.

How do I terminate the contract?

Because your best source of future direct contracts is referrals from satisfied clients, you should do everything you can to keep your clients happy. This means that you should never terminate a contract prematurely unless you have a very good reason to do so. The client's failure to pay you is one such good reason. A major health crisis at home might be another. Getting a better deal elsewhere is not!

If you feel that a client is eating up too much of your time and that you are missing out on valuable contract opportunities elsewhere, rather than drop a client entirely, you might explain that you are broadening your practice to make it more entrepreneurial and henceforth will be serving several clients at the same time.

Then gradually scale back the amount of time you dedicate to that client's project. Most entrepreneurial consultants *do* serve more than one client at a time, and once you begin doing this, defending you IC status becomes a lot easier.

If you do have to terminate the contract prematurely, do exactly what your contract specified in its termination clause. Usually you will have to give written notice some period of time before you leave, often thirty days. You do not need to explain to the client why you are terminating unless you want to. Do your best to keep the relationship cordial, no matter what stresses you might be under, so that you don't make an enemy who will give you the kind of negative word of mouth that can destroy an independent consulting practice.

INVOICE

SOFTWARE SOLUTIONS
123 Pleasant Street
Leominster, MA 01456
Phone: 789 123-4321
Fax: 789 123-4773

CLIENT: Industrial Coatings, Inc.
4732 Enterprise Parkway
Lunenberg, MA   01462

INVOICE: IC231   INVOICE DATE: 12/18/98
                            TERMS: DUE ON RECEIPT

DATE	HRS	DESCRIPTION	RATE	AMOUNT
12/14-12/18	40	Customer Database upgrade, Dept 203	$65	$2,600
			Total	$2,600

A Direct Contractor's Sample Invoice

CHAPTER 9
HOW DO I HANDLE THIS?

How do I give notice at my old job once I've found a contract?

First, be sure you really *have* the contract. At a minimum, you should have the signed written contract in hand before you give notice. It is also a good idea to verify with the consulting firm that the client has signed their contract with the firm, since that contract is the only contract that guarantees that you actually work.

Many contractors suggest that you give your notice in writing. When you give notice it is not necessary or even advisable to explain why you are leaving. Merely state that you are resigning, note when your resignation takes effect, and leave it at that. If you feel you have to give a reason, keep it vague. For example, say that you are resigning to take on an "exciting new opportunity." It never hurts to conclude with some polite fluff about how much you have enjoyed your work at the employer's firm—whether or not you really have.

Some companies have a policy of terminating employees immediately when they give notice, rather than letting them stay around for the last two weeks. Because of this, before you give notice, you should bring home any code listings you want to keep for future reference. You'll also want to remove any personal valuables from your office so that they don't get overlooked if you have to make a sudden exit.

If you are a highly valued employee, your employer may prod you for information about your new job in order to make you a counteroffer that might persuade you to stay. (Counteroffers are discussed further on Page 183.) But don't feel that you have to answer questions about where you are going or what you will be paid on your new assignment unless you feel like it. Your old employer does not have a right to this information.

As you prepare to leave, resist the temptation to blurt out all the pent up frustrations you've been holding in because you had to keep silent to keep your job. The thrill of the well-placed zinger is not worth the potential harm you might do yourself.

When someone from the HR department invites you to an exit interview, don't tell them the real reasons why you are leaving the company if those reasons include your bosses' incompetence. HR staffers have no ability to affect how the company is managed. All you will do by complaining to them is ensure that your criticisms are relayed back to the people you mentioned. Because computer professionals move around the IT community, it is quite possible that the person you insult when leaving this job will turn out to be the interviewer when you apply for a plum contract somewhere else next year.

Leaving on a positive note also makes it more likely that you'll get referrals to contract work from ex-managers and coworkers in the future, and these references and referrals can keep you working when times are tough. So treat everyone in a friendly, upbeat manner when you make your exit and keep your negative thoughts about the job to yourself.

TIPS ON LEAVING YOUR OLD JOB

"Write a resignation letter. Keep a copy. Example:

```
March 31, 1999
Dear Ms. Jones,
I regret to announce my resignation,
effective April 15, 1999.
It has been a pleasure to work on the
HR 2000 project with you and the team.
Please accept my best wishes for a
prosperous future.
Very truly yours,
```

"Carry the letter with you when you see your supervisor and give it to her after you break the news. You want to be remembered for your tact and professionalism. Be polite!

"Do not offer to help them out for nothing after your departure. Do not let them bother you daily at your new job with phoned in questions.

"If they try a counter-offer, you should almost certainly decline. People who allow themselves to be talked into staying usually get burnt. Once you've expressed an intention to leave, follow through."

—Scott Horne

How do I start my new contract?

On the first day of your contract, you will usually report to your new supervisor at the beginning of the business day. Someone from the consulting firm may also show up and make a big production out of checking up that you got there. This has little to do with you. The consulting firm is merely taking advantage of another opportunity to get face-to-face with managers who might need more contractors.

If you are a W-2 contractor, the recruiter may bring you a stack of time cards too. You'll need to get your supervisor to sign one of these at the end of each week. Then you will send it to the consulting firm so you can get paid.

Don't be surprised if it takes a day or two before the client gets around to getting you the badge necessary for entry to the building or a user ID you need to log on to some system you will be working on. It may even take a few days for the client to figure out where you should sit and what computer you should use. Relax and be patient no matter how chaotic things appear. With what you are being paid, the client should be motivated to get you working as soon as possible. Meanwhile, no one will think badly of you because you are waiting for other people to get you set up.

How long do I have on a new contract to figure out what's going on?

As a contractor you are expected to be an expert in the languages, databases, and platforms you work with. But no one expects you to know the details of a client's specific implementation of those tools. So you usually have at least a week or two before anyone expects you to be productive. The more experience you have, the less time it should take to get oriented, since an experienced contractor will have worked on enough systems in the past to know what kinds of questions they need to ask to get oriented to a new one.

But the operative word here is "ask." The more questions you ask in your first days on the job, the faster you'll become productive. And among the first questions you'll need to get answered is this: of all the people you've just been introduced to, which are the ones who really understand the client's systems?

It may take some persistence to find this out, since the system experts may not be the people your new supervisor has told you to rely on for help. Managers may not know which staffers have mastered the technical issues involved. Or they may want to keep you from pestering busy system experts, since the last thing they need is to have to take time out to help a new and unknown contractor come up to speed. So in your first few days on the job you will have to use diplomacy and tact to identify the people who have the answers you need and to motivate them to help you when you need help.

The best way to accomplish this is to give signs early on that you are a competent professional who respects the project experts and understands that they are busy. Do as much as you can with available resources before you ask them for help.

Read documentation and listings. Poke around the system on your own. Collect the questions you come up with and then schedule some time with the project expert–at their convenience–to get your answers. Once you've convinced the competent technical people on the project that you are an asset and not another burden your work will be a lot easier.

The work isn't what was described at the interview. I'm out of my depth. Help!

Consulting firm recruiters and high level managers often have a sketchy grasp of computer technology. Because of this, through no fault of your own, you may occasionally find yourself placed on a project that demands skills you don't have. Perhaps you were told at the interview that the contract would involve Y2K work on a COBOL system, something you have the experience and skills to do well. But once on the job you find out that the team leader expects you to know IBM mainframe Assembler which you've never used before.

In a case like this the very last thing you should do is try to wing it. There are some things you can pick up on the job because they are very similar to languages or tools you already know. But you'd be foolish to try to fake knowledge of a whole new operating system or first generation language. As soon as you determine that you have been the victim of a bad placement, talk the situation over with the consulting firm that placed you and let your supervisor know that there has been a mix-up. This gives the client the opportunity to decide whether they want to use you elsewhere or whether to let you go in favor of someone who can do the job they need done.

The biggest mistake new contractors make in this kind of situation is to keep silent and let a few weeks go by during which they frantically try to come up to speed. When something inevitably occurs that makes it clear that the contractor is incapable of doing the job, the client feels tricked and angry–quite rightly, since they have now lost precious time and must start out from scratch in finding someone to do their work. The contractor ends up getting the blame for the mistake made by the consulting firm or the hiring manager and may wind up out on the street with a bad reference. It is much better to be honest about a mismatch as soon as it becomes obvious so that the client can take the steps necessary to get their job done properly.

There's nothing for me to do!

Strange as it seems, it is not unheard of for contractors to begin new contracts only to find themselves sitting around with nothing to do. This may happen because anxious managers staff projects weeks or even months before they actually need people in order to avoid being caught short-handed when the crunch hits. Or it may happen because political forces have put the brakes on a project and management itself is waiting to find out if the project will be canceled or if they will still need the contractor.

If you find yourself in a situation like this, relax! As a new contractor, no one expects you to do anything but wait to be told what to do. Make sure that the lack of work is real and not the result of a misunderstanding with your manager or team leader. If it is real, ask if there is anything you can do to better prepare yourself for the time when the work does arrive, for example, familiarizing yourself with the details of the systems you will be working on.

If this request does not result in your being given something to do, put your time to use learning something that can help you on your next project. Study for a certification exam. Master a new language—on your own laptop if the client doesn't have the compiler installed.

If the situation goes on for more than a week or two, it's legitimate to put out feelers for a new contract even if the one you are on is supposed to last for several more months. Dead calms of this sort are often a sign that a project is about to be canceled.

The employees here work a thirty-five hour week. Does that mean I can only bill for thirty-five hours?

If you work forty hours a week you can usually bill for forty hours unless your contract explicitly stated otherwise. Take a shorter lunch than the client's employees or stay a little later. Just make sure that you really do put in the hours you bill for. Clients resent the contractor who bills for an eight hour day after arriving at 8:30, taking an hour lunch and leaving at 4:15.

The manager asked me to compete in the United Way Bowlathon. Do I bill for the time I spend on that?

Contractors who spend a long time on projects may find themselves treated just like employees by their supervisors. They may get invited to company picnics held on company time or be asked to participate in charity events. As a general rule, if your supervisor invites you to a company event that takes place during regular work hours, you can bill for it. But you should not bill for extracurricular activities that take place outside usual working hours. If you have a question about the billability of an event, bring it up with your supervisor before you go.

This project is headed for disaster, help!

The more badly managed a project is, the more likely it is to need the help of outside contractors. So you should not be surprised if once on the job you find yourself confronted with a situation where chaos rules and the system that was described to you as "90% complete" turns out to be so flawed it will never make it out of testing.

Managers under the gun to meet impossible deadlines often hire herds of contractors to show that they are doing something. Sometimes that "something" is finding a scapegoat—you—on which to place blame for an unavoidable disaster.

If you find yourself in this kind of situation, the important thing is to stay cool and remember, *it's not your problem.* Your responsibility is to do as good a job as any serious professional could be expected to do under the circumstances. But this does not include walking on water or making up, single-handedly, for a years' worth of stupid decisions by others.

In situations like this, you must keep yourself aloof from the emotions that run rampant in drowning projects. Remind yourself that you are a hired gun. While employees may be worrying about losing their jobs and having their careers go down in flames, these are not relevant concerns for a contractor. You'll be losing *your* job in a few months whether the project succeeds or fails, and the effect on your contracting career of participation in a disastrous project is no different from that of participating in most successes. No one outside this particular company will have ever heard about this project or care what happened to it. All they'll want to know is what languages you used and what rate you were paid.

I could save this project! Why won't anyone take my advice?

If you see how to make improvements in the project you're working on, by all means, share this information with the person you are reporting to. But once you've shared your ideas, let it go. Don't keep badgering people if you don't see them making the changes you've suggested. Sometimes your innocent suggestions might look to others like attacks on the way they've decided to proceed. Sometimes your ideas might not take into account factors you have no knowledge of. Sometimes your supervisor is simply a fool.

Whatever the explanation, it doesn't matter. As a contractor, your only responsibility is to do what you are told to do by the person to whom you report, fool or not. Getting overly involved in the details of a project that is outside your control is among the biggest hazards contractors face.

With my high rate, it's hard to justifying taking time off. How can I stop working so many hours?

Workaholism is easy to justify when you are earning very high hourly rates but only get paid for the hours you work. However, if you don't learn to pace yourself, you are going to burn out—or to burn out the people who have to live with you.

The simplest way to handle the tendency to work too much is to plan ahead and set aside several weeks' worth of time, spread throughout the year, which you will use to cover holidays, sick days, personal days, and vacation days. Make a promise to yourself that you will use *all* of these days as days off, come what may. Then, if something unexpected comes up that forces you to miss a day, simply take that day out of the fund of off-days you've already set aside. That way you treat time off as a normal part of your schedule, not as time and money you're stealing from yourself.

If you're worried that you may not get a new contract once the current one is over, work solidly for your first three or four months on a new contract and save as much as you can so that you build up an earnings cushion. Adjust your spending to the income you'd have if you worked only nine months, rather than a full year. This way, you'll build up some reserves so that you will be able to experience down time without panic.

PLAN FOR TIME OFF

"What I do is take 10% of my take home pay and put it aside into a separate checking account that I use only for time off. When I work OT, I put 25% of the OT extra money in the account. This takes discipline. but it also gives me 4+ weeks per year of 'paid' time off."

–Larry Girouard

The client wants to hire me as an employee, should I do it?

When you do good work on a contract, it is not uncommon for clients to offer to hire you in permanently. Before you decide whether to accept the offer, spend some time defining your career goals. What benefits would you get by converting to being an employee? What would you be giving up? Most importantly, where would you end up in a year or two if you took up this offer and the company then laid you off?

Most contractors who take offers of permanent employment do so because they were accidental contractors, rather than people who had decided that contracting made sense for their long-term career plans. Perhaps they started contracting because they lost an earlier permanent job and saw contracting as a bridge until they found something new. Often their skills aren't strong and varied enough to support a long-term contracting career.

Other contractors may convert to employees because they have seen enough companies in their contracting travels to know a good thing when they see it. They may like the way the company is run and enjoy the work there enough that they'd like to make it a permanent part of their lives. Like many long-term contractors, they may be burning out on the "hired gun" mentality that contracting requires and be looking for a situation in which they can take some ownership for the work they do.

Sometimes employers entice contractors who have very strong skills and leadership abilities into becoming full-time employees by making them offers that are simply too good to turn down. They may appoint them to upper level management jobs or give them the chance to do high level design on projects that use the latest in technology.

Whether it will make sense for you to shift back to being an employee is something only you can know. For people still in the early years of their professional careers, taking a job as an employee may offer benefits that contracting can't, most notably the chance to get experience managing projects. A salaried job that gives you an opportunity to learn skills that will enhance your value in the future is well worth considering.

But caution is in order. Many salaried jobs do not improve your value over time. Many salaried jobs, particularly those that involve management, lure you into focusing on problems unique to your employer's company and mastering its political environment, rather than learning skills that could be of use in other companies. Should you be laid off later, these company-specific skills have little value in the marketplace.

If you are tempted to take a salaried job because you like the feeling of security you get from having a "real job" this too may be an illusion. The layoffs of the past decade should have made everyone aware that there is no such thing as job security for any employee, and that any claims an employee might think they have on an employer's loyalty melt away as their salary rises and their age increases. Unfortunately, young people coming into the job market in the booming late 1990s may have to learn this lesson all over again, the hard way.

It is also worth remembering that some cynical employers convert highly-paid contractors to salaried employees to save money during the life of a project, only to lay off the employees at the end of the project when their services are no longer needed.

I am going to miss my deadline. How should I handle the situation?

Don't try to hide problems from your supervisors! The faster you can report a serious problem, the faster they can bring in additional resources to save the situation.

Explain the situation clearly and objectively. Don't attempt to lay blame on others—even if others are to blame—but do explain the reasons why delay is inevitable. Make whatever suggestions you can that might point to solutions for the problem at hand. Then relax and let the managers decide what to do next. Remember, they are the ones who will take the career hit if the project fails, not you.

If this strategy results in your losing the contract, take it philosophically. You may have been hired in to give management a scapegoat onto which to load the blame for some higher-up's mistakes. This is not at all unusual. If that is why you were hired, console yourself with the thought that you've been paid well for doing it. Then pull up your socks and go look for your next contract.

I have been assigned to work with another contractor who is an imbecile. How can I keep his mistakes from making me look bad?

Very, very carefully! The most difficult situations contractors encounter are those that involve poor performance of *other* people on the job. Because you are new and unknown, you have to be very careful when dealing with conflicts of this type, because lodging any type of complaint early on can result in your being labeled a whiner or troublemaker, no matter how valid that complaint might be.

The best thing you can do is to clarify exactly what your responsibility is and carefully distinguish your responsibility from that of the other contractors you must work with. If necessary, document your understanding of your responsibility in written memos.

For example, if you're working with another contractor who is way behind on his part of the project, you might send a weekly status report to your supervisor which says, "Next week I'll be testing the customer database update module I've completed against the new customer database that Yuri is supposed to deliver by then. Please let me know what you'd like me to do with my time next week if the database takes longer to develop than expected." This subtly gets across to the supervisor that there may be a problem with Yuri's work, without making you look like a whiner or blamer.

Usually, if you keep communications open with the client's staff, ask intelligent questions, and do a good job with the work you have been given, it will not take long for the client's staff to pick up on your competence. Management will usually take care of other less competent contractors as their problems become evident.

I've been assigned to work with a client employee who is an imbecile. What do I do now?

Proceed even more carefully! You do not know what political reasons have led to the company employing the imbecile. They may be related to the CEO. They may be having an affair with the Director of Marketing. They may be recovering from an automobile accident that killed their spouse and left them brain damaged. Or, more likely, they may have been very good at doing some other job which resulted in their being promoted to a new level of responsibility which they can't handle. Whatever the explanation, your only concern should be to do the best job you can, to be polite to everyone, and to keep the definition of your own, personal responsibility very clear.

If getting your work done is dependent on the work of the problem employee, discuss any concerns you have with your supervisor but do it as objectively as you can, avoiding the perception that you are dumping on the employee. For example, rather than saying, "Gladys is incapable of writing a single Perl script that works!" you can simply say, "Gladys might really benefit from some additional training in Perl. She is working very hard but seems to be having a tough time understanding how to write CGI scripts. I know she did a great job designing web pages in the past, but I think she needs some help here." Then let go. You've identified the problem for management. Now it is up to them to deal with it.

In a few weeks the term specified in my contract will end. What should I do?

You should have a frank talk with your supervisor right now about whether your contract will be extended. This is true whether you got your job through an agency or directly. Unless the client makes it clear that they will be extending your contract, you should begin hunting for your next contract immediately.

Behave exactly the way you did when you began to hunt for your original contract. Do some research to update yourself on current rates and then contact a few well-recommended agencies or use your network of business acquaintances to find a new contract. If you are happy with the consulting firm that placed you on this job, you can call them and ask them to start looking for something new.

Just be aware that, if there is any chance that your client might want you for an extension, your current consulting firm is unlikely to send you on interviews for other contracts, since that could result in clients making offers for you that the consulting firm would have to turn down should the current client decide that they do want you to extend. Since clients often delay making decisions about extending contractors up until the very last minute, it's a good idea to work with more than one firm. That way, you can go on some interviews before your current contract ends and can avoid ending up with downtime should your current client wait until the very last moment to tell the consulting firm they are going to let you go.

Do I have to be secretive about finding a new contract when my old one is coming to an end?

Since you are not an employee, there is no need for the secrecy that usually cloaks job hunting while you are employed. You can make job hunting calls from you desk at lunch time and you can take time off to go interview for new positions—though, of course, you don't bill your current client for this time.

In fact, broadcasting that you need another contract while still on your old one may pay off if you've done good work and built a fine reputation. Your current supervisor can be an invaluable resource in finding a new contract. They can recommend you to managers elsewhere in the company who are staffing up or to friends at other companies that are looking for people with your skills.

I'm stuck in a contract that just seems to go on and on. Should I take a third extension?

If the client decides to extend your contract, it's up to you to decide whether to take them up on it, unless you've unwisely signed a consulting firm contract with wording that obliges you to extend.

Consulting firms love to have the client extend your contract month after month and year after year. Many contractors like extensions too, since they get paid high contracting rates while enjoying many of the benefits of permanent employment like being able to build friendships with coworkers or schedule vacation time months in advance. But while the endless contract might seem like a contractor's dream come true, all too often the comfort it provides comes at a very steep price. By staying in one place for a long time contractors may let their skills atrophy and lose the edge they must maintain to keep their contracting career viable.

So before you decide to accept an extension of an existing contract, you need to evaluate it the same way you would a new contract. Will it add to your skills? Will it give you a chance to learn something new?

Sometimes contractors extend a contract for too long a time because they are afraid of irritating the consulting firm that placed them on it. But even if your leaving does annoy the consulting firm, as long as you have skills there are plenty of others that will be happy to hire you. Should you stay on one contract too long and let your skills atrophy, the very firm that pressured you to stay on that assignment will be the first to tell you that they're sorry, but without up-to-date skills, they can't place you.

DANGER SIGNS!

"The client would have loved to have kept me to maintain an Access app they had done that was mission critical. The problem is, VB/SQL Server is my main skill set. One day, one of the permanent staff approached me asking for help on a SQL trigger problem. It had been so long since I had dealt with triggers in SQL Server that I couldn't help her—and I'm certified in SQL Server, for Pete's sake! All this because I had been doing Access for so long that I had forgotten how to deal with the finer points of SQL Server.

"You can't let your high-dollar skills atrophy just to satisfy one customer. There is a day coming when they will not want you anymore."

–Eric Lynch

Can I ask the client about what they are paying before I negotiate an extension?

This is a controversial question. Some contractors suggest being honest with the client manager and saying something like, "I'm about to reenter negotiations with my consulting firm and I'd very much appreciate it if you could give me some idea of what rate they are billing you, so that I can get an idea of what kind of margin they have and can negotiate a reasonable raise." They say this helps them ask for a raise that is fair to everyone.

But others think this is a poor idea. They suggest that you leave the client out of your negotiations with the consulting firm, because if you don't handle this rate discussion diplomatically, you may irritate the client and cause them to complain to the consulting firm. In some cases, contractors report that dragging the client into their rate negotiations got them fired.

What kind of paperwork should I expect to see if I accept an extension?

Once you and the consulting firm have agreed on the terms of an extension, the consulting firm should fax or mail you a single page addendum to the original contract that spells out how long the extension will last and what rate you'll receive. After you receive this, sign and return it.

Be wary if the consulting firm makes you an oral promise about getting a raise with your extension but delays sending you the paperwork. Contractors who have begun working extensions without seeing the paperwork have gotten nasty surprises when the paperwork finally shows up. Sometimes the raises were missing, or the term was different from what the contractor had been promised. Because you aren't in a strong negotiating position once you have started working into the extension period, make sure you see a contract guaranteeing that the extension terms are what you were told—before the extension begins.

Today, without warning, the client terminated me. I had five months left on my contract. Can they do this?

Yes. As we mentioned when we discussed contract clauses in Chapter 7, "What's In My Consulting Firm Contract?," the time period spelled out on your contract is not binding because the clause defining it is almost always accompanied by another clause that allows the client to terminate you at will. It is partly because you offer the client this kind of flexibility that they are willing to pay you your high rate.

If you do get terminated without warning, your immediate and very natural reaction may be to feel anger or shock—particularly if you were counting on the income from the contract to pay impending bills. You may be tempted to call up the consulting firm and give them an earful or even feel like suing the client. But resist these impulses! Sudden terminations are part of contracting. As you will find when you talk to others at work or online, almost all contractors who have been in the business for any amount of time have run into a sudden unexpected termination somewhere along the line.

It helps if you can manage not to take the termination personally. There are many reasons why a client might suddenly let you go, most of them unrelated to your performance on the job. Clients may hide the fact that they are about to let you go because they think you'll slack off if you know you are leaving. Or they may have been fighting up until the last minute to get money restored to their budgets that would have allowed them to keep you on.

An unexpected termination should not make a difference in your ability to find a new contract. Get on the phone and inform past clients and recruiters that you're free to take a new assignment. You'll feel a lot better about the termination a few weeks later when you've landed a new contract at a rate $10 higher than the old one.

Can a client or old employer give me a bad reference?

Employers are so worried about being sued for damages that they rarely, if ever, give out a bad reference. If you really screwed up on the job, when someone asks the client or ex-employer about you, they will simply confirm the dates you worked for them and your role on the project you worked on, adding nothing else. The reference's lack of praise for your work may suggest to another client that all did not go well, but unless your old client or boss is really off the rails, they are not going to tell anyone the details.

I just discovered that the rate the consulting firm is billing my client is four times what they are paying me. Can I do anything about this?

It is very difficult to renegotiate a rate once you are working on a contract. In a boom market where consulting firms are scrambling to find talent, it may be possible to get a small boost in your rate by threatening to leave for another contract, but this strategy doesn't always work. Sometimes it merely gets you fired. And contractors who have been offered "squeaky wheel" raises report that they were offered only $2 or $3 more per hour after complaining because their rates were $20 or even $30 per hour lower than the market rate for their skills.

Experienced contractors suggest that you should only attempt to negotiate significant a raise if you are prepared to quit if you don't get it. Otherwise, wait until your contract is due for renewal, when the consulting firm may be more open to negotiating a higher rate. But if the disparity between what you are being paid and what you could get elsewhere is really huge, why keep working for a firm that insists on taking that kind of advantage of you?

Is there any way I can get out of my consulting firm contract?

Most contracts have some provision for ending the contract early. Often all that is required legally is that you give the firm some prespecified amount of notice.

However, the reality is more complex. Though you may legally have the right to walk away whenever you choose, if you terminate a consulting firm contract early, you may find yourself the target of considerable intimidation. Consulting firm staff will do all they can to make you feel guilty or scared since once you leave they will be left with an unhappy client. And remember, consulting firms stay in business only by keeping their *clients* happy.

If you do leave before the end of the contract, you aren't likely to get another contract through the same consulting firm that placed you there. They may also bad mouth you to the client, making it harder for you to get subsequent work with that client—though this isn't a huge consideration, since few clients would want to rehire a contractor who quit in the middle of a project. But if you have a good relationship with the client and have decided to quit because of unethical behavior on the part of the consulting firm, you should inform the client of the details of that unethical behavior *before* you tell the consulting firm you are leaving, so that you can salvage your relationship with the client firm.

If your contract does not have provisions for you to terminate early or if, worse, it specifies that you must pay penalties for early termination, you will need to get the help of an attorney to determine your actual situation. Some very restrictive clauses in consulting firm contracts may look impressive but be legally unenforceable. Others may look illegal but be completely kosher. Because laws having to do with your rights to work and terminate work vary from state to state, only an attorney versed in the relevant laws will be able to tell you the best way to proceed.

The recruiter says I'll be blacklisted if I leave this contract early. Can they do this?

Don't worry about being blacklisted throughout the IT community because you got on the wrong side of one consulting firm. Consulting firms compete with each other for staff so one firm's loss is likely to be another firm's gain. As long as you have hot skills and good references from other jobs, you should be able to find another contract.

But it is not smart to make a pattern of leaving contracts early. People in the local business community know each other and they gossip. If you make a practice of ditching clients or getting into dramatic confrontations with consulting firm after consulting firm, word will eventually get around that you are unreliable and you will find it difficult to get work.

You should also give some thought to the impact your leaving will have on the client if they have treated you well during the course of the contract. When your long-term goal is to find your own clients without having to rely on consulting firms, your existing clients are a precious resource that must be treated with respect. If remaining on your existing contract for another few months will provide you with a client who might hire you directly in years to come and who might refer you to others who would hire you too, it would be foolish to leave them without warning and destroy that good will just so you could earn a few dollars more per hour.

The client wants to hire me direct and cut out the consulting firm Can we do this?

If your client has signed a contract with the consulting firm, it is almost certain that it contains some wording that prevents them from hiring you directly without paying the consulting firm a finder's fee. By the same token, your contract with the consulting firm probably includes some kind of noncompetition clause that prevents you from working directly for the client for some period of time after you end your relationship with the consulting firm.

Be very careful if the client suggests some sleazy way around these contract terms. These terms are likely to be binding and consulting firms do go to court to enforce them. Even if they don't, you should be on guard with a client who suggests that both of you violate your contracts with the consulting firm. What does this tell you about how they'll honor their contract with you?

I found a new contract that pays a lot more than my current one. When I told the consulting firm I was leaving they offered to match the new rate. Should I stay?

There is resounding unanimity among consultants and consulting firm recruiters that once you have given notice, it is a mistake to stay on, even if your money demands are met.

One recruiter reports that, "Statistics show that 87% of individuals who accept counteroffers are either fired or leave voluntarily within one year." She believes that this is because "the trust factor is immediately gone and both sides feel it."

Managers who have hired contractors directly report that while they may offer a counteroffer to a contractor to induce them to stay after they've given notice, afterwards they take an increasingly negative attitude towards the contractor. They may now perceive them as being greedy or a troublemaker, so the contractor is likely to be the first to be let go as the project winds down.

ACCEPTING THE COUNTER OFFER WAS A MISTAKE

"Last year I was offered a tasty-looking and better-paying job which I was poised to accept. I stupidly felt obliged to tell this to the company whose long-term project I was about to finish.

"A counter-offer was immediately issued. I opted to stay with the devil I knew, and we split within 3 months. The rancor on both sides was eye-opening. Apparently, they thought their counter offer was a license to take advantage of me in ways that were clearly unethical and, lawyer friends tell me, probably illegal. It wasn't worth the extra money."

–G. Green

The project is over and my client is very pleased with my work, how can I make the most of this?

You can do several things to turn a happy client into a source of further work. Don't be shy about asking for referrals. Tell your client, "Please pass my name on to anyone you know who might be able to use my services." Give them a few business cards. If you feel a bit more aggressive, you can ask, "Do you know anyone who might need my services?" Write down whatever names and contact information the client will give you. Then you can call the prospect and begin your conversation by saying, "So-and-so, the director of SAP implementation at MegaCorp, suggested I give you a call about helping with your upcoming SAP pilot."

Another approach that works for some contractors is to ask a satisfied client to write you a letter of recommendation on company letterhead before you leave. Explain that you will not show it to recruiters but just use it to reassure other clients who may be interested in your service. Because managers and employees move around so often, and because companies themselves may disappear without warning, some contractors suggest that when you get a particularly good letter of recommendation, you also ask the happy client for a personal email address. That way you can still refer potential clients to that person even if they no longer work for the company at which you did your work.

I want to take a vacation before I begin my next assignment. How do I do this?

It may be difficult to line up a new job if you want to take a few weeks off. That's because clients usually want contractors to start immediately and may balk at waiting more than the two weeks it takes to give notice on a previous assignment. Some contractors report that they have had contracts lined up before they left for vacations, only to find that while they were gone the consulting firm had replaced them with another contractor who could start immediately.

The best approach to enjoying your vacation is to put a few months of living expenses in the bank before you take off. You may very well line up a new job the day you come home but if you don't, you won't face a crisis.

Another approach is to take your vacation while you are in the middle of working on a long-term contract for a client who appreciates your work. Give the client a lot of notice. Then take your unpaid weeks off, secure in the knowledge that you have work awaiting you on your return.

The consulting firm won't pay for my last invoice. How can I make them pay me?

This frequently happens if you get into a dispute with a consulting firm or direct client near the end of a contract. If calls to the firm's accounts payable department don't help, call up your local Small Claims Court and find out what their limit is for small claims law suits. If the debt owed you is under the limit, simply write the consulting firm or client a letter threatening to take them to Small Claims Court and pointing out that the costs of a small claims suit are borne by the losing party. Mail the letter by registered mail.

If the debt is over the Small Claims limit, pay an attorney to write you a "lawyer letter" briefly citing your case and threatening to sue. In most cases, the threat of a suit the firm can't win is all that is needed to free up your check.

CHAPTER 10

HOW CAN I DO BETTER?

How can I improve my earnings as a contractor?

The best way to improve your contracting earnings is to improve the quality of the skills you have to sell. Though it's not easy, it is possible to upgrade your skills while working as a contractor. Learning how behave more like a businessperson than a technician can also raise the rates your current skill set can command. Getting certified in the skills you have already mastered may also help you raise your value in the marketplace. If your career is stagnating because of a poor local economy, you may be able to revive your career by relocating. Finally, if none of these approaches work, shifting your focus to another specialty or returning to a properly chosen salaried job may help you prepare for a more successful stint of contracting in the future.

I need new skills. Can I get them by signing on as a consulting firm employee?

It is no secret that there are some technical specialties that pay a whole lot better than others, even though the work needed to master them may be much less than that required for less well-paying specialties. Usually these highly paid specialties involve mastering packaged software applications like PeopleSoft, and SAP. These are expensive high end applications found only in large corporate IS shops, and because there are few people who have mastered them, the people who can list these skills on their résumés can earn very high rates.

Consulting firms frequently tell contractors that they will train them in these in-demand specialties because that promise makes an irresistible bait. Unfortunately, few consulting firms deliver on these promises. Contractors who sign up at low rates hoping to get valuable training usually only get the low rates.

That's why 99% of the consultants who make themselves more competitive by upgrading their skills do it on their own, using hardware, software and industrial strength corporate training classes that they pay for themselves.

185

Indeed, the most striking quality of the contractors I've interviewed who earn rates of $100 per hour or more is their willingness to invest heavily and continuously in their own education. It is only by doing this that they can present themselves to clients as being experts in the buzzware of the minute. If you wait for clients or employers to buy you new software or pay for your training, you will wait a long time. Only by taking matters into your own hands can you develop the kinds of cutting edge skills that commend the highest rates.

It costs a fortune to buy all the hardware and software I want to master! How can I pick up new skills?

It does cost money to buy the hardware and software you need to upgrade your skills. But if you want to be treated as a small businessperson rather than an employee, you should start acting like one, and that means you should start making the investments that will keep your business alive and growing. Buying cutting edge software, hardware, and training is by far the best thing you can do to keep your contracting career alive as you move beyond the first few, easy years where you can you coast on the skills you picked up as an employee.

Contractors who learn only on the company's time and work only on the companies systems—including that small but persistent hard core who still don't own their own computer systems—are continuing to think and behave like employees. They are resigning their fate to chance, rather taking control of the direction in which their technical skills will develop.

If you lack an aggressive commitment to training yourself, during the first few years of your career you may luck into projects where you pick up enough new technology to keep your résumé attractive to clients. But when the inevitable business downturn comes around, and contracts become hard to find, it will be people who have picked up new skills on their own that will keep working.

Only a handful of packages require the kinds of setups that you can't duplicate at home—if you're willing to pay what it costs. Right now, consultants looking to upgrade their skills can get a good start in learning industrial strength development languages like C++, Java, Smalltalk, Visual Basic, or Delphi simply by buying an $1,800 mail order computer and a couple hundred dollars worth of compilers and books. For a little more, they can buy Oracle or set up a network in their home. If they want to learn to code under Unix, they can download a copy of Linux and run it on their own machines or rent web space on an ISP that gives full access to a Unix web server using a telnet connection. This can be done for as little as $20 per month!

I already know an in demand language and operating system. So why should I worry about upgrading?

Even if you are already working in a relatively in-demand technical niche, for example, C++ or Java programming, if you want to command top rates, you will have to keep up with the very latest developments in your niche. It's easy to get swamped with work and stop reading and keeping track of what's going on in the software marketplace when you're working fifty hours a week, but that's what the consultants who charge the highest rates manage to do. Many of them have an almost obsessional level of interest in the latest release of whatever it is that they code in, and if you're serious about improving your technical skills you will need to develop some of that kind of obsession yourself.

One way to do this is to get active online in the forums, newsgroups, and mailing lists that discuss your chosen languages and platforms. Reading fifty or sixty messages a day about your specialty and the problems others run into using your chosen software tools is a great way to hone your skills and to hear important bits of news that might be buried in the avalanche of trade magazines piling up on your desk.

As you network with other people who keep up with the very latest in your niche, you'll start hearing about sign-ups for beta testing of new product releases of the software you specialize in. Sign up for these betas! Doing that will make it possible for you to master new releases before they hit the market. Though it can be annoying to debug software for vendors, doing this gives you a hefty jump on others and allows you to put a documentable six months of experience with something "brand new" on your résumé.

HE BUYS HIS OWN

"Over the 14 years I have been an independent I have purchased at least 12 PCs. I currently own 3. I work on DEC software so I have owned 2 PDP-11s, 4 VAXs, and I just ordered my 3rd DEC Alpha Workstation. I have also owned such add-ons as a reel tape drive.

"Most of this was done to support my customers at my site rather than theirs but I have brought in to a client site a DEC terminal, VAX workstation, and a high powered PC when the client could/would not provide me with adequate hardware."

—Stephen C. Jackson

What about the packages you can't install and teach yourself? How do you add them to your résumé?

You can earn high rates working with some large-scale packages that can only be learned working for the large corporations who are the only ones who can afford them. SAP and Notes are examples. Mainframe-based client-server environments fall into the same category. The secret to getting training in these is to get selective about the contracts that you take. Wherever possible choose contracts where, though you may be hired to do work that uses only your current skill set, once on the job you will be working in an environment that features the hot new technology that you want to learn.

Let's say your résumé shows that you've spent ten years as a mainframe COBOL programmer and you're yearning to move into client-server processing. You know that Sybase has been a relentlessly hot client-server database for years so it seems to be worth mastering. Since you have had exposure to DB2, you already know how to write SQL database queries and have an understanding of the principles of relational database design. Since Sybase is another relational database using an SQL command set, you know you could easily make the transition to working with it if only you could get some training and hands on experience with Sybase to put on your résumé.

As an experienced mainframe contractor, the only contracts you're going to get offered are ones where you write or maintain mainframe COBOL applications. You won't get hired to write Sybase database queries because clients will want to see Sybase already on your résumé before they hire you to work with it. But there is still a way to pick up Sybase on the job. When you sign up for your next contract, hold out for a COBOL contract that puts you in a smallish, reasonably friendly shop that has Sybase running elsewhere in the department that you're going to be working on.

Then come in, do the best job of COBOL coding you can possibly do. Establish a reputation as someone who gets the job done fast and done right. Read a couple "Teach Yourself Sybase" books and work through the coding examples. Hit the manual shelf at work and read more. Look at the code listings for the Sybase part of the system you're working on and ask the local guru about the things you find in the code that you don't understand. Let the client know that you are learning Sybase, while you keep delivering top quality COBOL code, since this is what they're paying for.

Eventually, with any luck at all, when you get ahead of the work you've been assigned, the client will let you work on some Sybase code. Do a good job and, a few weeks later, you can legitimately put "Sybase" on your résumé and get interviewed for higher paying client-server projects. This is how most contractors upgrade their skills.

What is certification?

Certification usually involves passing a set of exams, after which you can add some initials to your résumé. Certificates can be awarded by just about any organization, though the ones that appear to have the most value in the marketplace are those that are provided by certain vendors. The best-known certifications are Novell's CNE (Certified Network Engineer) and several certifications developed by Microsoft, including the MCSD (Microsoft Certified Solution Developer) and MCSE (Microsoft Certified Systems Engineer.) Vendor certifications are also available for packages, like Lotus Notes, and for hardware, like the Cisco certification (CCIE).

Less well known, though they have been around for a much longer time, are the career certifications offered by a non-profit group that does nothing but offer certifications, the ICCP (Institute for the Certification of Computer Professionals.) Their best-known certification is the CLP.

HOW ONE OLD-TIMER RETOOLED

"Find a reason to use the 'tool du jour' in your current job. For example, In 1993, I took a job that consisted of continued development on a lame and orphaned DOS based application. I recommended to my boss that we re-target for Windows and re-develop in C++. He agreed, so I did so. So Windows and C++ went on the résumé.

"Use the tool for a small scope purpose, such as development of a prototype of an application program. For example: a client wanted an app developed in C++. I recommended that he pay me a flat price to develop a crippled prototype in VB so that we could do a reality check on the concept. So, VB exposure went on the résumé."

–Don Wallace

How useful is certification?

Certifications vary in their usefulness. Some appear to exist mainly to enrich the vendors who underwrite them and charge high fees for buying study materials and taking their exams. Other certifications can significantly improve your likelihood of getting hired and may enable you to charge a higher rate.

As with everything in contracting, the most valuable certifications are those that are rarest, yet involve in-demand technology. When certificate mills start cranking out certified individuals, many of whom have little or no paid experience using the technology involved in the certification, the value of the certification usually drops. This has been the case with the Novell CNE and some of the Microsoft certifications. You will only find this kind of certification useful if your résumé is full of relevant experience that reinforces the value of the certification.

Studying for certification exams may be a good way of plugging up holes in your knowledge of some specialty. However, paying huge sums to have a trade school coach you to pass an exam in a technology where you don't already have hands-on real world experience may be a waste of time. One reason for this is that many certifications are vendor specific and require only that you understand the use of a single product or product suite, rather than demanding that you understand all the different vendors' products that you would encounter in a real production environment. If your certification only covers the use of a single product, it may not prepare you for working in the multi-vendor environments you will find on the job.

The value of non-vendor certifications, like the CLP issued by the ICCP, are also a matter of debate. The biggest problem with them seems to be that the people in the business community who hire contractors are unaware of them and hence not impressed with their value.

CERTIFICATION CAN HELP YOU LEARN THE RIGHT THINGS

"What certification does for me and might do for you is give you a concrete set of steps to gain specific knowledge on a product.

"For instance I'm right now looking at learning Java. I could spend months and months reading books and messing around with it, but the hard part for me is knowing *what* to learn. Sun's Java certification sets out certain steps that you must follow to gain their certification. In other words they give you a start to *what* you should learn."

—Brian Harris (MCSD and MCSE)

What does the Real Rate Survey data show about the value of certifications?

Our Real Rate Survey showed no clear cut link between vendor certifications and higher rates. The median rates for contractors who cited vendor certifications as part of their "experience" entry were slightly higher than those of the group as a whole. The best certifications as far as rates go were the Novell CNE, and Microsoft's MCSE and MCSD. But rates for people with all these certifications were spread over a very wide range and the median rates for contractors with a MCSD or MCSE were not much different from that of the group as a whole.

It is also difficult to know if the higher rates these certified contractors earned were due to their being certified, or whether they were certified because they were the kind of people who were already earning high rates that invested in certification the same way that they might invest in new equipment or education—as part of their ongoing commitment to developing their careers.

HOW TO GET CERTIFIED CHEAPLY

"Certification is *not* overly expensive or time consuming. Community colleges often offer certifications for a fraction of the cost of flashy fly-by-night technical schools (disclaimer—not all such schools are shysters, but if you're not a careful consumer you'll get burned). Check with [the vendor]. If the community college is certified, you'll get top notch training just as good as if you'd paid premium $."

—Lee

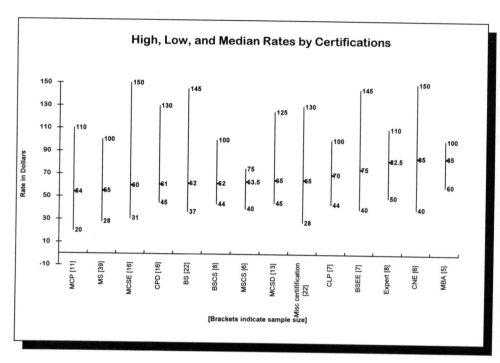

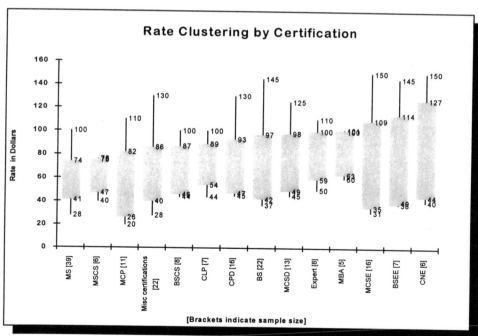

How can I find out if it is worth the bucks to get an expensive certification?

Talk to a few experienced recruiters before you invest thousands of dollars in a certification program. Briefly describe your résumé and then ask what kind of value the certification would add to it. This is a topic where you can probably trust what you hear from recruiters as they have no stake in misleading you about the value of a certification the way those who profit from selling you certification programs do.

Other useful resources are Ann Martinez' book, *Get Certified and Get Ahead* and the associated certification web site at `http://www.gocertify.com`.

A RECRUITER'S VIEW OF CERTIFICATIONS

"I've been recruiting many years and not once has a client ever specified 'Certified' when it comes to Oracle. Networking is a different thing—Certification is requested a great deal. I have also never seen a rate increased because of certification.

"It does however give you the edge if you are competing for a contract with another individual who is not certified. Even then, it can come down to who has the most experience, the certified or non-certified consultant."

—Lisa the Recruiter

Why does it sometimes seem like the biggest b-s artists get the best rates?

What you're calling "b-s" is actually a mastery of business communications skills. Unfortunately, many, if not most, technical people have mediocre communications skills. Computer professionals tend to be poor at listening and at relating to the subtle non-logical stuff that is going on in many business conversations.

How poor? The psychiatrist author of a recent book, *Shadow Syndromes*, spends several pages explaining why, in his opinion, many successful computer professionals are borderline autistic! By this he means that they tend to miss 80% or more of the cues that "normal" people use in conversation. They interrupt others constantly, or monologue, and worst of all, they often miss the point of the conversations they are involved in.

This author is a bit extreme—but his argument is not as extreme as I wish it were. An awful lot of programmers are extremely concrete in their thinking—these are the people who answer the conversational opener, "How are you?" with a detailed status report. This is what we call "missing cues" and while it isn't autism, it does disconcert people who don't miss cues—among whom are most of the people who can afford to pay high rates for contract work.

PAPER NETWORK ENGINEERS

"There will be an oversupply of what I like to call 'paper network engineers,' people who can pass tests but when it comes to solving real day-to-day network issues, these same paper engineers would most likely fail if their NT and UNIX network crashed.

"Most networks at least where I have worked are not just NT or Novell but rather a mix of many different systems like some NT, UNIX, Novell and Mainframe. One must master the basics and skills common to networks. Many so called MCSE or Novell CNE's may know something about Netware or NT but little about the hardware and networking devices like routers, switches and sniffers."

—Ben Prusinski

How can I improve my communications skills?

If you have a problem with your communications skills—if you do miss cues or have trouble getting your point across, there are several ways to help yourself. The quickest, if most brutal method, is to tape conversations you have with other people and listen to them. Listening to yourself this way can often help you pinpoint your worst communications problems. Group therapy can also help by giving you a safe place where you can get feedback from others as well as help in improving the way you interact with them.

How important is image?

Computer people tend to be inner-directed logical problem solvers with little interest in the superficial political posturing they see around them, but the people in management who have the money to pay you $75 or $80 per hour have mastered superficials, politics and posturing and take them very seriously. If you're going to sell yourself to them as a high priced resource, you're going to have to relate to them where they come from.

This means that you are going to have to take seriously the whole question of creating a businesslike image. There are plenty of contractors who have earned high rates while wearing long hair, sandals, and T-shirts. But before you can be one of them, you need to understand that creating a standard business image is one of those things you can afford to ignore *only* after you know how to pull it off.

It is one thing to know how to dress for success and then decide to wear sandals to work because you know that you have earned the kind of reputation where no one is going to care what you wear as long as you do your usual brilliant work. It is quite another to show up at a prospective client's office when interviewing for your first contract wearing sandals and a T-shirt because no other garb occurred to you.

At a minimum you need to be able to dress in a way that will signal to the executives who hire you that you are a highly competent professional, though different articles of clothing will do this in Columbus, Ohio than would work in Silicon Valley.

You also need to know how to send out business correspondence that looks professional, with a businesslike letterhead on the first page and a properly formatted envelope. You also need to remember to use your grammar and spellchecker on every résumé, client list, or business document you send out. Good programmers are often far too logical to spell English words correctly, but displaying poor spelling on your business letters or emails will not convince others of your technical abilities. All you will do by sending out letters, emails, and bulletin board postings filled with misspellings is turn off potential clients who will think you are either ignorant or still in a high school.

If you don't know how to write a proper business letter, there are plenty of books on the market full of examples. If you have reason to believe that others find you less than articulate, take steps to improve your ability to speak on your feet. For example, you can join a local Toastmasters group and learn from the people there how to better express yourself.

IMAGE IS FOR EVERYONE!

"I was introduced to a fellow who had Tourette's Syndrome and was forced to use a wheel chair and had a tendency to drool. He was very brilliant but couldn't really present himself well.

"His mother knew that I was in the computer field and asked for my help, I met the guy and told him what I thought. I said 'Well, wear a damn good suit and carry a monogrammed hanky to dab at any drool. Get a good hair cut and shine up that chair. And smile.'

"He did what I said. Bought an $800 tailored suit. Cleaned and shined the chair, etc. He went on one interview and landed the job."

—Charles Crizer

What are some ways to build a better image?

One simple way is to use what for lack of a better term we will call "props." Props are the sorts of objects that an actor would use to immediately establish that they were playing the part of a computer expert in a TV commercial. For example, when you go into an interview, bring along your late model laptop and use it in front of the client even if there really is no need for it. Keep copies of interesting articles relating to your specialties in your briefcase and hand them out where appropriate. Don't forget to have a good-looking business card made up. Nonchalantly hand out your card whenever you meet others in business situations.

These props establish your professionality and give clients subtle confirmation that you are worth the money you are charging, even though, to you, they might seem unnecessary. Many of the people who are hiring you don't have the technical knowledge to judge your skills or competence and so they will rely on things like image and props, as well as their gut feelings, when making the decision of whether or not to hire you. Make their job easier by showing them the symbols they need to see in order to believe you can do the work they need done.

I'm finding that my programming skills aren't good enough for me to make it as a contractor. What do I do now?

Unfortunately, after a contract or two, some people find that skills that were strong enough to make them a successful employee are not enough to let them succeed as a contractor. Some people aren't able to come up to speed in a new environment in two weeks. Others aren't able to handle the stress that comes with working on crunch mode project after crunch mode project.

Some contractors can do the work but dislike the fact that on most contracting assignments no matter how well paid, they find themselves shoved into a corner and expected to code forty hours a week. The lesson contracting teaches them is that what they *really* enjoy doing is meeting with users, doing design, or leading projects.

If you're dragging along as a contractor and hating it, the solution may be to go back to salaried employment. But before you throw in the towel, consider whether another solution might be to make a radical shift in the way you present yourself on your résumé. There are many other kinds of computer contract work besides programming which can also be pursued on a contract basis, and it may be possible, by rewriting your résumé and downplaying your coding skills, to find one that may be more in harmony with your nature.

Systems administration, network support, tech writing, software testing, and web site design are just a few of the other options that might be open to you if you already have a solid background in programming. Ask yourself what kinds of work you have most enjoyed doing in the past and then strengthen your skills in a direction that lets you do that kind of work.

It may be necessary to take a salaried position to get the training you need to be able to move into doing systems administration or network support. It may also take a couple of years of garnering further experience until you are ready to try contracting again with your new specialty. But when you do, you'll be doing something you enjoy, which will make contracting a far more pleasant experience.

SHIFTING GEARS

"I am a computer network engineer who used to be a lousy computer programmer. Networking experts are in high demand right now and it is more fun to me than programming. Maybe you can learn NT and UNIX networking? Its different than programming and lots of fun!

"Don't focus on what may be a passing fad like SAP or BAAN unless you have thoroughly investigated this area and unless you are really gonna enjoy working with SAP and BAAN. If you don't check it out, you will be *miserable* doing what others told you was hot and in the end you will be a lousy professional. Pick something that interests you and become good at it!"

—Ben Prusinski

Would relocating to another city be a good way to revive my contracting career?

The demand for particular skills varies greatly from city to city. So if you are having trouble finding contract work locally you may be tempted to answer job postings from agencies in distant cities that claim to have lots of work in your technical specialty.

Relocating can be an effective way to find good, high paying work. But moving to a distant city is not a trivial undertaking. Indeed, psychologists report that relocation can create almost as much stress in your life as divorce or the death of a family member. Besides having to deal with the normal stresses of relocation, contractors must face additional problems because of the innate insecurity of contract work. Every now and then a contract will evaporate without warning. If this happens when you've just relocated, it may turn a once reasonable move into a nightmare.

How can I decide if I'd like living in a distant city?

When considering a move, it is a good idea to split the issues you must consider into two groups. The first set of issues involves deciding how much you'd like living in the new location. The second centers on your long term career potential in the new location.

You must visit any city you are considering moving to before make a commitment to take a job there, because it is impossible to know if you would like living somewhere new without first visiting. Don't make the common mistake of relying on a company-paid interview trip to give you the information you need. If your only visit is a two-day interview trip, you may end up seeing little more than the business district, a restaurant or two, and your motel. If possible, plan to spend a week in the city you are considering before you make your decision.

Before your fact-finding trip, do some research, so you can make the most of the time you have to spend at your destination. Start your research a month of two before your trip. Read all you can about your destination, but take what you read with a grain of salt. Much of the information you read about what it is like to live in a city comes from local business boosters who hope to attract new industry.

Resources like *Places Rated Almanac* or *Money* magazine's survey of the Best Places to Live, which rank cities along various categories like cost of living and cultural offerings can give you some idea of what you will find in a new location. But these often fall short in real-world situations because they depend exclusively on statistics and ignore more subjective but important factors. As a result, these resources may rank a town in the midwest that features a Pincushion Museum, a petting zoo, and a summer theater festival starring local performers higher on a "cultural offerings" list than a town in Connecticut that doesn't have local facilities but is an easy drive to New York or Boston.

In a similar vein, the cost of living figures you see in such publications (and in those you get from local boards of Realtors and Chambers of Commerce) are also misleading. That is because they usually average together the price of housing in inner city slums and that of prosperous suburbs to come up with a "cost of housing" figure. Because it is an average, this cost of housing figure usually turns out to be half of what it really costs to live in the kind of upscale neighborhood with adequate schools that most computer professionals consider essential.

You can find out more about the real cost of living in a new area by browsing the Real Estate classifieds in the online version of the local daily and Sunday newspapers. To find out where the most desirable neighborhoods are, look for ads that brag about a home being in a specific school district. These will usually point you to the better neighborhoods. If you are a renter, pay close attention to the costs of rentals. Get a map of the area and see how far it is from the areas where you can afford to live to the parts of town where you'll find employers, entertainment, and cultural offerings. In cities like Boston or New York, you may find that the only housing you can afford, even with a contractor's salary, is located more than an hour away, perhaps even in another state!

Look at the job classifieds in the area you are considering too. Do you see a lot of ads for people with your skills in the paper? Do you see ads from employers or only ads from consulting firms? How do the salaries you see mentioned in ads compare with what you are used to seeing in your local paper?

Tour available housing with Realtors or rental agents. Interview for several contracts with several different consulting firms to see how strong demand really is for your specialty and what kinds of companies you'd find yourself working for. Read local newspapers. Listen to the radio. Visit online friends who live in the community. And, if you have children, visit schools or check out the availability of day care.

What specific dangers are involved in relocating to take a contract?

The biggest problem with relocating to take a contract is that doing this puts you at the mercy of the consulting firm and client. When you have just spent $7,000 or $8,000 to move your stuff and set up a new home, you are dependent on your job in a way that you aren't when you take a local contract. You are unlikely to have a network in place in the new city that can help you find another contract quickly if something goes wrong and you're far from your old friends and support system too. So you are much more likely to put up with poor treatment from either the consulting firm or the client than you would be if you took a local assignment.

When looking for work in a distant city, you should try to find not one but two or three contracts that you could qualify for and that you would want to take. Look for several consulting firms that seem interested in placing you. This ensures that if the original contract falls through or turns out to be intolerable, you can continue your contracting career in your new home with a minimum of disruption.

Another big problem when you take a contract in a distant city is that it is a lot harder to find out the truth about the quality of the consulting firms you deal with. At the same time, the damage that an unethical firm can do you is considerably greater when you relocate. Contractors have relocated to start long-term contracts only to discover when they arrive in their new destination that though they have signed a contract with the consulting firm, the client never signed one, so they are out of a job. They have arrived to find the firm has given "their" job to another contractor. They have had problems getting the rate they've been promised orally, and some contractors who have relied on verbal promises of reimbursement for moving expenses or the costs of flying to an interview have found it impossible to recover these costs from the distant consulting firm.

Clients can be a problem when you take a remote job too. Companies with terrible local reputations may hire contractors from far away simply because those contractors aren't likely to know that the firm is a sweatshop.

This makes it imperative that before you commit to a move you use the resources of the Internet to find experienced contractors in the city you are considering moving to. Get as much information as you can from them about the consulting firms and clients that you are thinking of working for.

Can I get paid extra for taking a temporary contract away from home?

Consulting firms may offer to pay you a daily expense payment, called a "per diem" in addition to your regular rate when you accept a W-2 contract located more than 60 miles from your home. The per diem is supposed to help cover the cost of food and lodging you must purchase while living away from your home.

The amount of any per diem is negotiable. Some firms pay a fixed daily amount, some pay an additional hourly amount, and some pay for actual expenses or a percentage of actual expenses. A per diem may be tax deductible, as long as it falls within guidelines given by the IRS. However, to qualify for a tax deductible per diem, your assignment cannot last longer than a year. If it extends longer, any past payments you claimed on your taxes will be disallowed and you will have to refile your taxes for the previous year and pay taxes and perhaps penalties on the amount you deducted in the past.

For information on the maximum allowed per-diem rates by city and or county visit:

http://www.govexec.com/travel/wrlddiem.htm

How can I find a contract overseas?

The best way to find a contract overseas is to find a consulting firm located in the United States that places contractors abroad. Some of these are consulting firms that have their own offices in foreign countries. Others place personnel on US military bases around the world. Be extra careful to get references for any firm you consider using when looking for work overseas.

WHAT TO WATCH OUT FOR WHEN TAKING A CONTRACT OUTSIDE OF THE USA

"HIDDEN COSTS There are several hidden costs associated with performing business globally. Europe, for example is extremely expensive by comparison with the US in simple things such as food, gas, travel, and just about everything else.

"CURRENCY Always work in the local currency when negotiating rates (considering the local living expenses, etc.) unless there is international travel involved. Never keep converting back to dollars and comparing the rates for similar US work. This doesn't work!

"AGENCIES Watch out! There are more shady types of agencies than legitimate and professional ones both in Europe and the States. Many agencies will promise you the moon just to get the business. *Very important point: everything should be in writing!*

"CULTURE Americans have a general stereotype of being too aggressive, too confident, too obnoxious (in a business sense), too demanding, too opinionated, too self-promoting and overall headstrong (by European standards). The key is to be sensitive to each set of local business customs—to listen more carefully and try to adapt. Even from country to country within Europe there are several stereotypes and culture differences."

—Robert Fox

Do I need to speak a foreign language to work abroad?

Because English is spoken by educated people around the world it is possible to find positions abroad that do not require mastery of another language. However, if you don't have at least a beginner's knowledge of the language spoken in a country where you intend to work, you will miss out on a lot. You may become overwhelmed or isolated or spend all your time with other Americans rather than getting to know the new country. You will also strike your coworkers as arrogant and the worst kind of "Ugly American" if you don't make some attempt to speak their language, however clumsy.

Do I have to be a gypsy to get the best rates and opportunities?

Some young contractors who are not tied down by family responsibilities adopt a gypsy lifestyle, moving from city to city following the hottest opportunities in their niches. This can be a great way to spend your twenties but is not practical if you have a family. Fortunately, it is not necessary to live this way to have a vibrant contracting career.

What is necessary is that if you settle down in one place, it be one that has enough companies that use the kind of technology you have mastered to support an ongoing career. This tends to rule out the small towns and resort areas where many people would prefer to live.

Unless you can cultivate an active clientele of direct clients who are willing to keep sending you work remotely, you'll probably have to settle for one of the thirty large urban areas scattered around the US where most computer contracting jobs are located. Fifty-four percent of all the rates reported to the Real Rate Survey over the first six months of 1998 came from the 15 urban areas listed in the table below:

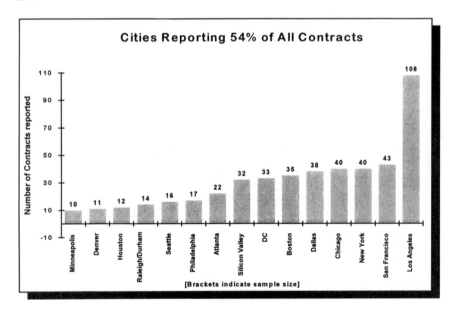

MORE ON CONTRACTING ABROAD

"I've been contracting/employed overseas since 1993, and would like to contribute some of my experience:

1. Negotiate rates in $. Local currency swings can wipe you out. Use US State department info for cost of living and per diem: (www.state.gov/www/services.html#living) for overseas rates.

2. For US per diem negotiating use http:/policyworks.gov/org/main/mt/homepage/mtt/perdiem.

3. The best positions are with international firms like KPMG, PW, E&Y, etc. It is very hard to break in since many new hires cannot take the living conditions, work pressure (vastly more responsibility), and "stranger in a strange land"ness of it all and quit, which is very expensive and disruptive to the firm and project. I took short term documentation projects for my 1st assignments, even though I am very senior.

4. The real job is rarely what the firm's managers in Washington/New York think it is. It is up to you to do the real work and explain things to your management and the project's sponsors.

5. You will really miss your significant other/newspaper/favorite coffee.

6. Take vitamin pills, a first aid kit, swiss army knife with corkscrew, toolkit, 3 in 1 oil, electrical plugs and transformers (usually 50 cycle 220V sources), small world band clock radio. Negotiate that your employer will forward books and magazines to you via air courier

7. Tax tricks can be very valuable or costly, and are not completely understood by anyone human. Basically:

A. Per diem at the State Dept. rate is tax free to the individual (1099 or W2). You must break continuous per diem before 180 days (a trip home or on vacation will do it) to maintain eligibility.

B. You get a $72K US income tax exclusion if you work and live out of the US for 330 of any 365 consecutive days, or all 12 months of a calendar year. This exclusion can be applied retroactively. There are lots of ways to screw this up.

C. Normally your employer pays hotel or rent for you. Rent is taxable income per some weird rules up to about $9K if you are a permanent resident.

D. Negotiate for the "post differential" for those garden spots given hardship differentials by the State Department. For example Sarajevo is 25%, so you should negotiate a 25% bump on your compensation after 43 consecutive days in Sarajevo. This is taxable compensation but falls under the $72K exclusion rule."

–Conrad Clark

Does it ever make sense to go back to being a regular employee?

Sometimes the best thing you can do for your contracting career is give it up in favor of a regular salaried job. This is particularly true when you are in the early years of your career. That's because many computer professionals get lured into contracting by the high hourly rates, before they have a broad enough base of experience to sustain a long and challenging contracting career.

If you find yourself stuck doing routine maintenance, minor fixes, and drudge coding on contract after contract, the only way to find more interesting projects may be to look for a company that will hire you as a salaried employee on a project where you'll be able to expand not only your technical skills but also your role on the project.

Many contractors make this move. By doing so, they pick up valuable skills and business contacts that allow them to reenter contracting at a later time when they are able to command higher rates and work on more interesting assignments.

How can I convince employers I'd take a salaried job. They say my contractor's earnings are too high!

You must be very careful about how you describe your contracting earnings on the job application form when you are trying to switch back to being a regular employee after a stint of contracting. That is because most HR departments are convinced that an employee who takes a job that pays less than they were earning in their previous position will quit in a few months. As a result, they often won't hire anyone who is already earning more than what an open position would pay.

This means that if you put down "$65 per hour" in the "current salary" field of the application form, HR staffers are likely to multiply your rate by the number of working hours in a year, 2,000, and conclude that your current salary is $130,000. This will cause them to throw your application away if the job you are applying for only pays $90,000.

So to make sure that your job application gets taken seriously give prospective employers an adjusted, annualized net figure as your "current salary" rather than telling them your hourly rate. Calculate this adjusted "salary" by adding up all the hours you've actually worked and deducting all the time you've lost while waiting for work in between contracts. Also deduct the cost of sick days, vacation days, and holidays, and of business and health insurance, as well as that of any training you've purchased for yourself. That way your $65 per hour comes out looking more like $80,000 than $130,000 and you will still be in the running for a salaried position.

I'm burning out on contracting but I don't want to be an employee. What are my other options?

If you have burnt out on selling your time, you will have to find something else to sell. For contractors, there are two obvious choices: software and the services of other contractors.

If you are a software developer, you may be able to use what you've learned while developing custom software to create a software product you can sell. It's possible to do very well writing niche software that solves problems of users in a specific industry, like insurance agencies or petroleum engineers. If you've spent your contracting years working in a variety of industries, you may have run across business problems that cross industry lines. Can you develop a software product that solves them? If you really want to aim for the big time, develop a mass market product like a game or a utility. Mass market software development is a tough path, but if you can make it work, you can retire wealthy while you are still young.

The other path many contractors take is to take the business friendships they've built up with other contractors and hiring managers over the years and use them as the basis for starting their own consulting firms. This is no longer as easy to do as it was a decade ago because of the competition that now exists in the contracting industry but it still can be done.

Other businesses that contractors have switched over to successfully are training businesses where they hire other people to teach classes and publishing companies that produce manuals, books, or magazines which can be sold to technical professionals through mail order or over the Internet.

The burgeoning growth of Web offers contractors career possibilities that were unimaginable in the past. Contractors can use their technical skills to write software that makes possible new types of commercial Web sites. There are fortunes waiting for the people who can do this. Just look at the people who invented the first Web auction sites and Web bookstores! The Web is still young enough that there are many other niches left that have not yet been fully exploited.

Whatever path you choose as you move forward from contracting, the key is to build on what you have already accomplished. Use everything you've gathered in your travels through the business world. Draw on your technical skills, your business contacts, and on what you've observed about how business works to identify unmet needs and to fill them. The possibilities are there. Now use the intelligence and insight that have gotten you this far to find them.

And in the meantime, here's wishing you the very best of luck with your ongoing contracting career!

INDEX

MASTER ENTREPRENEURIAL CONSULTING

The Computer Consultant's Workbook

277 Pages

TECHNION Books

ISBN 0-9647116-0-5   With 10% Direct buyer discount: **$36.00**

The Computer Consultant's Workbook leads you through the steps it takes to decide if you have what it takes to succeed at consulting and design an effective marketing plan. It helps you identify your clientele, set rates, develop a marketing message, locate potential clients and convince them you can do the job. It includes meaty discussions, worksheets, exercises, fact sheets, sample letters, contracts, proposals and more.

Computerworld's reviewer wrote, "Although the volume of information Ruhl provides is tremendous, it's easy to absorb and can be immediately useful. Even experienced consultants will find ideas to savor. But those who will benefit most from The Computer Consultant's Workbook are individuals with good technical skills who need a short course in entrepreneurship and self-management. In fact, it's hard to see how someone following Ruhl's savvy suggestions can go far wrong. Almost every page can be quickly translated into a to-do list or the outline of a plan of action. And it's easy to find the information you need, when you need it."

Promote Yourself to Expert

TECHNION Books Audiotape   **$12.95**

60 minutes

Big name consultants don't just appear out of nowhere. You know their names because you read about them in the trade press. This tape shows you how to raise your visibility by placing the right kinds of articles and books in business publications. Learn how to turn yourself into an expert!

Raise Your Rates

TECHNION Books Audiotape   **$12.95**

60 minutes

Learn the secrets of charging a premium rate from consultants earning rates of $100 per hour and more. You'll learn how to improve your skills and image, how to improve your ability to negotiate and how to find the right agency. Reinforces what you've read in this book!

ORDER TODAY FROM TECHNION BOOKS!
800-972-3665

or use the handy online order form you'll find at:

http://www.realrates.com/books.htm

ORDER THE LATEST
REAL RATE SURVEY REPORT!

The charts in this book include the data found in the July 1998 Real Rate Survey Report. Now you can order the latest, most up-to-date Real Rate Survey and find out what is happening in the current market!

The Real Rate Survey Report will include most of charts you've seen in this book (plus a few others) updated with data collected over the previous six month period ending in July or December.

People who have bought our earlier Real Rate Survey Reports tell us they are useful not only in helping them set their rates, but also as a tool for educating prospective clients about the rates that real computer consultants are charging.

Bring a copy along on *your* next interview with a consulting firm or client so that you have an instant authoritative response for any questions about why you charge the rate you do!

YOU CAN FIND OUT MORE ABOUT THE
REAL RATE SURVEY REPORT
AND ORDER IT ONLINE AT:
http://www.realrates.com/orderrr.htm